The Big Bucks Guide to

Shipping Out as a

Merchant Seaman

**Live Where You Want,
Work When You Must,
Earn What You Need**

Capt. Jonathan Allen

Cover design: Rob Johnson, www.johnsondesign.org
Book design: Linda Morehouse, www.webuildbooks.com

Illustrations by Shauna Crandall

Printed in the United States of America
First Edition
ISBN: 978-0-9839075-2-7

Published by
Prodigious Press
P. O. Box 537
Driggs, ID 83422
www.thebigbucksguide.com

Dedication

This book is dedicated to the memory of Captain Al Thoma,
the finest man I ever sailed under.

Acknowledgments

I thank my wife, Tammy, for not laughing when I told her I wanted to write books, and then for not crying when I told her she had to market them.

I thank all of the Master Mariners I have sailed under, first for your instruction, but mostly for your patience.

Lastly, I thank Linda and Matt Morehouse of Paradise Cay publishing and webuildbooks.com for making the seemingly impossible task of publishing a book quite possible.

Table of Contents

A Seaman's Life

- *Running Away to Sea*

- *So How Do You Get Started?*

- *The Next Issue is Choices*

- *Lifestyle*

- *Cons*

- *Working Conditions*

- *Women at Sea*

Running Away to Sea!

Sounds pretty exciting, doesn't it? Sailing through the Singapore Straits or putting ashore in Antarctica it can be one heck of an adventure, or it can be an endless drudge. It depends on the choices you make, your expectations, and the luck of the draw. But one thing for sure: short of joining the French Foreign Legion, it's the best way I know of changing your luck and starting over. With the Legion you get a new name and new French citizenship; with the Merchant Marine you get a new lifestyle, a new career, and perhaps even a new world view.

With experience and thoughtful career guidance merchant shipping can be quite lucrative with generous benefits and annual salaries into the six figures. Some of the more specialized maritime careers (such as piloting) top out at around a half million dollars a year. That's not bad for an occupation that may provide six months paid vacation a year and a free ticket to some of the world's greatest cities. Trust me, it's nice to have the day off in Hong Kong, Colombo, or San Francisco.

So what is the down side? There are plenty and they're substantial. Remember the six months of paid vacation? Not all employers pay nearly that much, and even when they do you only get it because you'll be unavailable the rest of the year. If your daughter is in a car accident, there is nothing you can do. When your son makes the pee-wee football all-star team you probably won't be there to see it. Your girlfriend may have a problem with your being gone so much and you may not have a girlfriend, or wife, when you return; that may be a problem.

Another issue to ponder is living where you work. Have you ever had to work with people you couldn't stand? Now you get to live with them too. It can be a challenge.

> I once had a watch partner who I thought was a pretty nice guy. He was kind of hippy looking, with gold granny glasses and a banjo he took ashore with him. He would find a friendly bar and start to play. He said it was a great way to make new friends. Then one day, right out of the blue, he told me he thought incest was a good idea, that people were being unfair when they condemned it so harshly.

I interrupted him. "Look, you stand over there (this was before the bridge watch was allowed to sit) in the far corner of the bridge and I'll stand over here in this corner. We'll only talk when business requires it, OK?" He soon took vacation and left, but it was creepy for a while.

This is an extreme example, but it happened and sometimes you have to be able to coexist and work with people you can't stand. Not everyone can do it, and if you can't this isn't the right industry for you.

Extensive government regulation is another issue you'll have to accept. You will be subject to random drug testing while you work, which will often make no sense. After the Valdez oil spill terminal security came up with a plan where returning mariners had to prove they were sober before they were allowed to return to their ships. The terminal was quite proud of preventing many drunken seamen from returning to their ships where they could despoil the environment.

OK, fair, right? Well, actually no. Last time I looked at their score sheets the only seamen Valdez terminal kept off of their ships were cooks and steward utilities, with a few entry-level engine and deck seamen thrown in, who might have been headed to bed for six or eight hours anyway. So they saved us from burnt eggs and sloppy hospital corners but "saving the environment" is a stretch.

The merchant marine suffers from a lot of these types of silly regulations; if you can't deal, don't waste your time.

Your papers are subject to renewal every five years, which can become a real headache if something turns up, such as a DUI or a health condition. The Coast Guard will even want to vet whatever prescription medicines you're on. They really get in your business and there is no way to avoid it.

If you decide to pursue a license, the federal government will become even more involved in your life. Each time you upgrade, the Coast Guard evaluates you before you're allowed to test for the next license. This drives some people to distraction; if you can't cope with the intrusion don't waste your time shipping, it isn't the industry for you.

So How Do You Get Started?

We should probably start with an explanation of what the Merchant Marine is, as most people don't seem to know. It has nothing to do with the Marines; it's not part of the military, though it often works with the military. It is civilian mariners operating all kinds of ships and boats all over the world. Sometimes these civilian seamen are working for the Navy, sometimes they've working for other government organizations, and sometimes they've working for private companies, either American or foreign. Rarely, mariners own their own vessel they're working on and are working for themselves.

To join the Legion you need to fly to France, pass a medical exam and a background check ,and you're in. Joining the American Merchant Marine is a little more complicated, particularly since Corporate America discovered how much money there was to be made generating security programs for the merchant fleet and the United States Coast Guard discovered how much additional funding they could generate by expanding their security requirements. You will have to jump through a lot of redundant, nonsensical hoops before you can even think of reporting aboard your first ship. It is as if the TSA baggage screeners at your local airport are your new career counselors.

But there is good news in the governmental regulatory muck you will have to slog through. If you have a clear, well-marked path and you stick to it, you will eventually reach your goal while the other guy sinks screaming into the quicksand. This little book will show you the way.

The Next Issue is Choices

Deck department, engine department or stewards department, which is the right one for you? Make the right choice and you're on your way, make the wrong one and you're spinning your wheels. Without some planning it's easy to grab the first job available and either get stuck in a dead end or start climbing the wrong ladder.

This can be a bigger problem in the shipping industry than in others because advancement in the maritime world depends on credentials. Credentials depend on sea time in the correct department. If your ultimate goal is to sail Master, then you're wasting your time in the engine department. If fixing engines is your forte, then don't take a job working on deck. If taking tests isn't your thing and you like working inside cooking and cleaning, the stewards department has a place for you.

We will discuss all three departments in greater detail later on to help you make the right choice. But first we'll cover the many different types of ships in the Merchant Marine and then we'll run through the different types of hiring systems: government, union, and non-union.

There are a lot of choices to be made while working in the Maritime industry. Should you get a license or would you be happier working unlicensed? Which would be better for you, joining a union or working non-union? Which union? Which department? What kind of ship appeals to you? Would you prefer inland or deep sea work? Helping you make sound, informed choices is the purpose of this book.

I told one union official I was writing a book about how to go about joining the American Merchant Marine. He asked me "How can you get a book out of that? All you do is get a TWIC, MMC and join SIU. Sit in the hall and take the first job offered."

That certainly is one way. It is probably how many of us got started, with minor variations, but it isn't always the best way. If you plan your career a little bit, if you know what most of you options are before you start you'll make better choices and wind up in a better place. Hopefully, I can help you with that.

Lifestyle

This is the single biggest attraction and the single biggest disadvantage of working in the American Merchant Marine, so we'd better discuss it. Six months of paid vacation a year sounds pretty good, doesn't it? Well, you most likely won't get that for a while. As you move up the ladder the perks get better and better, so you may have to become a licensed officer before you get day-for-day vacation, because the unlicensed crew often don't do as well. Typically the senior officers get a couple of more paid vacation days per month worked than do the junior officers.

But you usually have the option of taking extra days or weeks or months of unpaid vacation each year. This can be very advantageous if you have another seasonal job, such as ski instructor or fishing guide. I've also seen it work for entrepreneurs as well; they put in a few months at sea, or even a half a year, and the rest of the year is theirs to do what they will. Sometimes they rebuild a house or construct a website, shut it down for a couple of more months, take vacation, and go back to work. I've seen seamen who work harder on their vacation than they do at sea. Usually that's something you don't want to brag about on the ship, though.

I've only known of one person who put himself through school by going to sea. But he already had a BS degree and was working on his doctorate while shipping. Another reason it's difficult to continue with school once you start shipping is the money. It's tough to continue with your studies once you realize you'll most likely be taking a pay cut upon graduation. No doubt there are exceptions, but usually it's pretty hard to land a job just for the summer on a ship. The timing doesn't usually work out and the first few years of getting established are by far the hardest, so going to sea to pay for school doesn't usually work—unless you have some kind of an "in," in which case you probably don't need this book. If you're looking to fund your schooling, read *The Big Bucks Guide to Commercial Fishing in Alaska.* Summer processing and fishing work tends to work out well for students trying to raise cash for school.

It doesn't have to be all drudge, though. A seaman friend of mine on a two-month-on, two-month-off schedule bought a world almanac. For a year, every time he took vacation he looked up an international festival and dropped in. In a year he visited Rio for Mardi Gras, Munich for Oktoberfest, Pamplona for the running of the bulls, Monte Carlo for the Gran Prix, and Montana for trout season. That was a good year.

So how did he afford it? Glad you asked. He had no car payment and no apartment rental expense; he only had to cover the rest of his living expenses half of the year. His plane tickets worked out to less than rent, and he got pretty good at working the frequent flyer miles. I used to spend a lot of my time off in East Africa as I found it the most interesting and exciting place on earth (though I have to admit I've never run into any other seamen who share my enthusiasm for Africa). South East Asian vacations are presently very popular with professional seamen. If you need more freedom, go to sea.

This isn't going to happen in your first year of going to sea. More than likely your vacation will be spent attending professional classes or looking for your next job. But it is a lifestyle that you'll work into eventually. When I was younger I did a lot of third world travel, which tends to be very cheap. I invested my shipboard earnings and lived on my vacation pay, so it may even be possible to travel the world—avoiding Stockholm, Paris, and Singapore, of course—and save money.

It might not be a bad idea to pick up *The Four Hour Work Week* by Tim Ferriss. It's a favorite of mine and it will help you get used to a truly alternate lifestyle that has nothing to do with transgender or anything like that. The book is full of ideas for both business start-ups and inexpensive world travel. I mention it only because merchant shipping lends itself to the way of life Tim Ferriss advocates: one with plenty of freedom and plenty of money.

Merchant shipping provides another freedom, as well: the freedom to live anywhere. I have coworkers who live in Thailand, Florida, Maine, and elsewhere, all working on the same ship. I live in the middle of the Rockies and commute 3 times a year. I pay a little bit of a price in that I usually leave a day early to compensate for flight delays that aren't uncommon in the mountains, especially in the winter. Find the most beautiful, inexpensive, private, exciting place on earth to live; you won't have to worry about the local employment opportunities anymore. I've worked with captains who live in small towns in Maine and made a better living than anyone else in town. So if you want to ranch cattle in New Mexico or surf in Hawaii but need a well-paid job to pull it off, this may be just the ticket.

So how much money can you make? Well, it depends… Obviously, some companies and jobs pay more than others. The big union ships tend to pay the most, the smaller research ships or oil response vessels pay the least. Yachts sometimes pay nothing at all. You are going to have to take some responsibility here; keep your eyes out for a better deal and jump when you find one. You may need to take one of the lower paying jobs to get the sea time you'll need for an Able Bodied Seaman's (AB) papers or a Junior Engineer's ticket, then once you've got that in your pocket, move up to a better paying job.

When I quit commercial fishing in Alaska I thought I'd lock down a great job running boats on San Francisco Bay. I was tired of beating my brains out all winter long in the Bering Sea and running a tugboat or ferry on the bay sounded a whole lot better. In the space of less than a year I found and quit six jobs. First, the openings were all with bottom feeder companies. Second, they never told me the truth during the hiring interview: either the hours were fewer than promised or the raises slower than indicated or the new boats never arrived. Third, no one else thought my boat handling skills were as valuable as I did. I wound up with job after job paying $14 to $18 an hour, with never enough hours.

> Question: How do you live in San Francisco on $14 an hour?
> Answer: In your car or with your parents.

So I kept quitting. I quit a dredge company, an oil skimmer company, a burial at sea company, and a whole bunch of charter boat companies that gave their clients boat rides around San Francisco Bay. Since I had a Coast Guard Deck Officers License I was eventually able to join the Masters, Mates, and Pilots Union and I shipped out my first day in the union at about a 400% raise. I've been here almost fifteen years now.

The point is; there are a lot of low-paying jobs out there. Take them when you need the sea time and drop them as soon as you find or qualify for something better. Actively manage your career and you should do well.

There a lot of jobs out there on the water. I've looked into most of the maritime training programs and I've investigated the placement rate of their graduates. It's pretty close to everybody. As I write this, the real unemployment rate is upwards of 16% yet I've talked to union officials, governmental recruiters, and private companies and they all seem to have plenty of vacancies. They can't find enough labor with the required paperwork.

The paperwork seems like a pain, but it is actually a good thing; if it were easy, everyone would do it and it wouldn't pay much at all. Do the work, take the time to fill out the forms, spend the money on the documents, be patient, and eventually you'll have more options for a good paying job than you can believe.

Cons

This is where I try to talk you out of going to sea. It isn't a perfect career and it's not for everyone. When I'm trying to make my wife feel guilty, I tell her, "Going to sea is like going to prison, with the added risk of drowning." Actually, I've never heard of a merchant mariner drowning—ships just don't sink as much as they used to—but some things never change: for example, seasickness.

A very long time ago, as a cadet on my very first merchant ship, I made a trip from Seattle to Anchorage, Alaska over Christmas. On the way back to Seattle we ran into a storm with seas so big the first row of deck containers were all punched in. For days we ran at about 4 knots, or about 4.5 mph. I was so seasick I thought, and hoped, I would die. The only place I wasn't violently ill was lying flat on my back with my eyes closed or standing on the bridge with my nose pressed against the window. I can still remember rushing past the Christmas buffet without a glance, bouncing off of both bulkheads of the passageway, trying to get to my room before I humiliated myself.

I thought storms of this type were an everyday occurrence and seriously considered another line of work, at least until the seas calmed down. Well, in over 30 years of going to sea that trip may well have been the worst.

Ships today have all kinds of weather routing equipment and are pretty good at avoiding the worst of the weather. They still rock and roll; anything not tied down hits the deck and breaks and the new guys still get seasick. But modern technology gives a surprisingly accurate weather picture along the vessel's track four days into the future, making the master's weather avoidance strategy much easier than it used to be.

Seasickness can still be a problem, though over time people tend to become immune to it. Rarely, some people never become immune, even with medications, but I've never seen that on merchant ships, only Alaskan fishing boats. Usually if the vessel encounters some rough weather early in the voyage, some of the rookies get sick. Staying outside in the wind or at least watching the horizon through the window helps; so does eating soda crackers and drinking 7-Up. Bananas are also good, because they taste about the same coming up as they do going down. Marizine and Dramamine tablets both work but will make you sleepy, especially Dramamine.

The Transderm Scop patch is the best seasickness medication. Since it's a patch you place behind your ear, you can't throw it up. It requires a prescription and is usually not carried on board ship. But if you have some it is good for about three days, which should get you through most storms. It's not healthy to wear one for more than three days in a row since it has some side effects, but it usually won't put you to sleep like the other seasickness medications.

Another annoying aspect of joining the American Merchant Marine is the time frame required to get started. It will take weeks, if not months before you set foot on a ship. You'll need Coast Guard papers, which require physicals, background checks, and completed applications. You'll most likely need a class in Basic Safety Training. Finally, you'll need find a union or company looking for seamen. We'll walk you through the process and we'll get you there, but it will take a while.

Health issues should also be considered. Very few ships carry doctors, though they do usually have a hospital room. But if you have a serious medical condition, don't go to sea. It isn't fair to you, because you may not have access to real medical assistance when you need it, and it isn't fair to the poor deck officer who will do his very level best to help you, using the radio doctor, to stay alive. He will probably have the medical training of an entry level EMT, not really sufficient to deal with heart attacks or strokes.

The Coast Guard is making it harder and harder to get seaman's papers if you have a serious medical problem; on their website there are twenty pages of problematic medical conditions. If you have issues, take a look at the website and see if your condition is a deal-breaker before you invest a lot of time and money in pursuing a seagoing career.

I find it amazing that we even have to consider pirates as a downside to working in the American Merchant Marine. But there *are* pirate attacks taking place around the world—Nigeria and the Philippines come to mind—though the real action is taking place off of Somalia. It's been going on for a while, even though it only hit the American consciousness a few years ago. In 2003 I listened in over the radio as a group of armed men in a small vessel off of Somalia shot up a French sailing yacht, only to be sunk by a missile-launching helicopter flown off of a coalition warship. I heard the event unfold over the single side band radio, although it never made the papers.

I travel through the pirate corridor off of Somalia about six times a year, so I'm a little disturbed that the American Navy is either unable or unwilling to deal with the Somali pirates. The purpose of the American Navy is to project force around the world and keep the sea lanes open. Where else in the world are the sea lanes more under attack than in the Gulf of Aden, between the Horn of Africa and the Arabian Peninsula? The Navy would like you to believe that the reason they are mostly helpless is because the sea is so great and their ships are so small and few. Bullshit.

Every time we transit the pirate corridor we either see an attack or hear one over the VHF radio, which has a range of about 40 miles. And the American Navy can do nothing?

I'll tell you a story. Patrolling the corridor is a small fleet of coalition warships—judging by their accents over the radio, mostly from Europe. Unfortunately, each nation has its own policy when it catches pirates. The Germans and the Scandinavians confiscate the pirate weapons but then furnish the thwarted pirates with food and water and enough fuel to get home.

But there is one lonely little frigate, with one lonely little helicopter, the pirates are scared to death of. It's the South Korean contribution to the coalition fleet. When the South Koreans are on watch and a call comes in, the ship dispatches its helicopter to the scene. If pirates are observed attacking a merchant ship, the helicopter fires off a couple of missiles, sinks the pirates, and returns to base.

The pirates are highly indignant and put out a press release stating they have invested in an old Stinger missile to deal with the Korean helicopter. My hope, my prayer, is that some U.S. Navy admiral, who probably isn't any more thrilled with his navy's impotence than I am, sent over to the Koreans the latest and greatest electronics countermeasure package. I'm pulling for that lone, brave, South Korean helicopter crew. Thanks, guys.

Here is the issue. Somalia has proved to be unable to govern itself, much less patrol its coasts. Criminal fishermen, mostly from Asia, have taken advantage of the situation and destroyed the local fisheries by overfishing with factory trawlers. There are also reports of toxic waste dumping off of the coast of Somalia by criminal syndicates, which are less credible but possible. These crimes have been used by the pirate's public relations specialists as justification for their piracy, even though Somalia has traditionally been a nation of herders rather than fishermen.

Western Europeans have a dismal history around the horn of Africa. Only Ethiopia managed to fight off the European imperialists; consequently, westerners are very uncomfortable projecting force in the area. The pirates are all black and most of the navies arrayed against them are primarily white. Not a single African country has sent out a warship to confront the pirates. If pirates are attacked more aggressively they will very likely respond by packing their boats with women and children, a tactic the West has never been very good at countering. So countering the pirates effectively is a real public relations quandary. However, if you happen to be on a ship chased by pirates armed with rocket propelled grenades and assault rifles, the moral dilemmas are not nearly as perplexing.

Merchant ships are not allowed to carry firearms unless they are working for the Navy. But perhaps that is the solution; it worked for a couple of thousand years: Let merchant ships traveling through pirate waters carry weapons or security teams. Personally I think weapons are all that would be required. The pirates aren't very intimidating, except to an unarmed man. In the Gulf of Aden when the winds get above about 20 knots the pirates stay home, because it's too rough for ship boardings. Fair weather pirates. Some merchant ship security teams have started shooting back when attacked and that seems to always end the incident. My last trip through the Gulf of Aden we heard a pirate attack on a ship carrying a security team who reacted by shooting at the pirate boat. At first we thought the would-be pirates were screaming, "Beast, beast!" which would have been really hypocritical, but in retrospect I think they were shouting, "Peace, peace!" once the firing began.

Why do you think we can't carry guns? Why do so few ships carry security teams? Take a guess. Who runs the world? Insurance companies! Right on the first guess. Ransoms have been running around several million dollars a ship. One full-sized container ship carrying several thousand insured containers is probably insured for around a half a billion dollars. The insurance companies don't want any firefights that might destroy the ship and her cargo; it's just way cheaper to pay the ransom. I don't think the insurance companies are too concerned if the crew is held in captivity for many months. Presently, as I write this, there are about 30 ships and 660 seamen held by Somali pirates.

To be fair, the Maersk *Alabama* is the only American Merchant ship to have been seized by Somali pirates so far, since our ships tend to be too big and fast for most of the pirates. The pirates also know they have a very limited time to operate after seizing an American ship before the SEALs show up and start shooting. However, pirates, a new fly in the ointment that most of us thought the world was done with, are another downside to working in the Merchant Marine.

An anti-piracy security expert recently told me that the Somali pirates were scouring the world looking for fast-ship boarding experts willing to train their pirates for a large fee. He said it would have been completely legal for him to take the assignment and he would have been very successful as he is presently designing anti-piracy countermeasures used on large merchant ships. He told me he just couldn't bring himself to go over to the dark side, but who knows how long it will take the pirates to find less principled experts to improve their efficiency. Hopefully the U.S. government is considering the next generation of countermeasures; I suggest drones armed with Hellfire missiles.

Working Conditions

It's probably time to give you a rundown of the working conditions on a boat or a ship. There is a lot of variation from ship to ship and company to company, but some things don't change. Everyone works seven days a week. When you aren't feeling well you still have to go to work; taking sick days off is a rare thing.

Most ships, with a few government exceptions, run with the minimum crew required to sail the ship from one port to the next. Remove one crew member and the ship's efficiency drops dramatically.

> I only mention this because once when I was crewing up a large new fishing boat with greenhorns right off the street, some of the new crew were flabbergasted when they had to work while seasick or even on Sunday.

Work hours are either daywork (8 to 5, with an hour lunch) or watches. Most engine rooms are automated with alarms that ring in the engineer's staterooms or on the bridge when a problem is detected. This allows the engineers to work days with the duty engineer answering all the alarms that ring at night.

On the deck side the watches are usually divided into three watches that each stand four hours of watch with eight hours off. Any work done in the eight hours between watches is overtime. Some smaller vessels, research vessels, supply boats, offshore tugs, may run with two watches of six hours on and six hours off, usually with the captain standing a watch. Sometimes the captain will prefer to set up the watches for twelve hours of duty followed by twelve hours off.

One of the biggest problems facing mariners is sleep deprivation. There are international regulations from the International Maritime Organization (IMO) requiring the seaman to get eleven hours off a day. That's fine, but it doesn't guarantee a good night's sleep.

What if the vessel is rolling so much that you have to shove your life-jacket and survival suit under one side of the mattress so you don't roll out? You won't get much sleep; eventually you'll get tired enough to fall asleep, but it may take a few days. If the ship is arriving in the middle of the night, you'll most likely have to get up for a few hours; if it shifts four hours later you'll have to get up again.

> I've worked on survey vessels that detonated air cannons every minute or so as they tracked oil deposits with a sonic array. When the water was shallow and the bottom rocky, the detonation would bounce me right off of the mattress each time the cannon went off. Eventually I sort of got used to it, but I never slept really well when they were surveying.

Sometimes you have the option of turning down overtime work and resting instead. But your gross income takes a hit and sometimes the overtime is mandatory, such as tying up and letting go the ship. I'm not trying to talk you out of shipping out; I just want you to know how different it is than working in an insurance office.

Seamen working on a survey vessel or on many cargo vessels can spend extended time at sea. They are usually hired for one or more voyages that may last anywhere from a couple of weeks to a couple of months each. Often when they take vacation there is no job security after that; when the vacation is up they have to return to the hiring hall and wait for the next job. The length of time off between voyages depends on job availability and personal preference. Until enough seniority is achieved there is a lot of uncertainty and thoughtful budgeting is required.

About half of the job is living with your shipmates. You must be considerate of your fellow crewmembers or bad things will happen. Even really big ships start to feel really small when you're trying to avoid someone. Learn to go with the flow and follow the Golden Rule. Try to fit into the ship's system, rather than changing the system to something more to your liking.

The good news is that all professional seamen know how important cooperation is and will strive to make it work. They'll show up on time to relieve you, won't play their music too loud when you're sleeping, and will always pull their own weight. In short, they are considerate of their shipmates.

Keep that in mind, it's important.

Women at Sea

There was a time when most seamen thought the sea was no place for a woman; indeed, it was thought to be bad luck to have a woman aboard a ship. Women were not well treated aboard ships. That was a long time ago. Women have been working successfully aboard ships for some 30 years now. Most American ships now have at least one woman signed on as a crew member, in any capacity. The industry has evolved to the point where a woman who is competent and a good shipmate is welcomed.

Personally, I think it's a good thing to have some female crewmembers aboard; I appreciate the civilizing influence. It drops the cursing a notch and inspires the rest of us to hit the rain locker a little more frequently. I would encourage any woman who has an urge to go to sea to give it a shot, in either a licensed or an unlicensed capacity. The various maritime academies are always looking for qualified applicants to balance out their incoming classes. I've sailed with women with master's degrees who sail as Able Seamen because they make a lot more money at sea.

Long term, is going to sea a good career for a woman? That depends. It is difficult for a woman to go to sea and raise a family. It's hard for men too, but it's even harder for a woman. Mariners struggle to stay married. Many are successful, but it's more difficult than with a conventional career. Six months a year separation is a difficult nut to crack. (If you don't plan to have children then this isn't as much of an issue.)

But there are ways to do both. I've known women to advance to a senior officer's position aboard ship and then take a management position ashore when it seemed like the right time to start a family. The best movie I've ever seen about life at sea was the first *Alien* movie. Ok, I know it took place in outer space and the story was about fighting monsters, but except for that it was spot on. The screen writer must have been a former merchant seaman because he got the dialog and the crew dynamics exactly right. The female crew members are crew members and their sex has very little to do with anything—that is where the merchant marine is headed. Ships' crews today are so small that if someone is good they are truly appreciated, for no other reason than that they make everyone's life easier.

Ships and Shipping Company Information

- Cruise Ships
  - Hiring Partner Issues
  - Small Non-Union Cruise Ships
  - American-Flag Union Cruise Ships
- Offshore Supply Boats
- Ferry Boats
- Tugboats
  - Typical Day on a Two-Man, Tug Day Boat
- Tankers
  - Typical Day on a Tanker
- Bulk Carriers
- Great Lakes Shipping
  - Unlicensed Jobs on the Great Lakes
  - Licensed Jobs on the Great Lakes
- Container Ships
- Ro/ro's
- Breakbulk Vessels
- Military Sealift Command
- Research Ships
- Dredges
- Army Corps of Engineering
- Yacht Jobs

Cruise Ships

There are three categories of cruise ships: union American-flag cruise ships, non-union American-flag cruise ships, and foreign-flag cruise ships. All are very different; each has its advantages and disadvantages. We will discuss each category in detail.

> Let's begin this section with a quick warning. A friend of mine, with a United States Coast Guard Unlimited Chief Mate's License, thought he might like to work on one of the state ferries, being unemployed and tired of being away from home so much. He got hold of a number for the ferry company's Human Resources department and gave them a call.
>
> The woman who answered the phone jumped straight down his throat. "How did you get this number? Why are you calling me? What's wrong with you?"
>
> Taken aback, my friend told her he was an experienced mariner and had an urge to try something new, like a ferry boat job. She quickly calmed down and explained the phone was ringing off the hook because some jackass had written a book on how to find a job on a cruise ship and had erroneously included her number. She was upset because she had to explain all day long that ferries aren't cruise ships and all crew members were hired through the unions and they really didn't have anything for newbies, anyway. But the phone kept ringing.
>
> Let's try to avoid that scenario, shall we?

Many of the cruise ship companies have websites and do want to hear from you, if you have the qualifications they're seeking. But read the disclaimers and understand that it is very difficult for an American with no experience to break into the cruise ship industry on a foreign flag vessel without some sort of skill.

Under certain circumstances, cruise ships might be one of the few situations where it makes sense for an American to seek employment on a foreign-flag ship. Hundreds of foreign-flag cruise ships operate out of the U.S., sailing to the Caribbean, Mexico, and Alaska, and they hire Americans under certain circumstances. The problem is the Internet is absolutely loaded with scams. But I've got your back and I'll walk you through the process and tell you how to proceed if you want to work on a top-shelf cruise ship.

Royal Caribbean Cruise Lines, sailing primarily out of the U.S., employs 40,000 people worldwide. To me, that's a stunning number, and Royal Caribbean is not even the biggest cruise ship company in the world. Carnival is the biggest; Royal Caribbean is number two.

Foreign-flag cruise ships sailing out of America do have some positions that they are willing to fill with Americans, particularly since the vast majority of their passengers are Americans. But since foreign flag vessels do not have to hire Americans or follow American labor laws, these cruise ships are free to hire whomever they like. I think it is fair to say that a Guatemalan or a Honduran is willing to work for a considerably lower wage than most Americans.

> Carnival Cruises, the aforementioned biggest cruise ship company in the world, is owned by Mickey Aaronson, a longtime member of the Forbes 400 richest Americans list. The vast majority of his ships sail out of the U.S. and carry primarily American passengers. Yet none of ships are registered in America or are required to hire Americans or face the stringent inspections of an American ship. It is all quite legal, but keep this little tale in mind the next time you hear someone insisting the U.S. would be better off without the Jones Act.

The foreign cruise ships pay their manual labor—their maids, bus boys, and deck hands—far less than Americans are willing to leave home for. Presently, only the *Pride of America,* sailing out of Honolulu, is registered in America. Many of these enormous foreign ships are registered in Malta, a tiny island in the Mediterranean Sea that I suspect few of these ships have ever visited.

The cruise ship companies have "hiring partners" located around the world. These companies are recruiting agencies who locate, train, and service the low-cost labor that does most of the grunt work on a cruise ship.

These hiring partners never admit that they aren't much interested in filling most of their jobs with Americans. That's probably bad politics, but reading between the lines isn't difficult. For the most part, check the cruise ship websites more than the hiring partners (there are some exceptions); the better jobs are often listed on the cruise ship websites. Often most of the hiring partner jobs tend to be a grind and poorly compensated.

Hiring Partner Issues

Beware of scam hiring partners. Unfortunately, there are agencies and individuals that attempt to collect funds from job seekers by fraudulency representing themselves as being authorized to recruit for cruise ship companies. Beware of these scammers; many cruise ship companies post the names of all known scammers on their websites. The authorized hiring partners are also clearly posted on the cruise ship websites.

You know how the Viagra you buy over the Internet never seems to work very well? It is exactly the same with many scam cruise ship employment websites. Never pay anyone in advance for assistance finding a cruise ship job. You don't need to; there are jobs everywhere and the turnover is huge. The scam is charging for help when all you have to do is email the cruise ship company or their hiring partner at no cost (not a heinous crime, perhaps; certainly way less evil than selling bogus Viagra).

Usually the company websites have better job opportunities for Americans than the hiring partners, but not always, so check them both. The cruise ship website generally has an employment section for more specialized occupations, such as sommelier, or food and beverage director, or surf instructor.

My all-time favorite is cupcake supervisor (really).

These jobs tend to pay a lot better than the ones filled by the hiring partners. The downside is that you have to know what you are doing. If you don't already know wine they aren't going to hire you as a sommelier; if you don't already know cupcakes you can forget about . . . . You get the picture.

So if you already have experience as a sous chef or a food and beverage manager, the foreign cruise ships will hire you, happily. Just don't think you can hire on for unskilled work, such as making beds or washing dishes, because that's what the Third World is for.

A quick look at a cruise ship website shows openings for first officer, electrician, second assistant engineer, and all kinds of restaurant and hotel management positions. If you can get a job on a foreign cruise ship as a photographer or as a musician and don't need to make a lot of money, I say go for it. You'll probably have a blast and you won't have many living expenses—except for your crew bar bill, I would guess.

Here is a partial list of rough cruise ship wages, just to give you an idea of what to expect. Remember the wages will vary from company to company and factors such as experience, language skills, even citizenship will come into play. All wages are per month.

Cruise Director: $5,000 to $10,000
Host/Hostess: $800 to $2,000
Bar and Wait Staff: $500 to $2,000
Captain: $6,000 to $10,000
Deck Officer: $1,500 to $3,000
Able Body Seaman: $1,600 to $1,800
Gift Shop Manager: $2,500 to $5,000
Gift Shop Staff: $1,000 to $3,000
Guest Entertainer: $4,000 to $10,000
Dancer: $2,000 to $3,000

Start looking early, though; it may take several months from submitting your resume to reporting aboard your new ship. Also keep in mind that working in the gift shop or bar tending isn't going to count as sea time, so the chances of the Coast Guard counting cruise ship sea time is pretty slight unless you've been working in the deck or engine department, an unlikely event on a foreign cruise ship. You'll have a much better chance of earning Coast Guard sea time on an American flag cruise ship, both union and non-union—an important consideration if you're planning to continue as a merchant mariner.

Here is a list of foreign-flag cruise ship websites:

Celebrity Cruises: www.celebritycruises.com
Royal Caribbean Cruises: www.royalcaribbean.com
Norwegian Cruise Lines: www.ncl.com
Disney Cruises: www.disneycruises.com
Carnival Cruises: www.carnival.com
Princess Cruises: www.princess.com
Holland America Cruises: www.hollandamerica.com

Small Non-Union Cruise Ships

We move on to American-flag, non-union cruise ships, which tend to be much smaller than the usual cruise ship. Listed below are five American-flag small cruise ship companies. There are more, but these listed companies run larger vessels that require larger crews. They all actively solicit crew members on their websites and sound like a lot of fun.

I've never worked this part of the industry, but it may not be a bad place to start. Entry level positions pay around $100 a day, but it may be a long day. Check with the individual companies on how long their work day is before accepting a job. The sea time on these ships may count or it may not, it depends on what you need the seatime for and how big or powerful the ship is. These mini cruise ships are often under 100 GT, but keep track of your seatime here too, as it may still be useful. Some of these companies like hiring college students and will work with you to fit your trips in between semesters, which isn't the case in other areas of the industry.

Lindblad Expeditions

They run two small American flag cruise ships, the *Sea Lion* and the *Sea Bird*. Both carry around 60 passengers in 30 staterooms. Destinations include Alaska, British Columbia, Baja California, and the Columbia and Snake River. They've partnered with National Geographic to offer adventurous travel, using naturalists and other experts. Their website lists the jobs available. They require a six-month contract and the entry level positions are steward and deckhand. Entry level pay is a guaranteed $80 per day, but the tip pool usually adds $20 or $30 more per day. There are some other perks as well, including free air fare, free uniforms, and the usual free room and board. The ships are 99 GT.

866 819-5327

lexjobs@expeditions.com

Blount Small Ship Adventures

Three small vessels make up their fleet of small American-flag cruise ships. The ships are about 180 feet long and carry just

fewer than one hundred passengers each. They cruise the Mississippi River and the Great Lakes, the Erie Canal and the coast of Maine, the Chesapeake Bay and the Atlantic Coastal waterways. You'll have to pass a drug test and have no criminal record before they'll hire you.
(401) 337-9043
Personnel@blountsmallshipadventures.com

Alaskan Dream Cruises

Alaskan Dream Cruises features two small cruise ships. *American Dream* is a 104-foot-long catamaran that runs cruises of up to 11 days around southeast Alaska. It carries 40 passengers. *Admiralty Dream* is a 143-foot single-hull vessel with 39 passenger staterooms it offers trips of up to seven days touring southeast Alaska. Their website, www.alaskandreamcruises.com, has an employment section that asks for contact information and why you would be a good fit for their company.

American Cruise Lines

The company runs six small cruise ships that carry between 49 and 140 passengers. The vessels navigate all of the usual American inland waters, such as along the East Coast, the Mississippi, and the Inside passage to Alaska. They run an authentic paddlewheel up and down the Mississippi River.

The company features a really good employment web page on their site. They offer 12-week contracts, included room and board (everyone does, but they mention it so I'll pass it along), training, and are very friendly to college students taking a semester off. Pay runs around $700 to $900 per week and no previous cruise ship experience required. Entry level positions include deckhand, galley steward, and room steward.

Applicants must be high school graduates and be able to pass a drug test. You can apply on line or download an application from the website and send it to:
American Cruise Lines, Inc.
Attn: Personnel Dept.   741 Boston Post Rd, Ste 200
Gilford, CT 06437

American Safari Cruises/InnerSea Discoveries

Both companies hire through the same source, the website careers@innerseadiscoveries.com. American Safari Cruises runs three small vessels: *Safari Quest, Safari Spirit,* and *Safari Explorer.* They range in length from 145 feet to 105 feet and carry 12 to 40 guests. Crew sizes range from 6 to 15. These small ships look more like yachts than cruise ships and travel to Alaska, British Columbia, and Mexico.

Innersea Discovery consists of two slightly larger cruising vessels, *Wilderness Discoverer* and *Wilderness Adventurer.* They run 169 and 156 feet in length, carry 24 and 20 crew each, with a total capacity of 76 and 60 souls. Both of these ships only cruise Alaska.

American-Flag Union Cruise Ships

There is only one; it works out of Honolulu. If it weren't for the Jones Act there wouldn't be any—remember the Jones Act states that only an American-flag ship can carry cargo between American ports and passengers are considered cargo. That's not much of a restriction in the Caribbean where a foreign port is usually only a few hours away; things are a little different in Hawai'i where the closest foreign port is half an ocean away. If you want to take a cruise in Hawai'i, you either have to join the ship in Canada or Mexico or you have to book the only union American-flag cruise ship sailing, *Pride of America.*

The pay aboard *Pride of America* is nothing to get excited about but it's a place to start. I knew someone once who worked aboard another Hawaiian cruise ship that has since gone out of business; he didn't make much money, but oh the girls, he kept talking about all the girls, he couldn't get over the girls. Apparently it was just one big party. If the ship hadn't gone under I'm sure he'd still be there, working for next to nothing if need be.

Since *Pride of America* is American-flagged, the sea time in the engine and deck department should be as wonderful as the girls, so there are two good reasons to ship out on *Pride of America.* Whether or not those reasons compensate for the pay rate is something you'll have to decide.

The jobs are filled by Seafarer's International Union, the biggest maritime union in the U.S. We will discuss SIU extensively later on because it is very likely where you'll begin your seagoing career. It may even be where you end up; that is entirely up to you.

Pride of America has about a dozen entry-level jobs in both the deck and engine departments: ordinary seaman and wiper, respectively. Base wage for an ordinary seaman is $2,300 a month for an 8-hour day and a 7-day week. The overtime rate is $12.00. Base wage for a wiper is $2,600 a month for an 8-hour day and a 7-day week. Ordinary seamen and wipers usually match their base rate in overtime each month.

Now do you see the union advantage? The pay is about 50 percent higher than on the non-union ships, and more than twice the pay of the foreign cruise ships for the same job.

So how do you sign up? Fly to Honolulu? Not so fast, back her down, Hot Rod. If you fly to Hawai'i, figure on sitting in the union hall for eight hours a day, five days a week, for one to six months. You can do better than that.

I do have a bit of good news, though: *Pride of America* is doing very well, apparently, booked up months in advance. There is talk about bringing another American-flag cruise ship to Hawai'i. I hope it happens. If it does, there are going to a lot of jobs to fill. A few years ago there were three American cruise ships sailing out of Honolulu, and things were nuts: I think I remember crewmembers being shanghaied out of sleazy Hotel Street bars, but I could be wrong. Even with just one additional ship the union will be scrambling to fill the jobs—something I would love to see.

Offshore Supply Boats

A number of different types of vessels are lumped into this category: platform supply vessels (PSV); anchor handing tug supply vessels (AHTS); inspection, maintenance, and repair vessels (IMR); and crew boats. They are all used to support the offshore drilling industry, and are used everywhere offshore rigs are working.

A platform supply vessel, along with submarines and fishing vessels, is always referred to as a boat, no matter how big it is; they usually run between 60 and 300 feet in length. They are designed to service oil rigs, delivering deck loads of dry cargo and liquids such as fuel, water, and drilling mud in their large internal tanks. They are also used for firefighting, crew rescue, oil spill clean-up, crew transportation, or anything else that may come up. Mostly, though, they deliver goods to rigs that may be a long way offshore.

Supply boats require a good deal of seamanship because they have to work in all weathers. The captain backs the boat up to the rig so a crane on the rig can drop its hook on the back deck. The AB hooks on the cargo and jumps clear as the cargo soars off of the back deck of the supply boat to the main deck of the rig; it's easy in calm weather, harder in bad weather.

Anchor handling tug supply vessels serve as extra capable platform supply vessels that work with semi-submerged drilling platforms that can be moved to different drilling locations. The tug first yanks up a dozen or so massive anchors out of the seabed that hold the rig in place. Then the vessel tows the rig to the new location and precisely drops each anchor, spotting the rig in the best drilling location.

Inspection, maintenance, and repair vessels tend to be bigger than the others, often over 300 feet in length. They tend older oil wells that are starting to slow down. Some of these vessels are fitted out with heliports, 100-ton cranes, remotely operated vessels, a gym, a hospital, and even a movie theater. They carry a crew of between 50 and 100 and probably have more in common with a naval repair ship than with most supply boats.

Crew boats are smaller vessels designed to carry as many as 150 passengers and a small amount of deck cargo throughout the oil patch at speeds of up to 27 knots. Occasionally they're used in harbors to run passengers from ship to shore and back again.

In the U.S. the center of the offshore supply boat universe is in the Gulf of Mexico—Louisiana, to be more precise. This is probably because Cajuns have made the supply boat industry their own. Many of them have been driving boats since childhood and might be the best boat handlers in the world. I didn't say they were the best boat handlers to *work* with in the world, I just said they were the best boat handlers.

Which brings me to my next point, what's it like working in the Gulf?

Well, it's a little bit like surfing in Santa Cruz. If you're local, it's tremendous. If you're not, it can be an adventure, and not necessarily in a good way. As a Yankee you may have to low-key it for a while before you prove yourself; but on the bright side, the food is great and the people fantastic, once they get to know you (if they like you).

Some people hate it and some people wind up married to a local gal; hunting ducks, gators, and deer every year; eating like a king every day, and talking with an unusual accent. Personally, I love it down there, even if I don't speak French. Anyone who can't have a good time in New Orleans should just suck a bullet and get it over with; it may be the best party city in America. The best music in the world, the food is nearly as good, 24-hour bars, drive-through Daiquiri stores, are you kidding me? I probably need to fly down there to do a little more research... Of course, I've still got that outstanding warrant... I better just keep typing.

The chief engineer of a vessel I was working on decided one evening to drive his rental car into New Orleans for a little rest and relaxation. After a very enjoyable evening during which he may have imbibed a drink or two more than was good for him, he decided to find his car and drive back to the ship. Unfortunately this proved problematic, and in the course of his search just outside of the French Quarter he was set upon by a pack of hookers who cleaned him out. They took his wallet, his keys, his gold bracelet, his watch, even his shoes. A bad night.

So what is the lesson of this sad little story? Sometimes it's cheaper just to cab it? Naah, you guys already know that. Never go out on the town by yourself? That's good, but there is a bigger lesson here.

He should never have mentioned the hookers to us. He should have said he was robbed by a truckload of angry rednecks or a posse of gangsters, with their guns all held sideways. We would have believed him, and he would have lived a much better life for months afterward.

I'm starting to feel really good about this book, this is valuable information I have seen nowhere else in print, I'm a regular humanitarian. Don't forget, robbed by a pack of hookers? Lie.

Each company sets up its crewing rotations a little differently. Crews usually sign on to live and work aboard for several weeks followed by several weeks of vacation. If the boats are working overseas the on-and-off periods will be much longer because the company has to fly you home after each crew change. Most likely you'll work a twelve-hour day, usually six hours on and six hours off.

Some supply boat companies run only a couple of boats. Tidewater

Marine is the biggest supply boat company in the world, with 350 boats. They service the oil patch all around the world. They have boats in the North Sea, the Middle East, Asia, South America, and Africa. The smaller companies are family-run businesses and the bigger companies tend to be far more corporate.

As with every faucet of the maritime industry, some companies are gold-plated and some are true bottom feeders. It is a lot easier to sign on with a top company once you have some experience, so keep your eyes open and jump to a top company when you get the opportunity. Many PSV companies have vessels working around the world, which can also be a factor.

> A good friend of mine was running a supply boat off of Brazil for a while. I asked him once what it was like working in Brazil.
> "It's really hard to stay married and run boats out of Brazil," he said with a sad sigh.
> But if you're not married . . . . Just saying.

Appendix 1 lists most of the American companies servicing the off-shore energy industry around the world. They seem to prefer being contacted by email and provide a job application on their websites. Read the websites carefully, because some of the companies set up their application system a little differently, allowing faxes or resumes as well as applications. Many of the sites specify the positions they're presently trying to fill; others solicit applications and then file them. Some companies will hire first-timers; others claim to consider only experienced seamen.

If you're wondering what a platform supply vessel or crew boat deck hand's job description consists of, I'll lay one on you.

> **You'll most likely spend a lot of time in the galley if the crew is too small to carry a cook, either cooking for crew and any passengers or cleaning. After every meal you'll wash dishes and galley work surfaces, then sweep and swab the galley deck at least once a day. Clean the reefer out at least once a trip. Keep a weather eye on the sink drain. Clean the overheads and bulkheads as needed, but at least once a week. Manage both the garbage collection and the roach population by any legal means necessary.**
>
> **You'll clean and maintain heads at all times. Clean mirrors, commodes, lavatories, shower stalls, and decks daily. Handle the**

soap and paper issues as needed. Clean bulkheads and overheads as needed, but at least weekly.

Clean and maintain crew's lounge and passenger quarters in an orderly condition; sweeping and swabbing daily. Garbage cans emptied daily.

Now we're outside, at last. Clean and maintain the deck and superstructure. Everything needs a wash-down at least weekly. The skipper will let you know when the wheelhouse windows need washing, but it will be frequently. Keep the hand rails grease-free and replace all burned-out light bulbs. Stow all cargo transfer gear such as hoses and cargo slings. Keep the decks free of debris and keep any rust chipped, primed, and painted. Make sure all water-tight doors are closed at sea and check that the firefighting equipment is in good shape and stowed properly.

When the captain is running the stern controls, stand by for orders. Help the passengers on and off the vessel, insuring they follow the lifejacket rules. Keep them seated while under way and show the safety video prior to each run. Make sure the baggage is stowed properly and each passenger has signed the passenger manifest. Assist with all cargo loading and discharging, hooking up and letting go of hoses and cargo slings.

Inspect, splice and stow mooring lines as needed. Perform engine room inspections when the engineer is sleeping. Man the lines during vessel tie-up and let-go and assist in the transfer of fuel and water. Maintain safety equipment by stenciling, greasing, and replacing worn equipment. Wipe up any oil or grease on deck, taking care to let none over the side.

Report any dangerous or unsafe conditions to the captain immediately. While in dry dock, paint, chip, scrape as ordered. Assist other crewmembers in their duties as needed while maintaining a pleasant and cheerful demeanor, at least on the outside.

At the crew change, turn over a clean vessel and brief the relieving deckhand on the condition of the vessel and any outstanding issues.

Just between you and me, a good deckhand has probably more to do with the smooth running of a vessel than the captain does, but keep that to yourself and don't ever worry about running out of things to do.

Ferry Boats

Ferry boats are cool for a number
of reasons. Very often you get to go
home every night and feed the cat.
That may not seem like a big deal
now, since you've never been to

Antarctica or West Africa, but it may be in a couple of decades. Some ferries,
such as the Alaskan ferries, make trips lasting for several days, but that's the exception rather than the rule and even they aren't gone for all that long. Another advantage is most ferry skippers and chief engineers start out as deckhands
or wipers and work their way up; it's a pretty straightforward ladder to the top.

You're definitely dealing with the public, which depending on your per-
sonality can be either a very good thing or a very bad thing. They don't pay as
well as most deep sea jobs but they aren't the lowest paying jobs around either.

Wages and benefits of ferry jobs vary considerably, depending on the
operators. Some operators pay their entry level crew not much over minimum wage. Other ferries provide state jobs that pay a generous wage and a
full slate of benefits. Ferry companies hire captains, chief engineers, mates,
designated duty engineers, deckhands, QMEDs, and wipers in varying
combinations. Some ferries use union labor, generally either Inland Boatman's Union (IBU); or Master, Mates, and Pilots; Inland (MMP, Inland.)
We will discuss the maritime unions further on.

The Washington State Ferries operate the largest ferry system in the
U.S. with 10 routes crisscrossing the Puget Sound and Straits of Juan de
Fuca. Some of the routes are short, with terminals in sight of each other,
while others are longer, such as the run from Seattle to Victoria.

The busiest ferry in America is the Staten Island Ferry in New York
City, shuttling between Manhattan and Staten Island. Other smaller ferries
work the Hudson River, carrying passengers from New Jersey and around
Manhattan Island—a nice way to beat the traffic.

Massachusetts has ferries servicing the islands of Martha's Vineyard
and Nantucket, which are not bridged to the mainland. Some of the ferries
run year round, others do not.

San Francisco Bay has a number of different ferry lines running from
Alameda, Vallejo, and Marin to San Francisco. Alcatraz and Angel Island can
only be reached by ferry.

There are ferries in thirty states and three territories of the United States, some of which will take you across a small river in five minutes, while others are transnational. Nationally, ferries carry 108 million passengers a year. About half of American ferries are privately owned. About a third are publicly owned and operated, while the rest are privately owned and publicly contracted. About 70 percent of ferries operate year round.

Some ferries are state-of-the-art hydrofoils that ride like wide body jets when under way, others are considerably lower tech.

> I once filled a relief job running a one-hundred-year-old ferry across the Sacramento River. It was a double-ender that never turned around; just went back and forth, one side of the river to the other. Its large wooden ship's wheel was placed sideways in the wheelhouse, where you had to turn left to go left one way and turn right to go left on the way back. I never really mastered the technique. It was the most difficult watercraft to pilot I've ever encountered.
>
> The five-knot downriver current made every landing an adventure. The terminals featured large wooden vertical pilings arranged in the shape of a funnel on each bank. I kept the power on until just before I crashed into the pilings and hoped for the best. Occasionally I'd turn left when I meant right and things would get ugly fast.
>
> I'm sure the residents of Frank's Tract were at least as happy as I was when the regular ferry skipper came back to work.

If you don't live on the coasts or a major waterway, ferries may be a real alternative. You can get your feet wet, work on some of the required paperwork, and decide if you like boats. Then, when you apply for something a little more deep sea, you'll have some experience to brag about. Unless the ferry passes through Canadian waters you won't need a BST endorsement on your STCW, only a Merchant Mariner's Credential (MMC). We will cover all of these acronyms in excruciating detail in the Government Paperwork section. The sea time should count, even if it's only a five-minute shuttle across a modest river.

Except for my semi-controlled crash landings and having to turn left when I wanted to go right half of the time, I enjoyed working on ferries. You get to know the locals and are an important part of the community. Every day something interesting seems to happen, and working on the water without having to leave the country is always a good deal, to my way of thinking.

Appendix 1 contains a list of most of the North American ferries. Many of the websites don't have job application pages but they do describe the routes and the vessels. Often there's only a single small ferry with only one deckhand, so job opportunities may be limited. Other ferry systems employ thousands and are hiring constantly.

If you live near one of these ferries, check it out—you may be surprised by the opportunities you find. If the ferry system has a nice website but no employment opportunity page, that's a solid indication that they hire through a union, which means you'll have to join a union before you can work on one of the vessels. Each union has different rules. Some unions will help you find a job, others expect you to find the job, but you may have to join the union before they'll even tell you which companies they contract with. Clearly, some unions are better than others.

Tugboats

Tugs are small, slow, strongly built, powerful work boats used for a number of different tasks. Ship assist tugs ma-
neuver large ships alongside or away from berths and help the larger vessels safely in and out of crowded harbors. If a ship breaks down or has insufficient horsepower to navigate safely in inland waters because of wind or tidal conditions a ship assist tug will be summoned. A ship assist tug is incredibly maneuverable, able to move astern as easily as forward—or even sideways. They're a kick to drive.

Ship assist tugs are a good place to start for anyone interested in working as a harbor pilot, probably the highest compensated members of the maritime industry. Ship assist tugs and pilots work together to safely move big ships in and out of busy harbors, and practical tug experience is quite helpful to a harbor pilot.

Escort tugs follow big ships in and out of the harbor, ready and able to assist in an emergency. They are required to have a crew of at least four up and working, so they tend to have larger crews, but minus an emergency they can be quite boring, just driving back and forth, waiting for something to go wrong. Many tugs do a combination of tasks: escort, ship assist, and local barge moves. That can make for an interesting day.

If a ship breaks down at sea, an ocean-going salvage tug will be called. Salvage work is a distinct and interesting category of the Merchant Marine that I find fascinating. Its laws and customs date back hundreds, if not thousands of years. Salvage is the rescue of any valuable item lost at sea, except people. The saving of life at sea is required by both the legal and moral laws of the sea and is not compensated. Pollution prevention under certain circumstances, such as the removal of fuel oil from a sunken ship, can be regarded as salvage, the value being the prevention of pollution rather than just the value of the recovered oil.

Salvage tugs make their living rescuing lost or endangered property, which could be ships, oil rigs, lost cargo, even pirate treasure. Salvage tugs tend to be large, seaworthy vessels capable of working offshore for weeks at a time. Salvage tug work isn't nearly as common as work aboard some of the other types of tugboats.

Pushing and pulling ships, barges, or other types of floating objects that need moving is another common tugboat task. Some tugs pull barges across oceans; others push dozens of barges at a time up and down America's rivers.

River and ocean tugs look and work completely different from each other. A river tug has a flat, pusher bow, low freeboard, and wouldn't survive for long in the rough seas of the open ocean. An ocean-going tug is heavily built, with a big, flared bow built to protect the wheelhouse windows from heavy seas. It can tie up alongside a barge or pull from ahead, but it can't push as securely as a river tug.

An ocean tug may take months (they're really slow, under 10 mph) to pull a barge from the East Coast to Africa and back, or a barge to Point Barrow, Alaska (on the top) and back. The barge is generally towed behind on a huge line, called a towing hauser. The line, which is taken in or let out as sea conditions change, acts as both a shock absorber and a tow line.

These tugs tend to be cramped and noisy but require real seamanship to operate. Tugboat sailors have to be pretty tough to make it.

There isn't much port time on an ocean-going tug. A barge is made up in port, towed out to sea, and several weeks later landfall is made. The barge is dropped off, fuel and food loaded, another barge made up, and the tug heads out to sea again.

Another type of ocean-going tug is a notch tug. Its bow is designed to fit into a mirror-image stern notch on a barge. This allows for efficient pushing and is easy to make up. Sometimes the size of a combined notched tug and barge approaches that of a moderate sized ship.

Similar in design is the integrated tug and barge, or ITB, a tug and barge system where the two units lock together so tightly that the Coast Guard considers it a ship. The two units can be detached—but carefully, as the tug is barely stable by itself.

Other tugboats are day jobs, moving loads around the local bays, rivers, and harbors. They tie up at night or when the job is finished, and everyone goes home until the next job or day. These can be good jobs, particularly with a good tugboat company. Some of the smaller, bottom-feeder tug companies feature low pay and filthy boats (take it from me.)

But these crummy little companies aren't completely useless, because they always have job openings and can be a good place to start. Get what you need from them and move on to something better. Other tug companies run both ocean and local towboats; you'll probably have to start on an ocean boat and work your way up to an inside boat.

Getting a tug boat job can be a challenge. The crews are smaller than ships: some day boats run with only a two-man crew. A lot of seamen prefer to stay close to home, which makes a tug berth very desirable, particularly at a good union company that may pay nearly as well as a deep sea job. However, an entry-level deckhand job may only pay $12 or $17 an hour, so jobs are going to open up as crew members move up. Tugs sometimes carry a single engineer, with the deckhands assisting him as they are needed; conversely, on other tugs the engineer works on deck as well.

If the tug company is non-union, visit the hiring manager, talk to him, and drop off a resume. Ask if they hire standby guys to do maintenance while the boats are not working—that can be a good place to start.

If the tug company is unionized, the union will usually have a casuals list. You'll have to join the union to get on the list, but once there the covered companies will call the names on the casuals list when they need someone to fill in. I would also suggest dropping by the company and meeting the dispatcher, so he can put a face with a name.

Remember to look at these brief assignments as an opportunity to earn a full-time job. Each one is an audition, so do you best, put your best foot forward. Learn as quickly as you can, help out as much as you possibly can, and soon you'll be a permanent employee, hopefully.

There are many different ways to allocate hours. Most companies pay by the hour, so it's important. Some work week on and week off, with only the odd hour or two off of the boat during the duty week. On other boats you may work five days on and three days off. With call-out boats the dispatcher gives out assignments the day before and the crew goes home at the end of the work day. At some companies you may only work 40 hours a week; at a busy company you may average 80 hours a week, it all depends.

> Years ago I asked an old tugboat skipper how to be successful on a tugboat. He thought for a minute and said, "There's only two rules to working on a tugboat. Rule one, you have to be on time. Rule two, you have to be sobe— No, wait, you just have to be on time."

I would encourage you to try to be sober as well, but be on time, for sure; sometimes tugboats can't wait. If you work hard, show an interest, and the skipper likes you he'll often show you how to handle a boat. At first he'll let you drive between jobs and slowly work you into the more challenging aspects of the job. With luck, by the time you're ready to sit for your license you'll be fairly comfortable driving a tugboat. If you have to bring doughnuts in the morning to make this happen, bring the damn doughnuts.

Typical Day on a Two-Man, Tug Day Boat

The vessel is scheduled to get under way at 0600; the deckhand/engineer shows up 30 minutes early to get everything started and online. He arrives carrying his lunch, flashlight, and pocket knife. He unlocks the boat, starts the generator, flips the breakers lighting the vessel. Next he starts the air compressor, checks the starting air pressure, checks the engine oil, and starts the main engine. He makes a careful engine room round as the engine warms up, checking temperatures and pressures, looking for fuel leaks. He checks the bilges, looking for flooding; he checks the shaft packing on the shafts leading to the propellers, looking for the correct drip every couple of seconds.

The captain has still not arrived, but the deckhand is moving fast. He dashes through the wheelhouse turning on electronics as he passes: radars, navigation lights, radios, steering motors, down sounders, autopilots, and any other required electronic devices. Prior to the captain's arrival he must have the coffee brewing or there will be hell to pay.

Right at 0600 the skipper shows up, drops into the captain's chair and asks if the coffee is ready yet. Fortunately it is.

"Hey, Billy, if we're all ready to go, grab a radio and start letting the lines go from the stern, forward. What channel is the Head Bangers Ball on?"

The deckhand dashes out on deck, slacks the lines, jumps down on the dock, and flips the lines aboard, radioing the captain as each line is tossed aboard.

The captain radioes the deckhand. "Ah, Billy, you want to come up here and relieve me once we get away from the dock? I need to hit the head and I think I left some doughnuts in the galley yesterday."

The deckhand races up to the wheelhouse to briefly take over steering.

The captain climbs back up to the wheelhouse. "Billy, after you clean the galley and head, how about degreasing the engine room floor boards? The port engineer is supposed to come down to the boat today, so make me look good."

So the deckhand cleans the galley, head, engine room on the trip across the bay. As he feels the boat slow down he climbs back up to the wheelhouse.

"OK, Billy, we're coming up behind the barge, take your radio with and secure the wires to the cleats on the barge stern. I'll bring them up tight from here. Then start letting the barge lines to the dock go, working from aft forward. Call me on the radio as you let each line go and be sure to throw the line back up on the barge. It looks unprofessional to leave them dragging in the water. Take your raingear, too; it's starting to rain pretty hard and I can't see over the barge. So once we get moving, stay up on the bow of the barge as lookout and call me if it looks like we're going to hit anything."

The tug is secured to the barge, the barge is let go from the dock, and as the rain pounds down, the tug and barge make their way slowly across the bay.

The radio squawks, "We're here, Billy; I'll put the barge alongside, make the spring line fast first, then run up and secure the headline, then the stern line. Hurry, we've got a call to dock the APL *Thailand*—oh, the coffee starting to run a little low too."

The barge is secured at its new berth. The tug lets go from the barge, wires secured, a new pot of coffee is made, and the tug races over to the container terminal.

The captain can see ahead now, without the barge blocking his view, so the deckhand can continue with his cleaning duties. When he hears the engines slow down, he darts out to the bow, where he grabs the heaving line lowered from the container ship. He pulls it aboard until he can grab the messenger line, ties the messenger line to the tug's tow line, and stands clear as the captain pays out the tow line on the reel until a crewmember on the container ship signals "All fast."

"Billy, you got an ax handy by the tow line? All the watertight doors closed? Ahhh, you're a good man."

While the tug is working, the deckhand has time to grab a quick bite. He could go up to the wheelhouse and watch as the captain executes the commands of the bay pilot on the ship. The captain might even let him get a little stick time. But he'll also probably spend the whole time bragging about the size of his stock portfolio, or how good-looking his new girlfriend is—it may not be worth it.

"Well, that's it, Billy, easy day. We're headed for home. Did you get all of the engine room floorboards degreased? Good, don't want the port engineer thinking we're not on top of things."

As soon as the tug is tied up securely, the captain grabs his briefcase and hops ashore. "Good job today, Billy. Make sure you check everything before you leave."

The deckhand retreats to the engine room, where he writes down another round of readings in the log. He checks the shaft packing again and the bilges. He secures the main engines, the start air valve, the air compressor, as well as all the breakers before securing the generator itself. He locks up the boat and climbs ashore with a tired smile, thinking, "Someday I'll be captain and life will be phat!"

Tankers

A tanker is a ship built to
carry liquids in bulk—
usually oil or one of its

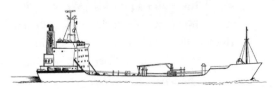

derivatives, though Guinness operates a fleet of beer tankers. The first tankers were built in the 1880s and have been evolving ever since. Just in the last few years all tankers have been required to have double hulls, which places the ballast tanks between the oil tanks and the sea, hopefully making the vessel more crash or grounding resistant. All the old single-hulled tankers have been replaced, vastly updating the tanker fleet.

Tankers are divided into three categories: crude carriers, product carriers, and beer carriers.* Crude carriers are huge ships, used to transport raw crude oil as it comes out of the ground. They often have large steam heaters in their tanks because crude sometimes takes on the consistency of molasses or tar when it cools sufficiently, making it difficult to pump.

Product carriers carry the many different products cracked out of crude oil, such as gas or lube oil. They feature multiple separate cargo systems on the same vessel so the different products don't contaminate each other: you don't want any gasoline mixed in with your heating oil. Chemical tankers are similar to product carriers, though even smaller with even more isolation between the different tanks. They often have a separate pumping system for each tank and special linings to resist corrosion. Some of the chemicals they carry, such as caustic soda and ammonia, are really nasty. Scare the heck out of me.

An under-way replenishment tanker is a very specialized vessel used to refuel naval ships at sea. They pass a hose over to a carrier or destroyer while steaming alongside. Once the hose is hooked up, various fuels can be quickly transferred, sometimes to a ship on each side of the tanker at the same time.

These ships used to be manned by the U.S. Navy, but no longer. The Navy determined it was cheaper to hire smaller, higher-paid civilian crews to run their non-combatant ships than to use Naval personnel. These ships are staffed by Military Sealift Command (MSC) and often travel with naval battle groups. Though civilian, they run a far more military-like system than most other civilian vessels. MSC makes up a huge part of the American merchant marine and we'll talk more about it later.

---

* I made up the part about beer tankers being their own category; they're just another small product carrier.

Ore-bulk-oil ships are designed to carry many different types of bulk cargo, both solid and liquid. This gives them a lot of flexibility as market conditions change.

> Once upon a time I worked on a non-bulk-oil tanker that after a thorough cleaning was loaded with grain bound for Pakistan. On the way home it picked up a load of oil in Indonesia. Unfortunately, the oil was loaded on top of grain sweepings that hadn't been properly cleaned out. The grain swelled in the oil and stuck together like chocolate Rice Krispy treats, clogging everything.
>
> For weeks during cargo operations I had to open up the cargo pump strainers every couple of hours and clean them out. Sounds pretty horrible, doesn't it? Nahh, it was great, I made so much overtime I bought a De Tomaso Pantera when I got home. Hopefully the ore-bulk-oil ships are easier to clean, though.

Floating production and storage units (FPSU) are a new development used more overseas than domestically. They're usually converted from unneeded supertankers and designed to anchor near a smaller offshore oil well, where they can either process the crude or store it until another tanker picks it up. It avoids the need for a pipeline, since when the well dries up the FPSU can be shifted to another location.

The world's fleet of 200 liquefied natural gas (LNG) tankers is expected to grow by 140 vessels over the next three years, which will double the world's LNG carrying capacity. Since 2002 there have been no American flag LNG tankers, but I think that is about to change.

These ships carry huge amounts of natural gas that has been chilled to a liquid. They are, in effect, huge floating bombs. There are only six LNG terminals in the U.S. and they are all quite aware of the considerable risks involved and so are their neighbors. These terminals would really prefer it if the LNG tanker crew members were vetted by the Coast Guard, but the Coast Guard only checks American seamen.

Some of these terminals are already planning to restrict foreign crews. They may start requiring American crewmembers on certain foreign flag LNG tankers or they may encourage new American flagged LNG tankers; either way, it's worth keeping an eye out. LNG tankers are very expensive, sophisticated ships that should pay well.

I worked on tankers, product and crude carriers for a while and never really liked it, probably because I wasn't very good at it. In fairness, many people have worked on tankers for their entire career and wouldn't consider sailing anywhere else. Tankers require special skills, especially for the bosun and chief mate. Once those skills are developed, they make the crewmember very valuable to the company.

There are both union and non-union tanker jobs. The oil industry has historically been anti-union, and it shows. There are a few tanker companies that employ union engineers and unlicensed personnel, but nothing like the dry cargo industry, which is far more unionized.

Tankers really came of age during WWII with the 16,500 ton T2 tanker. Thousands were built during the war, when they were considered to be quite large ships. I worked on one of the last survivors during the 1980s, the tanker *Suzanne*, but they're all gone now.

In the 1970s tanker sizes grew dramatically as the Suez Canal was closed after the 1973 Yom Kippur war and tankers had to round the southern tip of Africa to deliver to the U.S. and Europe from the Middle East. Some of the tankers were pushing 400,000 tons. Oddly enough, the huge ships began exploding spontaneously for no apparent reason. Some of the ships disappeared at sea without a trace; others came into port with most of their main deck peeled off. In time it was determined that an oil-tainted water droplet falling the height of an empty tank could generate enough of an electrical charge to arc and ignite the hydrocarbon-rich atmosphere in the dirty tank. Bummer. Tankers began venting their main engine exhaust gases into their cargo tanks to crowd out the oxygen and make combustion impossible; this is called an inert gas system.

The new closed systems where the cargo tanks are never open to the atmosphere except through a one-way high-pressure relief valve had another advantage. The crew now had to breathe far less carcinogenic hydrocarbons that had been killing off many tanker sailors.

When I began sailing in the early '80s, tanker chief mates often developed a nasty cancer by the time they turned 50. Thirty years of looking into the open tops of oil cargo tanks and breathing the gassy air will do that. I remember asking about it and being told to try and hold my breath. Research showed that benzene was the main culprit and we were told as long as we avoided concentration of 200 parts per million we should be fine. But tanker sailors kept getting sick and dying.

The data was rechecked and the word came down. Stay away from benzene concentrations of greater than 20 ppm and there's no risk. But again, crewmembers were still coming down with cancers.

The researchers went back, looked at the numbers again, and told us we now had to avoid 2 ppm and at that point I left the industry. Benzene contamination is cumulative and permanent. Once it enters your body it never goes away. Now, before you can work on a tanker you must have your benzene levels checked and if they're too high, find another line of work.

The closed system tankers are much safer to breathe on and explode fall less often than their predecessors, an improvement I heartily endorse. It's a lot safer to work on tankers now and they tend to pay pretty well at the good companies. When I worked tankers I sailed with a number of sailors who had done twenty years on Chevron tankers, earned their retirement, and moved on. One of Chevron's benefits was a stock purchase plan with company matching funds. Over the years the stock did very well and the prudent seamen who took full advantage of the program all wound up millionaires, a development I also heartily endorse.

Today working on tankers in the U.S. often involves loading crude oil in Valdez, Alaska and transporting it to the West Coast. American tankers deliver oil from overseas and move products and chemicals around the American coasts.

Tankers are big, powerful, steady ships that require highly trained crews to operate safely. They are usually crewed by highly trained specialists dedicated to their craft. If you get a chance to work on a tanker and enjoy the experience, I wish you well. The world needs good tanker crews as the potential damage from a mistake is incredible. I never quite got over the feeling that a single mistake could land me on the cover of *Time* magazine . . . . OK, so maybe I was a little paranoid, but tankers may be perfect for you.

I'll walk you through a typical day on a tanker, but remember there are a lot of different types of tankers and all of them do things a bit differently. We'll follow a large crude carrier picking up a load of crude oil in Valdez, Alaska for delivery to the refinery at Barbers Point, Hawaii.

Typical Day on a Tanker

The day begins in the early morning dark. The bridge watch, a deck officer, and two able-bodied seamen are standing watch together on the bridge. One AB serves as a lookout, watching for lights, either other ships or navigational aids or anything else out of the ordinary. He stands either outside on the bridge wing or quietly in the corner of the wheelhouse. The helmsman watches the compass and the autopilot and also looks for lights on the horizon. The captain and duty engineer have been notified prior to passing Cape Hinchinbrook, the entrance to Prince William Sound.

The bridge is kept as dark as possible to improve night vision, the glowing electronics the only light source. Radars show any approaching vessels and the nearby shoreline. The electronic chart system shows the vessel's progress down the track line and a picture of the surrounding land features, the same as a paper chart. The mate on watch is navigating the vessel, avoiding any potential collisions or groundings and carrying out a long list of required tasks and calls. The captain has left detailed orders on when he is to be called and where the ship should be at a given time to insure the vessel's timely arrival.

The three watch partners work together to keep the vessel safe. Lights are called out as they appear and are watched carefully until they recede. New course orders are given to the helmsman, who repeats them and carries them out either by turning the ship's wheel or dialing in the course on the autopilot.

Before long, the captain joins the bridge watch, where the mate gives him a rundown of vessel conditions and progress. He has a quiet cup of coffee while his eyes adjust to the darkness.

American ships follow a principle called bridge team management, where all the tasks required to safely deliver a ship to her berth are divided up among the bridge watch, the size of which expands and contracts as needed. Each member of the bridge watch has his assigned duties and also keeps an eye out for the other members of the team. This insures no one member of the team is overwhelmed and mistakes are quickly caught and rectified.

It's a cooperative effort at its best; I've seen helmsmen remind captains, "Captain, I'm still carrying ten degrees right rudder," and be thanked for their help.

I've seen a cadet point out to the helmsman last order was right five degrees rudder, but the rudder angle indicator is moving left. Cadets aren't usually thanked by anyone, for anything, but that was still a good catch. It is very satisfying to work as a part of a team of professionals where everyone knows their job; it's one of the most satisfying aspects of going to sea. A good helmsman or lookout is respected and appreciated.

In the engine room things are happening as well. Almost all merchant ships are diesel; steam turbines are just about gone, done in by the higher fuel efficiency of the diesels. Some of these diesel engines put out over 50,000 HP and don't slow down easily. As the RPMs drop, shaft generators are secured and diesel generators started. Heavy fuel is switched to a lighter marine diesel fuel. Compressed start air tanks are pressed up, batteries tested, and necessary members of the engine department are called out.

Once the harbor pilot is aboard, the pilot ladder stowed, the lookout moved to the bow, and the anchors made ready to drop in case of an emergency, the rest of the deck department is called out to tie up a tugboat on both ends of the tanker. The pilot conns the huge ship gently to the berth, issuing steering orders to the helmsman and engine orders to the mate on watch. As the tanker comes alongside her berth, pushed by the tugs on each end, heaving lines attached to mooring lines arc ashore. Half a dozen mooring lines are brought up tight on each end of the vessel and the tanker is secured.

As soon as the main engine is secured, the engine department will begin working on various types of engine maintenance that can only be done while the vessel is at rest, such as changing piston rings or replacing or repacking valves on the engine cylinders. There is always much to do in the engine room just to stay current on the preventive maintenance program.

A gangway is quickly landed by the deck crew, the pilot leaves, and a cargo surveyor comes aboard to check the cargo tanks. An empty oil tanker is never really empty—if it were, it would roll over or break in half. So when there is no oil on board, the tanker loads water, called ballast, to keep it seaworthy. If the water is stowed in cargo tanks it is dirty ballast and must be pumped ashore prior to loading oil. If the seawater is loaded into clean, segregated tanks it's called clean ballast and can often be pumped back to the sea.

The surveyor's job is to keep an eye on how much is loaded and discharged, keeping everything on the up and up. Without them the ship and terminal would apparently spend much of their time trying to cheat each other. In fairness, many millions of dollars are involved in a single load of oil and a small discrepancy can run into a lot of money.

As the surveyor is checking the ship's tanks, the crew is hooking up a flexible rig called a chick-san that bridges the gap between the terminal's piping system and the ship's piping system.

No oil can hit the water, really none whatsoever. A teaspoon of oil in the water in Valdez, Alaska is a problem. It could get cargo operations shut down and cause costs to the vessel to mount. The oil must be kept out of the water. It's not always easy, especially since it never seems to stop raining or snowing in Valdez and the rain water builds up and flows down the deck and into the harbor.

The ship's cargo system valves and pumps are controlled from the cargo control room, activated hydraulically by buttons and levers. The ship's officers will discharge the ballast and load the crude oil from the control room. They and ABs on watch will make frequent rounds of the deck and pumproom, to insure everything is working properly and no oil is spilled.

The ABs on watch keep a security watch at the gangway and carry a radio. If needed they can be called to help tend mooring lines, check for leaks, or anything else that may come up. Usually one AB is on deck while the other is taking a break in the galley, where he can be quickly reached. Whenever loading or discharging operations begin, everyone on watch will carefully walk the lineup looking for leaks. Once a flow is up to speed, things settle down a little. Some of the big tankers load at a rate of 100,000 barrels an hour. One barrel is 42 gallons. That's a lot of oil.

As the ballast is discharged and oil is loaded, cargo tanks are stripped out and finally topped off. The deck officers, usually the chief mate, will take care of that. As the vessel loads and discharges and the tides and winds change, the lines must be tended and the gangway tended or it will fall in the water or get crushed.

As the ship fills up, it's time to start thinking about getting under way. This usually seems to take place during meal times, so adjustments must be made and crew members called out.

Now everything happens in reverse. The cargo, once loaded, is checked by the surveyor. The pilot boards, the tugs appear, the lines are let go, and the ship heads for sea. Bligh Reef is dodged, the pilot dropped off, and the ship secured for sea. Say a prayer for good weather as you pass Hinchinbrook and you're on your way to Honolulu.

A tanker I once worked on lost its main engine just as it was departing Prince William Sound with a full load of crude oil in a massive storm. The huge seas and howling winds precluded any chance of a salvage tug arriving in time to render aid, even if one had been available. We were on our own.

Fortunately, the 110-knot winds blew the ship back down the long axis of Prince William Sound, which is really deep—except for Bligh Reef, as the *Exxon Valdez* once discovered. Hours passed as every member of the engine department worked frantically to restart the single main engine. Frantic distress calls had summoned a single ship assist tug from *Valdez*, who was standing by. Later we found out he had been forbidden by his company to leave port because the conditions were so dangerous. He came to our aid anyway and was later fired for his trouble.

As the tanker drifted down onto the rocks of Glacier Island, the captain finally told the third mate to call down to the engine room and tell them they had 30 minutes to get the engine started, or after that it wouldn't matter.

We never were able to get a line to the tug, but the engineers did manage to restart the engine with minutes to spare and maneuver clear of the island and an environmental catastrophe.

Tanker companies come in different shapes and forms. Some, such as Keystone Tankers or Crowley Marine, are oil tanker companies. Chevron operates four U.S. flagged, double hulled, product tankers; obviously, they're an oil company that also runs a few American tankers. After the *Exxon Valdez* fiasco most of the oil companies tried to hide their tanker ship ownership. Exxon Tankers became SeaRiver Marine and Conoco Phillips became Polar Tankers, Inc.

It's not always easy to establish who owns a particular tanker. Ships are required to post their ownership on the bridge. Sometimes it's simple, just the name of the company. With tankers it's often a full sheet of paper describing holding companies and other various legal entities, and after months of readings (bridge watches can get a little slow), ownership may still be unclear. This is because the liability of an oil spill is so great. Exxon spent billions on its Valdez spill; very few other companies have those kinds of resources. If something horrible happens, the lawyers will be as busy trying to blur responsibility as the oil recovery experts will be trying to clean up the oil.

Appendix 1 lists all of the American tankers and the companies that operate them. Some of these vessels are union, some non-union, and some a mix of union and non-union on the same tanker. If the vessel is non-union, then you need to contact the company directly. Their contact information is located at the end of the same appendix. If the vessel is union, then contact the union, obviously. These jobs tend to pay pretty well, for the most part.

Bulk Carriers

Similar to tankers in many ways are the bulk carriers. They look a lot like tankers, high out of the water when empty and low in the water when loaded, but the lack of a complicated on-deck piping system gives them away. They range in size from small to large but most are on the huge side. They're built to carry bulk loads such as grain, coal, scrape metal, cement, or various ores. They make up about 40 percent of the world's merchant fleet and are mostly owned by the Chinese, Japanese, or Greeks. Most of the American bulk carriers work on the fresh waters of the Great Lakes.

Some bulkers can load and unload themselves; others depend on shoreside equipment, such as conveyer belts or shovel buckets. They can be very interesting ships to work on because there is such a range of terminals. Some facilities are as modern and efficient as any in the world and are capable of loading nearly 20,000 tons of cargo an hour, loading a huge ship in around a day. In some Third World countries it's an entirely different story, where a load of give-away grain may take weeks to offload.

These can be dangerous ships to work aboard. In 1991 24 bulkers sank around the world and 154 seamen were lost. There are a number of cargo issues to consider. These ships require careful loading with no void spaces. If the cargo settles or the holds aren't filled completely, the bulk cargo can shift to the low side as the ship rolls, causing a list. This causes more cargo to shift downhill until the ship rolls over.

Condensation can accumulate at the bottom of a load, of, say, cement. A slippery mud forms, causing the cargo to really slide around. This problem is avoided by proper ventilation and keeping a close eye out for water accumulating in the holds. Condensation can cause another problem as well; if the moisture gets into an organic cargo such as coal or cotton, it can create heat until it spontaneously combusts, or bursts into flame for no obvious reason.

Because of all the sinkings, new safety of life at sea (SOLAS) rules came into effect in 1996 that make bulkers much safer than in the past. Since 2004 the largest bulk carriers are required to carry freefall lifeboats on the stern, specifically so the ship can be abandoned quickly should it start to break up—if that makes you feel any better.

Great Lakes Shipping

This brings us to a fascinating branch of the American Merchant Marine that many people aren't aware of. The American and Canadian interiors are linked to the rest of the world by the Great Lakes. Through a series of lakes, locks, and canals it is possible to sail from Duluth, Minnesota to the Atlantic Ocean on a large ship; that's a distance of over 2,300 nautical miles, the longest deep-draft inland waterway in the world. It's a fresh water industry that shuts down because of ice every January 15 and resumes again in early March. The ships are never out of sight of land for more than a couple of days, yet are some of the biggest in the world, reaching lengths of over 1,000 feet.

These ships, called Lakes bulk freighters or "Lakers," seem to last forever. Salt and warm water are the enemy of steel ships, so in the fresh waters of the Great Lakes they have an expected life span of about 50 years, double the span of a deep sea vessel. They range in size from 494 feet to 1,013 feet in length and operate with a crew of about 25. They're all diesel powered and make about 15 knots (a knot is about 10 percent faster than a mile per hour and means nautical mile per hour.)

The American Great Lake's fleet owes its survival to the Jones Act. Iron ore loaded in Wisconsin and shipped to Michigan must, by law, be shipped on American ships. Otherwise it would be cheaper to ship it on a Chinese ship, whose crew is paid a few hundred dollars a month each.

Keep in mind the Jones Act not only makes our jobs possible, it also insures that shipping on U.S. waters is governed by the world's highest safety and operational standards. The United States Coast Guard keeps a weather eye on every aspect of U.S. shipping, including ship maintenance and construction, and crew qualifications; foreign ships are also inspected but not to the extent that American ships are.

The Great Lakes U.S.-flag fleet numbers about 65 large ships and tug/barge units in the dry and liquid trades, with another 20 or so smaller tug/barge units working as tankers. In a single season the fleet moves over 115 million tons of cargo. There are no cargo subsidies for these operators; they compete with the railroads and short haul truckers for the business.

The steel industry built the Great Lakes fleet. Iron ore is shipped out of six ports on Lake Superior and sent to foundries throughout the northern Mid-West and Canada. Steel makers can stockpile only so much ore; consequently, the industry depends on Coast Guard ice breakers to keep the channels open early in the spring. Stone and coal are the other big cargos, with smaller amounts of cement, salt, and grain also being shipped on Lakers.

There are job openings available during the shipping season—usually "relief jobs" spelling the regular crew as they take vacation or are injured. There are also permanent jobs available as well, just not as many. Just as with the deep sea jobs, you must have an MMC to work on the Great Lakes. Since Canada shares about half of the Great Lakes with us, a STCW would be a good idea as well. There are 17 main Great Lakes shipping companies. All of their jobs are unionized, though with a great number of different organizations.

Unlicensed Jobs on the Great Lakes

Many of these companies contract with SIU for their unlicensed crew. For information call (810) 794-4988. The following companies are contracted with Steelworkers Local 5000, but hire unlicensed personnel directly:

Central Marine Logistics, Inc. (219) 922-2644
Great Lakes Fleet/Key Lakes, Inc. (800) 535-2321
The Interlake Steamship Company (800) 327-3855 ext. 1140
Liberty Steamship Company (a subsidiary of American Steamship Company) (800) 828-7230
Grand River Navigation Company is contracted with Masters, Mates and Pilots for both their unlicensed and licensed personnel, but hires directly. (440) 930-2024
Lake Michigan Carferry and Pere Marquette Shipping Co (231) 843-1509

Licensed Jobs on the Great Lakes

Most of the Great Lakes companies contract with American Maritime Officers to supply licensed officers. Individuals with a Deck or Engine license should call (800) 221-9395. Grand River Navigation Company is contracted with Masters, Mates and Pilots (MMP), but hires directly; Call (440) 930-0224. MMP can be reached at (216) 776-1667. Marine Engineer's Beneficial Association (MEBA) represents officers on Interlake Steamship vessels. MEBA's Lakes' agent can be reached at (216) 771-9830.

This hodge-podge of unions illustrates one of the major problems with the American Merchant Marine. How do you think all the different unions sign up different companies? They poach from each other. When a contract comes up at a company, all of the different unions race each other to offer the lowest rates to the company and lowest pay to the union members. Whoever offers the lowest pay and worst benefits wins the contract.

I know the name of this book is *The Big Bucks Guide to Shipping Out as a Merchant Seaman,* and going to sea still *is* a well-paid profession—it just isn't nearly as well paid as it used to be. In 1980, on my first union tanker, the

BT *San Diego*, I made about $10,000 a month. That was a lot of money back then; it was more than Harvard Law School graduates made on their first job out of school, it was more than the Major League minimum, and it was good money. Maybe even too good money. I remember my first year when my union voluntarily gave back a contracted-for raise. When is the last time you hear of that? And the union members didn't even object.

Then one union started undercutting the next union, which justified the next round of poaching until we arrive at where we are today, with hardly a wage gain in 30 years, with each contract signed at a lower rate than the previous one. A few years back Matson Navigation Company built some new ships and began negotiating with Masters, Mates, and Pilots, the union that had been supplying them with deck officers for nearly one hundred years. No problem, right? They demanded a 36 percent pay cut, telling MM&P they would sign with AMO if MM&P didn't agree to the wage cut.

Matson and MM&P finally settled on a 30 percent pay cut, and I haven't worked for Matson since. We are not overpaid anymore, though perhaps we were 30 years ago.

One of Matson's ships is called the *R.J. Pfeiffer*; named after a great man who built Matson into one of the best American shipping companies. He cared deeply for his seamen, and we cared for him. He refused to promote any deck or engineering officers who suffered from "likeability issues," which turned Matson into one of the coolest shipping companies on Earth to work for.

I remember that Captain Toma, another great man, the Master of the Matson *Lurline,* always blew the ship's whistle as the ship turned around at the foot of Aloha Tower at the end of every voyage. One day I asked him why. He told me, "R.J. lives in that penthouse. I'm just saying Hello."

Then Mr. Pfeiffer died, Matson cut our wages at the next contract negotiation, and everything changed.

I'm not saying Matson is a bad company now, it's not; it's just not a special company anymore, it's the same as everyone else. Too bad.

Container Ships

For thousands of years dry cargo was carefully stacked below deck, one piece at a time; it was a slow, intricate process that if done incorrectly could sink the ship if the cargo shifted in a storm. The work was done by large groups of longshoremen that could take weeks to complete. Ahhh, the golden days of sailing.

Those days are completely gone, save the odd government ship. Today dry cargo operations on a container ship take hours to complete, rather than days or weeks, to the point that it is difficult to find the time to shut down the main engine long enough to get all of the required maintenance done. In China it's not unusual to see six container cranes all working the same ship. That's six cranes moving 30 containers an hour; in 20 hours that 3600 moves, which is a pretty good-sized ship loaded and discharged in under a day. While the cargo is flying on and off, repairs have to be made, ballast adjusted, stability checked, stores loaded, inspectors dealt with, stowaways searched for, and so on. It makes for a busy day.

But I'm getting ahead of myself. Let's go back to the beginning of containerization and Malcom McLean, a true big thinker. This was back in the day, before American business mostly consisted of moving massive amounts of debt around while taking a rake-off, or manipulating ones and zeros in new and creative ways. Malcom McLean was a trucker who in 1956 decided to park 58 truck trailers on the deck of a modified T2 tanker named the *Ideal X* to see how efficiently they could be shipped from Newark to Houston. It must have worked out pretty well because it revolutionized shipping and it made Mr. McLean's company, SeaLand, one of the biggest shipping companies in the world.

Malcom McLean was an innovator for his entire career. In the early 1970s he built the fastest cargo ships ever seen. When even to this day a 23-knot container ship is considered very fast, his SL-7s could do 33 knots. He was going to revolutionize shipping again.

A few months after the first SL-7 was delivered, the oil embargo was declared and the price of bunker fuel skyrocketed. The SL-7s made their speed through sheer horsepower and not a single fuel-saving device had been designed into the vessels. They never made any money and were finally sold to the Navy, who loved their speed and didn't care about how much fuel they burned.

Having learned his lesson, Mr. McLean struck again in the 1980s. This time he built a class of huge ships that topped out at 18 knots and were very fuel efficient. Unfortunately, fuel prices were dropping as the ships were delivered. As the fuel prices dropped and dropped, no one wanted to ship their cargo on the slow ships, even at discounted rates. The big ships made a complete voyage around the world, nearly empty, until United States Lines went out of business in a few years. Even with all of the ups and downs, Mr. McLean continued to innovate over his entire life. He remains a hero of mine.

Containerization of cargo presents many advantages over the old palletized system. Not only does it vastly speed up the loading and unloading process, but it also eliminates most of the pilferage problem. Under the old "breakbulk" system, a remarkably high percentage of the cargo was stolen during cargo operations. As a cadet I can remember being cautioned by an old-school chief mate to never go down in the holds as they were being loaded in certain Third World ports. I remember one story where the mate did go down in the hold at the wrong time, in Indonesia, and was stabbed through his eye and hung up with a cargo hook for his trouble. I heard that story 35 years ago and I'm still not going down in the hold in Indonesia on a breakbulk cargo ship, ever.

Now, with sealed metal containers it's a lot harder to even know what's in a container. Except for dangerous and hazardous cargo or reefer cargo, none of the longshoremen or ship's crew knows what's in the container; it could be smart phones, or it could be empty paper bags.

To successfully rip off a container ship takes inside knowledge and it doesn't happen very often. Containers are now tracked so closely and container ships arrive on time so reliably that goods shipped to a factory or a Wal-Mart can be timed over a two-week voyage for an arrival with an accuracy of under a half an hour. But I have to tell you, the accuracy is a lot better in the summer, spring, and fall, than in the winter when the North Pacific weather just blows.

This efficiency reduces the need for holding large inventories and cuts costs. However, after a few bad mid-Pacific storms, the rice and toilet paper can thin out on the shelves in Honolulu. But a modern container ship is so large a single ship's arrival can do wonders to stock things up. The containers come off of the ship, are backed up to stores' loading docks, and the goods are rolled in, hanging on racks, already sized and tagged, right onto the showroom floor.

Over 90 percent of the world's non-bulk dry cargo arrives on container ships. These ships come in all sizes, from tiny to huge. They haul cargo all over the world, but the biggest container ship trade route is a virtually one-way trade from China to the U.S., with China to Europe not far behind. The U.S. military ships much of its cargo in containers to its bases all over the world on American ships.

Container ships require container terminals to operate. They need large blacktopped areas to store the containers that are loaded and unloaded. San Francisco was one of the biggest ports in the world prior to the advent of containerization, with wharfs built out over the water to handle the cargo. Once containerization came in, the terminals moved across the bay to Oakland as there was no room for a container terminal on the San Francisco waterfront.

A set of container cranes is also required, at about six million dollars per crane. These cranes feature a boom that is lowered in place over the ship once it's securely tied up. The crane operator sits in a cabin suspended under the boom and travels back and forth on a trolley, lining up over the container to be moved. The operator lowers the spreader from the bottom of the cabin to the container, where it is locked remotely to the top of the container. The container can now be quickly moved on or off of a ship. An average crane and driver can move about 25 containers an hour.

The biggest container ships in the world are owned by Maersk Line, a Danish company and the biggest container ship company in the world. Their biggest ships are 1,305 feet long and 185 feet wide and can carry 14,770 TEUs (a TEU stands for twenty foot container; most containers come in 20', 40' and 45' lengths, so a single 40' container is two TEUs).

That is a really big ship that brings with it big problems and opportunities. On the up side it can deliver much more cargo for the same crew costs as other smaller ships. The fuel cost per container is also lower on large ships than smaller ships. On the down side, what if there isn't enough cargo to fill the ship? It's better to have a full small ship than a half-empty big ship.

Then there are the terminal issues. As the ships get bigger so do the terminals; their berths need to be dredged out to 50 feet deep, or more. The container cranes require replacing with higher cranes with a longer reach to fit over the larger ships. The very biggest ships can only be accommodated at a few ports around the world, and they certainly can't pass through the Panama Canal, which can only service ships 110 feet wide and 1,052 feet long.

Most American ships are smaller, a size or two down. These American container ships compete with foreign-flag ships that pay their crews roughly nothing—not an easy thing to do. There are fairly small operational subsidies for some of these American ships, but other ships receive nothing.

There are no non-union container ships. If you want to ride one you'll have to join the SIU, SUP, or the MFOW. These are the unions that supply entry-level labor to the container ship companies. SIU supplies both engine and deck labor. SUP and MFOW service the same ships, with SUP handing the deck department and MFOW doing the same in the engine department. All stewards' department personnel are hired through SIU.

Which union to join? That's the question, isn't it? They all have their strong points and faults, just like humanity in general. First I would decide which department I was interested in. If it's the steward's department, you're done. If you want to work in the engine department you'll need to decide between two unions. Call them both up and see what they have to say. It's easier to get started with the SIU because they have an excellent training school at Piney Point, but over the long run you'll probably make more money with MFOW or SUP; so, that's not an easy choice.

Both the MFOW and SUP have no hiring halls on the East or Gulf coasts. If that's where you live the choice is much easier. On the West Coast I would suggest you visit halls from all the unions and see if one has a better vibe than the others. Spend the day, talk to seamen waiting for jobs. See how the union officials treat you. If they say there are no jobs for newbies and not to wait around, you have your answer. If a low-paying ship is crewing up, you may get lucky and have a shot at that first job, always the hardest one to get. I would suggest you talk to a number of seamen at the hall, hopefully in private, maybe at lunch, before you commit to a particular union. Ask them how long it took before they were able to make a good living shipping out. How often does a low-paying job come up? (Your best shot at getting that important first job.) Is there any standby work? (Lasts only a day or two, but better than nothing.)

A couple of points to remember: Seamen, with notable exceptions, are good guys, far more decent human beings than most bankers or brokers. They'll often give you the information you need to get started just to be helpful, rather than trying to take advantage of you. Sometimes the union officials are your best friend and will lead you through the process like a wise uncle; other times they'll just take your money, knowing there will never be a job available for you. Talk to the seamen; buy them a beer at lunch and it may be the best money you ever spend.

Go in with the understanding that you're not going to get a very good job on your first try. The best you can hope for is a job no one else wants; it will probably be low-paying, or it may be on a ship cursed with horrible officers, or it may be on a ship bound for a place no one wants to go. Take it, don't think twice.

This seems as logical as to not be worth mentioning. Yet I've seen new guys hesitate, as if something better may come along. It won't; just take the job. As soon as you've worked a union job your status improves and the next job is easier to get. You may also start your eligibility for union benefits, such as schools or insurance. The work duration requirements to receive benefits vary from union to union and benefit to benefit, so you'll need to nail that down in a discussion with a union official. Again, some of these guys are great, achieving near surrogate dad status; others are less so. Good luck. I hope they treat you right.

> Now I'm going to go off on a rant. A union job is a wonderful thing. It allows you to work when you want to, once you've achieved sufficient seniority. It usually pays more than an equivalent non-union job and if you get yourself in trouble the union will usually defend you with some really smart guys. Once you've worked your way into a solid position with the union you've worked your way in to a solid middle class lifestyle, something that seems harder and harder to do as I write this. Union jobs are beautiful things—some non-union jobs are as well, but I'm ranting about unions now.
>
> So, that's what the union does for us. What do we owe the union in return? What do we owe the company that supplies the job through the union? I think a lot. I've seen companies come and go; I've even seen unions disappear. I think seamen need to stay informed, vote for politicians who support their interests, and should try to contribute extra money to the union political funds as they are able, since, unfortunately, money translates

directly into political power in this day and age. We also need to keep a weather eye on our union leaders and hold them accountable. When they work for the membership, support them; when they work for themselves, vote them out.

Our most important contribution we can make to the union is how we conduct ourselves aboard ship. Contracts have been worked out over the years that are quite detailed. Learn the contracts and follow them.

Having said that, the contract can also be used as a weapon against the company if it is manipulated. I've seen seamen stall a job until the work slipped into overtime and a two-hour minimum plus a penalty meal hour. I've enjoyed long and convoluted arguments about how one class of work should be interpreted as another class of work and must be paid at a higher rate. It is in everyone's best interest if the contract is followed honestly and comprehensively. We don't want to kill the goose that laid the golden egg. It is in all of our best interests if we work to insure the company remains profitable; it's vital for job security. Help me keep these union companies happy, solvent, and in business, at least until my pension vests, and I'll be your friend forever.

Ro/ro's

Several cargo handling systems evolved around the same time to replace the age old "breakbulk" school of cargo stowage. Lighter aboard ships (LASH) carried big barges that could be offloaded into a harbor with the ship's cargo gear. The barges could then be delivered with the help of local tugs to any local berth. It's a slow, complicated system that has just about died off as container cranes have sprouted up around the world; container cranes cost about 24 million dollars for a group of four so it took a couple of decades.

Another system designed to overcome the lack of container cranes is the ro/ro system, meaning roll on and roll off. Cargo is driven or towed on and off the vessel. Ro/ro ships feature many linked decks like a floating parking garage with a huge ramp, usually located on the stern that is lowered to the dock as a bridge for wheeled cargo to be moved on and off the vessel.

Originally ro/ros tried to compete with straight container ships by loading containers still attached to their rolling chassis. The system just isn't efficient enough to compete as a transporter of containers, though it has survived and thrived delivering wheeled vehicles in certain niche markets. You can't deliver an army tank or a road grader in a container—they won't fit and they're too heavy for the cranes. Normally two passenger cars will fit in a single 40-foot container, but if a fleet of rental cars needs to be shipped, it's cheaper to drive them on a ro/ro.

Ro/ros can deliver just about any wheeled object, from huge cranes to trailers of circus animals, but some ro/ros have evolved into even more specialized vessels called pure car carriers (PCC) that take only passenger cars and pickup trucks.

PCCs are often chartered by car manufacturers to deliver their products all over the world. They are remarkably ugly ships—as sleek as any vessel afloat underwater, but shaped like a match box above the waterline. This allows them to store their entire load of up to 7,000 cars under deck, out of the weather.

Their construction allows for rapid loading and discharging due to wide open decks running from bow to stern with as few intervening watertight bulkheads (walls) as possible. The cars are driven aboard through large doors in the hull, not far above the waterline.

It is an excellent idea on a car carrier to make sure the big watertight doors are properly closed and secured before getting under way. If water is able to enter through an improperly secured door, the lack of those watertight bulkheads vastly increases the danger of a sinking, to the point of changing the acronym to roll on/roll over. These ships do occasionally capsize; as with all vessels, it takes eternal vigilance to keep floating, for going to sea is a deadly serious profession.

A number of American companies run ro/ros and pure car carriers—Central Gulf and Maersk are a couple of the big ones.

Military cargo lends itself to ro/ro ships. The military doesn't like to be limited to container terminals. A ro/ro can tie up to any dock it can reach, drop its ramp, and start discharging cargo. A Marine division utilizes thousands of vehicles, all of which can be transported on a single large ro/ro vessel. There are American preposition ships packed with military vehicles stashed all around the world near potential flash points, preloaded with all of the vehicles needed by a rapid response division.

In a pinch, an American ship, crewed by American civilian mariners, can be alongside a berth, offloading tanks, artillery, fuel tankers, bulldozers, and Humvees in under a week. The Marines are able to fly out from the U.S. and join the equipment as it comes ashore.

This ability to quickly project force around the world is unmatched by any other nation. It's a heck of a deterrent that has no doubt avoided bloodshed around the world. These ships are usually staffed by Military Sealift Command (MSC), which are civilians working for the Navy.

Breakbulk Vessels

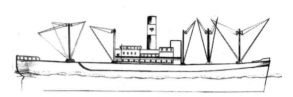

This is the last type of dry cargo vessel and there aren't many of them left. Except for a few stashed away by the government, the only American breakbulk freighters that I know of still working are operated by Coastal Transportation out of Seattle, Washington. These small freighters, ranging in length from 176 feet to 237 feet, service many of the small coastal communities of Alaska, such as Chignik, False Pass, St. Paul, or Adak.

This is a non-union company and these are old-school jobs. The weather is usually bad, the hours usually long. Most of the crew, except the cook and the chief engineer, work cargo, which includes running the crane and stacking heavy blocks of frozen fish in the freezer hold, some packages of which weigh up to 100 pounds. It makes for a long day. The work on these small freighters isn't much easier than on the fishing boats that offload to them. To be successful working on a small Alaskan breakbulker you need to be young and tough.

> I had a friend who used to work on these vessels as a mate. On his vacation time the ship would drop him off on an uninhabited Aleutian Island alone, with a backpack and a rifle. Two weeks later he'd get picked up again. Last I heard the Kodiak bears still hadn't managed to eat him yet. These ships attract tough, adventurous people who are a match for most any Alaskan commercial fisherman. If you want to test yourself, this is one place to do it.

Coastal Transportation has a nice website at www.coastaltransportation.com. It has all the information you need to apply for a job. Look under "Company" and then "Jobs". The pay starts at $185 a day and goes up from there. You don't even need an MMC to work as a deckhand, wiper, or cook on these ships.

The website has downloads for job applications and a background check authorization. There's a good description of the work on the website, as well. I used to offload to these small freighters when I fished in Alaska and I found much to admire in their crews. There used to be a number of small non-union freighter companies servicing coastal Alaska; I think this is the last one remaining.

I can't find any other small freighter companies, though I'm pretty sure there must be more. If you run across another one, give me a heads-up and I'll send you the new corrected edition of this book.

Military Sealift Command

MSC is one of the single biggest employers of American civilian mariners. It operates about 110 noncombatant, civilian-crewed ships that replenish U.S. Navy ships, conduct special missions, and strategically preposition combat cargo at sea around the world. In the event of a war, over 90 percent of the required war fighting equipment will come by sea.

Out of WWII came the Military Sea Transportation Service, a government organization responsible for military transportation around the world. During the Viet Nam war it was renamed MSC and came of age. MSC transported over 50 million tons of combat supplies and almost 8 million tons of fuel to Viet Nam between 1965 and 1969. That was also the last war that American troop's rode ships to war; today there are no troop ships left.

After the Viet Nam war MSC was a player in the Cold War, spying on Soviet missile launches and continuing to support American naval battle groups. Under-way replenishment was developed to a high art as nuclear ships bypassed the need for fueling more than every couple of years. Their aircraft still needed aviation gas and their crews still needed beans. MSC supply ships allow the Navy to keep its fighting ships at sea for months at a time.

During Desert Storm, the first Gulf war, MSC proved itself to be the world's largest and most effective military transporter, with over 230 ships.

It successfully delivered over 12 million tons of armored vehicles, helicopters, ammo, fuel, and other supplies to the theater. It was a good time to advance in the industry; they were just about knocking on doors to find ship's crews. But it wasn't as bad as during the Viet Nam War, when local judges were giving convicted criminals the choice between jail time and shipping out on a merchant ship bound for Viet Nam. The Gulf War was too short for that.

The September 11, 2001 attack galvanized MSC, which again moved millions and millions of tons of military supplies, equipment, and fuel in support of the wars in Afghanistan and Iraq. This sealift function is ongoing and carried out by a number of different types of vessels all around the world. Two chartered tankers, the MT *Empire State* and the MT *Evergreen State,* carry almost all of Department of Defense fuel from commercial refineries to storage and distribution facilities worldwide.

Much military dry cargo moves by container on commercial container ships, but if the cargo won't fit in containers it moves by MSC's ro/ro ships. Most of these are large, medium-speed, roll-on/roll-off ships (LMSRs); they are government owned and contractor operated. They can make up to 24 knots and carry all of the equipment of an armored battalion of 1,000 soldiers.

LSMRs are perfect for carrying armored vehicles and other rolling military cargo. Each ship has a stern ramp and a movable side ramp that can be deployed either to port or starboard. The ramp weighs 80 tons and requires a fair bit of seamanship to rig. Interior ramps allow access to all of the ship's cargo decks. Some of the decks can be raised or lowered hydraulically to allow for different-sized vehicles. Two big deck cranes allow for cargo movements to the dock or to a barge on the offshore side. These big, capable ships are normally kept secured to a dock on reduced operating status with a skeleton crew. They can be crewed up and ready to move in as little as four days.

The U.S. Ready Reserve Force (RRF) consists of 48 ships that can be activated as needed. Many of these ships keep a nine-man crew and are activated for a couple of weeks a year with a full crew to test their readiness. The RRF consists of fast sealift ships, more ro/ro's, LASH ships, heavy lift ships, crane ships, and tankers. The program is quite cost effective with ships laying up when they're not needed and upgrading to full operating status as they are needed.

We've already briefly discussed MSC's Prepositioning Program. It consists of 30 ships preloaded with military equipment and supplies in key ocean areas. These ships can be used during natural disasters for humanitarian purposes, but their main purpose is to supply the Army, Navy, Air Force, Marine Corps, and Defense Logistics Agency in case of war.

These ships have similar layouts and capabilities as the sealift ships and are able to discharge their cargo quickly, even with minimal port facilities. Prepositioned ships are a combination of government owned, chartered U.S. flagged ships and vessels activated from the Maritime Administration's Ready Reserve Force. All of the prepositioned ships are crewed by American civilian mariners working for private companies.

These Maritime Prepositioning Ships are divided into three squadrons located in the Mediterranean Sea and Eastern Atlantic Ocean, Diego Garcia in the Indian Ocean, and the Western Pacific Rim. The ships move about a bit, sailing from one friendly port in their area to the next. The Diego Garcia ships spend most of their time anchored or moored in the Diego Garcia lagoon, with occasional brief training cruises to some of the surrounding islands.

I did a contract on a Maritime Prepositioned Ship anchored in the middle of the Indian Ocean at Diego Garcia. The money wasn't very good, less than $10,000 a month for a Second Mates job, but it was my first job in the union and it got me enough union seatime to qualify for the union schools I needed to attend to qualify for the big money ships.

Diego Garcia was a kick. I shot a round of golf and a round of trap almost every day. I stood the midnight-to-eight watch every night, which left me all day to entertain myself. A half day of big game fishing for tuna, dorado, and occasionally marlin cost $50, which I split with a buddy about once a week. There was a softball league, dart and pool tournaments, snorkeling, the biggest gym I've ever seen. Even walking down the beach picking up shells was a trip as each little cove produced a different type of shell. Beer cost less than a dollar, which made it too easy to drink too much. Most seamen on the island became either sportsmen or drunks.

The ship was anchored out in the lagoon, so I'd take the launch in at noon every day after a short nap. If I was still tired I'd take another short rest in a coconut grove, usually under a picnic table to protect me from the coconuts the size of bowling balls dropping out of the trees whenever the wind came up.

I haven't been back to Diego Garcia since—the money just wasn't good enough—but I learned how to golf a little and I still have the skeet shooting trophy I won. It was a good time; maybe I'll do it again someday.

There are 26 Special Mission Program ships from the Navy; they carry out an impressive number of functions for the American government. These ships conduct oceanographic, hydrographic and acoustic surveys, underwater surveillance, missile tracking, command and control, and submarine and special warfare support.

Most of the special mission ships are crewed by civilian mariners working for private companies contracted to MSC. Some of these ships require secret and top secret clearances and are probably up to all kinds of sneaky activities. MSC is steadily taking over more and more axillary ships. Some of these ships operate with a hybrid crew of both civilian and military sailors under the command of a Navy captain. The civilians handle the navigation, deck, engineering, laundry, and galley, while the military crew handles communications, weapons, and security. Submarine Tenders and the command ship USS *Mount Whitney* operate under this new system.

Civilian mariners make a much better wage than their military counterparts, but civilians are trained to do more with less and can run a ship with a much smaller crew than the Navy can. Civilian crewing is cheaper than naval crewing, making for lower operating costs. This may be a continuing trend as the Navy continues to turn over noncombatant ships and functions to the higher paid, but in the long run cheaper, civilians.

The Naval Fleet Auxiliary Force (NFAF) consists of 42 ships that are the supply lines to U.S. Navy ships at sea. These ships provide everything Navy ships need, including food, fuel, spare parts, mail, nuclear bombs, and other supplies. NFAF also conducts salvage, rescue, and towing operations or serves as floating hospitals. All NFAF ships are government-owned and crewed by civil service mariners. Making up the NFAF are fifteen fleet replenishment oilers, one ammunition ship, four fast combat support ships, eleven dry cargo/ammunition ships, four Fleet Ocean Tugs, four Rescue and Salvage ships, and two Hospital ships.

There are two ways to find work on an MSC ship. One way is to join a union—either SIU, SUP, or MFOW—and ship out on a vessel contracted to MSC. But that's not what we're talking about here. That's a union career, not an MSC career.

MSC also hires civil service mariners, called CIVMAR, federal government employees who pursue a civil service career while working aboard government-owned MSC ships. I know what you're thinking: which is better? I know what you don't want to hear: it depends. They both have advantages and disadvantages:

The union will give you a lot more freedom, allowing you to pick your ships and how often you want to work. But it will be tough for a few years; you may give up before you can work enough to support yourself.

Once MSC hires you, you're on your way; you get paid from the beginning, every month. But you have very little control over which ship you work on or how much time off you get.

Which is better? That's up to you.

The web site www.sealiftcommand.com describes how to hire on with MSC. As with any sea-going job, you will need a MMC and a TWIC card. Next you fill out an information request form (IRF). This starts the process and an application will be sent to you. MSC only accepts applications for current vacancies, which can be found on the "Now Hiring" page of their web site or by calling (866) JOBS-MSC.

One cautionary note: It's going to be tough to get hired by MSC if your finances are a mess. If you owe a lot of money and you can't pay your debts or haven't been filing tax returns, you won't qualify for a security clearance or a job. Civil Service Mariners need to get at least a secret security clearance to get hired. Get your bills under control before you apply and be sure to answer every question on the IRF, the personnel security questionnaire, and your application accurately. The FBI does the security clearance investigation and they're pretty good.

I've heard a lot of different opinions on working for MSC over the years, some good, some bad. I worked for them a long time ago and I liked it for the most part, but I was young and single. Here's the deal: MSC wants you to sail a lot, like about ten or eleven months out of the year. The money is not bad and you'll get plenty of seatime, probably more than you want. You just don't get much vacation, only about a month per year.

There are ways to mitigate this problem a bit—leave without pay, family emergencies, or attending various training schools. MSC will send you to a lot of schools ashore: firefighting, damage control, small arms, helicopter landing, or any one of a bunch of different schools. That gets you some extra time off of the ships, but unless the school is located in your neighborhood you still won't be home.

Fortunately, it's not quite as bad as it sounds, since many of MSC's ships spend more time tied up to the dock or anchored than they do at sea. I worked on an MSC research ship out of San Diego where many of the crew members hadn't taken a vacation in years. They lived in San Diego, were home almost every night, and were making a tasty living. I'm not saying it always works out like that, only that sometimes it does. Often the ship's schedule can be predicted by reading the New York Times; a natural disaster or an international incident can change everything. With MSC you often get to watch history close up.

Make the call. MSC is a good place to start, they have openings regularly, you'll get a lot of seatime, you'll make good money, and MSC will pay for a lot of your training. You'll see a lot of the world too, with MSC.

Research Ships

My first job was on a research ship. I didn't know anything and yet I didn't get fired so they must be a  good place to start, right? Some research vessels are run by supply boat companies, doing private research for the oil companies looking for more offshore oil. We won't talk about them here because they're really closer to a supply boat and probably are run by a supply boat crew with a supercargo (passengers on a non-passenger vessel) to run the sonic array and recording equipment.

Other research ships are run by schools. There are 21 research vessels located at 16 operating institutions in the University-National Oceanographic Laboratory System. These university-run vessels tend to be non-union, low paying, and fun. They have a completely different "vibe" than a typical merchant ship. The crews tend to be young, literate, and smart, which is probably why I don't work on them anymore.

Usually about half of the crew is responsible for running the vessel and helping the scientists as needed, and the other half are the scientists making an annual trip. On some vessels the science party changes every trip, while on others they hardly ever change. I've been on ships where one of the biggest days of the trip occurs in port when the new group of scientists boards the vessel and most of the crew finds an excuse to lean against the rail and evaluate the young lady scientists as they board the vessel. Of course, I find that demeaning, sexist, and I would never do that—at least I wouldn't where anyone could see me. Some seamen enjoy the academic feel, others don't; it's a matter of personal preference.

These ships are not a bad place to start. They're often half female, which has an enormously civilizing effect on the rest of the crew, who suddenly begin bathing regularly and communicating with far less profanity—or at least it had that effect on me.

The silver lining to low paying jobs is they tend to have frequent openings. My very first job out of school was on a research ship working in Alaska. I learned a ton, got four months of seatime, and made what I thought at the time was a pretty good wage.

> On my first research ship my room was right at the head of the ladder (stairs) over the steward's department berthing areas. It was like living backstage at a Grateful Dead concert; I got a contact high nightly and never left my room.
>
> I never complained because they were so good. When you walk by the galley and see the chief cook toasting the Baked Alaska with a cutting torch, you know you've got something. They would serve a raw bar with shellfish on the half shell on a bed of ice for no particular reason. And I'm going to complain about a little pot smoke?
>
> OK, it was a whole lot of smoke, but I still didn't say anything. On one trip the chief steward ordered three full prime ribs, and then he scratched it out and wrote four full prime ribs.

They read it wrong in the office and sent the ship thirty-four full prime ribs for a month-long voyage in the Gulf of Alaska. We were awash in prime rib, which was quickly traded for fresh salmon, king crab, halibut, and probably a few other things. That was the best I've ever eaten in my life.

I've worked on a few research vessels since, and they have all been fantastic feeders. Maybe I've just been lucky, though.

The best and the worst part of working on a research vessel are the scientists. Some of them are great—excited about what they're doing, very professional, and about as bright as a human can be. Others are awful—smart but barely able to navigate their way from the bow to the stern without a guide. Some of them believe anyone who doesn't have a doctorate isn't qualified to tie a bowline. So it can be a challenge to work with the scientific party, especially after you've been to sea for a while. But if you try to keep an open mind and try not to judge scientists too harshly it can be a delight.

A long time ago, when all I had was a new third mate's license, I was working aboard a moderately-sized research vessel doing gravity survey work (gravity varies slightly all over the planet, which is a fairly important variable to know when programing intercontinental ballistic missiles) between Cuba and Florida. We ran back and forth from 20 miles offshore to as close to the beach as we were able. We then moved a mile north and did it again, for weeks at a time, while the machines recorded the data.

One night the new, young, ambitious chief scientist stopped by the bridge to tell me that he wanted us to get as close to the beach as possible. "In fact," he said, "keep coming in until we touch bottom."

He noticed that both my AB and I were staring at him like his head had just fallen off. "Oh, don't worry, it's a soft bottom and if anything goes wrong I'll just tell everyone it's my responsibility."

"I'd like you to leave the bridge now. Right outside the door is a license rack. If you take my license out and put yours in, I'll be glad to run the ship aground. If that doesn't work for you, the captain's stateroom is one deck down. Tell him I refused to ground the vessel. If he relieves me, you guys can park the ship wherever you want."

Sometimes you have to protect the scientists from themselves. Today I'd probably do it a little more gently, but I'm still not grounding any ships, on purpose or by accident.

These little university research vessels are non-union and usually hire through the university. Normally they try to maintain one permanent full crew but are always scrambling for relief crew members for whenever the permanent guys want to take some time off, which is perfect for our purposes.

The entry level positions are, as always: steward utility, wiper, and ordinary seaman. They usually work at least a 56-hour week with everything over 40 hours a week overtime; the monthly gross should work out to about $3,500, if all goes well. These details are fairly standard but not set in stone, so before taking the job, discuss the usual issues such as: pay, OT rate and expected number of hours, contract length, vacation days earned per month worked, who pays travel costs, health insurance coverage.

I would caution you, the research fleet is fairly tight. Don't blow it; if you can earn a lot of warm, fuzzy, positive feedback it will make finding the next job much easier. You may even get a panicky phone call at home begging you to race to the airport where a ticket to Bora Bora is waiting for you issued by a university you've never even heard of, let alone worked for. When research ship crewing managers get stuck, they start calling each other, so one good relief job usually leads to another.

No union, right? If the captain asks you to stay for an extra trip, do it. Hide your true feelings and convince the scientific party that you like all the scientists, not just the female college students.

A smile, a good morning, and a willingness to always help out goes a long way. You want the HR ladies to think of you with a smile. Be nice to them, even when they drop the ball—actually, especially when they drop the ball; they'll make it up to you. Get your seatime, your endorsements, and when you think you can do better move on. But you may think back on your research vessel days as the most fun you ever had afloat.

My very first job out of school was on a small research vessel working in the Bering and Chuckchi Sea. I did four months aboard the S.P. *Lee* and decided it was time to go home. The *Lee* was headed home in a few weeks and the company didn't want to send up a relief for just a couple of weeks.

Well, I whined more than I should have. I think I even threatened to quit. Bonehead.

I stayed, but I could have agreed to the inevitable with considerably more grace. I learned from my mistake, and I hope you do too.

The National Oceanic Atmospheric Administration (NOAA) runs an odd little assortment of hydrographic survey, oceanographic research, and fisheries research vessels. NOAA is a little-known governmental uniformed service similar to the Coast Guard or the Army. They operate small research ships all around the world. At one time all of the ships were run by NOAA officers who sort of acted as if they were military officers—except that NOAA isn't the military.

I've sailed with a lot of ex-NOAA seamen, and I've listened to a lot of NOAA sea stories. Think a combination of *Mutiny on the Bounty* and *The Caine Mutiny Trial*.

(Check out *The Caine Mutiny Trial* if you get a chance—excellent old movie. Humphrey Bogart demanding, "Who took the strawberries?" while manipulating his steel ball bearings, Fred MacMurray as a sneaky backstabber; just a tremendous flick. *Mutiny on the Bounty* is good because you just might end up at Tahiti or Pitcairn Island, and *The Caine Mutiny Trial* is appropriate because NOAA's ships are small and some of the officers might be a little shaky.)

To be fair, I've never worked on a NOAA ship myself, and all of my information is secondhand, but I sure enjoyed the stories.

Presently NOAA is starting to hire regular U.S. Coast Guard licensed officers to run their ships in combination with their regular NOAA officers, so no doubt things are improving.

I would consider taking a job at NOAA to start. They have nine ships on the East Coast and nine ships on the West Coast. As with all research ships, the money isn't great, you won't get any union sea time, but it will be an adventure and give you a chance to get your feet wet. Perhaps you'll spend your entire career there, get a license, and wind up as captain or chief engineer, you never know.

To check out NOAA jobs go to www.USAJobs.gov, a federal government website. Click on Advanced Search, in the Series Number Search enter "99", in Agency Search enter "Department of Commerce". In the Then sub-agency box enter "National Oceanic and Atmospheric Administration. Hit "Add" and "Search Jobs".

As I write this NOAA is looking for able seamen, oilers, and second cooks with a salary range from $36,193 to $39,975. These jobs are not entry level, but they're only one rung up. The AB position requires an AB Special (the lowest one). The oiler position requires an USCG endorsement of QMED, oiler or above (also the next step), and the second cook requires a Food Protection Manager Certificate. All require an MMC, a TWIC, and an ability to pass a physical and a drug test.

The entry level position on these ships is listed as general vessel assistants in all three departments and pays a little over $30,000 a year. (I took a peek at the top captain's pay too: $177,113.) There is a pretty good turnover in the entry level positions as crew members gain seatime, so the website is advertising for them about half of the time. You must have an MMC and a TWIC to apply. If you qualify you will be given a tentative agreement and sent out to see a doctor and pass a drug test. If you pass everything you'll be offered a job on a ship where you're needed and you're on your way.

Once you're hired you'll have to join SIU, which isn't a bad thing because you'll have a permanent job without sitting in a hiring hall, potentially for months. Your time will also count as union time, so should you decide to make a move to another SIU vessel, you'll already have some seniority. You'll also be paying union dues, but that's just the way it goes.

Appendix 1 lists the contact numbers for most of the research vessels around the country. Though this list is not exhaustive, it should get you started.

Dredges

There are dredges working all over the country at different tasks. They are used to deepen channels to keep existing facilities functional as ships keep getting bigger. Then they have to keep the channels from silting up—a job, like cutting the grass, that is never really finished. Maintenance dredging, the most common type of dredging, occurs in most harbors, nearly all of the time. It's often done by the Army Corps of Engineering, but private companies also do some of the nation's dredging.

The first step on a large harbor construction project is often to dredge some of the mud before the foundation work commences. Sometimes the harbor bottom is mined for construction materials such as sand or gravel, usually for a concrete pour. The last oyster in San Francisco Bay died a long time ago, but the southern part of the bay is still covered with at least a hundred-year supply of crushed oyster shells that are dredged and sold for plant and chicken food.

Some dredges are self-contained small ships, others are on barges moved around by tugboat. The job is about the same either way, but the seatime might be granted in a different category. There are hundreds of small dredging companies that barely use boats at all; some actually do their work from the bank.

The contact numbers for the larger dredging companies are located in Appendix 1. If you live nearby it might be worth getting in touch with them, because even a modestly paying job might be valuable if you earn enough seatime for an AB's ticket.

Army Corps of Engineering

The Corps performs maintenance dredging with its own four hopper dredges and contracts for maintenance dredging with 15 privately owned hopper dredges. These vessels are operated by civilians, not military personal. The Corps also maintains another eight dredges that aren't being used. They used to run a lot more dredges, but pressure from private industry has encouraged the federal government to privatize most of its dredging work. If you can hire on, being a civil service mariner is a good thing, with good money, good benefits, and security. As with NOAA and MSC, the jobs for Army Corps of Engineering are posted on www.USAJobs.gov .

The bad news about the government jobs website is that all of the various federal government agencies don't use it exactly in the same way; for instance, the entry level position at the Army Corps of Engineers is called a deckhand, but over at MSC the position is called an ordinary seaman. So it can be a little tricky to use, but if you keep grinding on it you'll get the hang of it.

It is an immensely powerful website. I typed in Deckhand into title search in the Advanced Search mode and BOOM, came the response:

Deckhand job in the National Parks Service in Seward, Alaska at $27.50 an hour. It's only a seasonal job, but it's in one of the most beautiful spots on earth with excellent cash and great benefits. I had no idea the National Park Service even offered deckhand jobs. Who knew? You just have to know how to use the site and you'll be way ahead of the game.

Here's how to make it work for you. First step, you have to submit your resume into the USAJobs.gov website. But it's not as simple as that; you will need to customize your resume to fit the job description. You're not trying to blow smoke up someone's backside, you're just trying to get the automated system's computer to pick your resume out of the pile. So the first step is to find the job that you want and that you believe you might be qualified for.

Let's look for a deckhand's job at the Army Corps of Engineers.

Go to www.USAJobs.gov
1.   Go to Advance Search
2.   Title Search "Deckhand"
3.   Agency Search "Department of Defense-Department of the Army"
4.   Then Sub agency "U.S. Army Corps of Engineers"
5.   Add
6.   Search Jobs

If the Army Corps has any deckhand openings they'll come up. If you want to check all of the U.S. Army Corps of Engineers jobs, just in case you got the title wrong delete "Deckhand" and start over. You'll have to reenter everything except Deckhand, but you'll get a list of all the Army Corps jobs.

Now suppose you want to check on any federal government deckhand job in the country. This time only enter "Deckhand" in the Title box and hit Search Jobs. There's that cool National Parks Deckhand job.

I want this job. This is where the customized resume comes in; I'm going to get this job. So on the Search Results page hit Quick View; then hit View Job. Up will come a nicely written overview of the job. It tells you the closing date, housing costs, lifestyle issues, even that you must be registered for the draft to be considered—if you're male, anyway. Somehow that doesn't seem quite fair.... I digress. Sorry.

The Duties section is what we're after. I'm going to copy the Duties section right off of the page.

Duties:

Primary duties as a Deckhand aboard the M/V *Serac*, a 53' live aboard park support vessel providing park personnel access to the remote coastal areas of Kenai Fjords National Park. Serves as a host to the numerous passengers on board, ensuring their safety, preparing Ship's menus, stocks supplies of food stores, prepares three meals a day for up to 10 passengers on multi-day trips (up to 14-days) without resupply.

You will maintain the interior and exterior of the vessel, scrub decks, fiberglass hull and deck house with appropriate brushes, buffers, and cleaning agents. Clean and sanitize galley, food preparation and eating areas, as well as vessel's head.

You will operate a small inflatable skiff to deliver passengers, gear, and supplies from ship to shore; serve as cargo loader, transporting heavy loads up and down steep sloping docks, from vehicles to vessel. Lift and load gear, supplies, and equipment onto deck from dock, and secure.

You will make many trips up and down ships ladders with supplies and gear for storage while underway, must access head while underway, often in rough seas.

Physical requirements: The work involves standing, stooping, bending, kneeling and climbing ramps and cramped ladders, which are often wet. Items weighing over ten pounds are lifted frequently, and cargo weighing over 100 pounds is often handled (winch assistance available in most instances).

Qualifications Required:

1. Ability to do the work of the position without more than normal supervision (screen-out element)

2. Driver's license is required (screen out)

3. Ability to prepare a ship's menu, stock food supplies, prepare meals, and maintain a clean workspace.

4. Knowledge of safe food handling practices and sanitation standards.

5. Ability to safely operate an inflatable skiff with outboard motor.

6. Work practices (includes keeping things neat, clean and in order).

7. Reliability and dependability as a deckhand.

Now we take our existing resume, the one we wrote at the start of this process, and customize it. I'll add the following Physical Abilities and Professional Qualifications paragraphs to my resume.

Physical Abilities:

I'm very capable of standing, stooping, bending, kneeling, and climbing ramps and cramped ladders, even when they are wet. I am able to lift items over 10 pounds and cargo over 100 pounds when a winch is available.

Professional Qualifications:

I take pride in my ability to work without more than normal supervision and I am a reliable and dependable deckhand. I have both a driver's license and am able to safely operate an inflatable skiff with an outboard motor. My work at McDonalds has given me knowledge of safe food practices and sanitation standards. I have the ability to prepare a ship's menu, stock food supplies, prepare meals and maintain a clean workspace.

Now, let me be clear about this: I'm not telling you to lie. If you can't operate a skiff with an outboard or cook, don't claim that you can. Alaska is a really long way to go just to get fired. But if you're confident you can fulfill all of the requirements, your resume should reflect that confidence. Remember, you're not blowing smoke; you're just trying to convince a computer that you have the abilities and qualifications. I know it seems a little cheesy, but that's how it's done.

Yacht Jobs

Are yachts considered part of the American Merchant Marine? Probably not, but there is a wide range of yachting jobs available, running the gamut from holystoning the decks for free passage to captaining a mega-yacht where part of your duties includes picking up the ex-president of a South American country in the ship's helicopter. I've heard that an experienced yacht captain with a helicopter license can ask for a salary of $1,000 per foot of ship per year. My limited super-yacht experience has never allowed me to confirm the numbers, though.

These jobs can be on private vessels or on charter boats, either sail or motor. The quality of job you find depends on your skills and experience or luck.

> I once ran into a friend of mine in Hong Kong who ran out of money (it's a long story) and took an unpaid position on a large sailing yacht to work his way back to the U.S. I visited the vessel and talked to the skipper and came away with a bad feeling because he didn't impress me with his knowledge. The captain was planning to take the shortest route back, a Great Circle course that would take them just south of the Aleutian Islands of Alaska in mid-February, not a good voyage plan for a sailboat.
>
> Later I found out "What's the worst thing that can happen?" had happened. They ran out of fuel for the axillary diesel fighting headwinds, got caught in a massive storm in the middle of the Gulf of Alaska that pitchpoled (flipped end over end) the big sailboat, which tore out both masts and the radio antennas. The emergency position indicator radio beacon (EPIRB) didn't work, and it took them over a month of drifting before they were finally rescued. On the bright side, my friend was over 50 pounds lighter when he finally made it home.
>
> Not all yacht jobs are created equal. Be very careful; don't take the job if you get a bad feeling.

Living conditions can be tough on a yacht for the hired help, with tiny, shared staterooms. It's not unusual for four small bunks to be located in the very bow of the vessel, in a single small stateroom. The living quarters are usually tighter than a merchant ship, so you'll have to be even more disciplined and considerate. To be successful you'll have to be clean, quiet, and thoughtful. Once the boat leaves port, walking off the job becomes problematic. Yacht owners and captains can have very high expectations, so things must be done right. The term shipshape means everything in its proper place and secured. It must become second nature on all vessels but particularly on yachts. Professional seamen are not always clean, but they are always neat; if you doubt me, wait until your first storm and you will see why.

Working on a yacht can be fun, obviously, or why would billionaires spend so much money doing it? But working on a yacht is also hard, serious, potentially dangerous work. Take it seriously, do more than is expected, maintain a cheerful attitude, pick the right boat, and you should do fine.

The best time to find yacht jobs depends on where you're headed. The two main yachting areas are the Caribbean Sea and the Mediterranean Sea. To walk the docks for a Caribbean voyage, try Fort Lauderdale, where the season runs from October to April. In southern Europe the season runs from May to September; try the high end marinas of Monaco, St. Tropez, Cannes, or Palma de Mallorca.

Once you arrive at a suitable departure port, try the following:

1. Go to the harbor and register at a crewing agency.
2. Locate the yachty-yachty bars and do some research. Talk to the yacht crews, ask about openings, boats to avoid; you'll learn a lot.
3. Talk to the marina locals: the harbor master's assistant, the chandlery counter help, the bar maids, everyone. People hear things, and if you present yourself correctly they are often willing to help.
4. Walking the docks and chatting up crew members working on the deck of a yacht can be productive; just be sure to be sober and looking particularly together. If the vessel has an opening, ask to speak to the captain. On an extremely large yacht the chief officer may do the hiring.
5. Marinas have fascinating bulletin boards to assist in communication. You'll find notes looking for crew members and notes looking for jobs. Check them daily and add your own. If you're overseas and don't have a cell phone, list a daily meeting place.

Online try: www.cruiserlog.com, www.floatplan.com and www.findacrew.net. At the very least you'll see what's out there.

As you acquire skills, experience, endorsements, and licenses, it will get easier. The jobs available include entry-level deckhand, stewardess, engineers, or chefs. If you know what you're doing you can get a real paying job through an agency. The money can actually be pretty good, particularly on a charter vessel, if you can work the tip situation correctly.

If you're just starting out, you may only get a ride and some experience. You may even have to kick in for food—it depends on the boat owner and how desperate he is; it's hard to sail a big boat alone. Often jobs are available when the season ends and the boats have to be repositioned to a new area or ferried home.

Once you have a job, some advice…

1. I don't mean to be a party pooper, but skip the drugs. The penalties overseas can be outlandish. In Singapore, for instance, drug smugglers are quickly and efficiently executed with no fuss at all. In other Third World countries, catching Americans with pot or other drugs is looked on as winning the lottery by the local police, so don't play.

2. The yachting world can be like a small town. Watch the gossiping, excessive whining, and backstabbing; it can get back to where it shouldn't, awfully quickly.

3. Send your money home as soon as you can. You don't need much on a boat and if the owner runs into trouble—well, you just want your money in the bank.

4. Make sure everyone's roles and responsibilities are understood in advance. Be honest about your abilities and fulfill your commitments. Let your intuition protect you; if it doesn't feel right, move on. The ocean can be a big lonely place; don't sign on if you have any reason to doubt your shipmates' competency or integrity.

5. If you're a woman, be careful of vessels with a small crew looking for females only, no experience required, must be between 18 and 30. You know the drill; just be careful. As I keep telling my daughter, "Men are pigs."

6. Always email the pertinent details to someone: Name of vessel; country of registry; planned itinerary; owner's name, address, and phone number.

I have a remarkably attractive friend who got a job cooking on a boat when she was seventeen. Once the vessel got under way, the captain adamantly tried to expand her job description into areas she had no intention of going. So she baked a large chocolate cake whose secret ingredient was an entire case of chocolate Ex-Lax, which apparently made the cake quite moist. Once the captain and crew were indisposed, rolling on the deck, fighting stomach cramps and worse, she nipped over to the radio, where she put out a distress call to the Coast Guard, who picked her up and took her ashore, as they were still in American waters.

I don't think a lot of mariners start out working on yachts; usually what happens is dedicated, skilled, amateur yachtsmen decide to make their passion their living. In a few years a license and a reputation can be earned and an exciting, fulfilling lifestyle may be the result.

I would caution you: don't try to move up too fast. Learn your craft; master your present position before you step up to the next one. According to Malcolm Gladwell's book *Outliers,* it takes at least 10,000 hours of practice before you can master nearly anything. I think that may apply to becoming a good seaman also, but only if you apply yourself.

This becomes a particularly important issue when you take a Master's job, your first command on any vessel. If can happen fast on yachts, and you may need to make the correct life-or-death decision your first trip out. Make sure you're ready, particularly if you're carrying passengers and crew; their lives depend on your experience and skill. Never take that lightly.

Union or Non-Union

- *History of the Merchant Marines*

- *Choosing Between Union and Non-Union*

- *American Seamen's Unions*

- *Joining*

    Seaman's International Union
    Seaman's Union of the Pacific
    Pacific Coast Marine Fireman, Oilers,
        Watertenders and Wipers Association
        (MFOW)
    Inland Boatman's Union
    MM&P United Inland Membership Group

History of the Merchant Marines

Before you can truly understand what the Merchant Marine is like today, you have to know something of its history. Knowing something of that history is going to help you decide between union and non-union jobs.

Working on ships could be the fourth-oldest profession on Earth. Hunting, farming, and hooking are all older, but not by much. In the Western Hemisphere, shipping probably dates back a millennium to Leif Erikson, who founded a settlement called Vinland in Newfoundland, Canada. Fish, timber, and livestock were transported back and forth to Scandinavia. But the colony didn't survive, so enough of that; we'll jump ahead nearly 800 years to the American Revolutionary War when the Merchant Marine actually predated the American Navy.

Since the earliest days of the American colonies, ships were carrying resources and goods between Europe and the New World. During the early stages of the Revolutionary War the new American government granted Letters of Marque to American merchant ships; this was a license to pillage British ships all over the world. American privateers (or pirates) were quite successful in annoying the British and enriching themselves. An early American merchant seaman, John Paul Jones, founded the American Navy (which is quite unsurprising, because to this day American seamen consider themselves to be vastly more talented than their naval brethren).

The life of an early American seaman was a difficult one. In 1812 America fought a war against England, who insisted on stopping American Merchant ships and kidnapping some of their crew, a hiring technique known as impressment. The hugely unpopular war ended in something close to a draw, with the White House burned but with the British agreeing to stop impressment of our seamen. However, seagoing conditions were still harsh—so harsh that crewing a ship often still required a kidnaping, called Shanghaiing. This occurred when a vessel's captain, needing a few bodies to fill out a crew, paid tavern-keepers to deliver intoxicated customers to the vessel. In San Francisco some of the waterfront dive bars were constructed out over the water, trap doors and all, to increase the efficiency of the process.

A seaman's pay was low, food was unbelievably bad, and working conditions were remarkably harsh. I've read stories of sailing vessels so intent on making an early arrival that crew knocked over the side were left to drown in the ship's wake. I've read of bugs in the bread constituting the protein component of a seaman's diet. Conditions, obviously, have changed, but history has left its mark on the industry. Things will make more sense to a potential merchant mariner if he understands the history of his chosen career.

Let's jump ahead a hundred years or so. Conditions are improving; flogging and impressment no longer exist. The Seaman's Act of 1915 abolished imprisonment for disobedience. It required most of the seamen to share a language with the ship's officers. Minimum crewing standards were set; hours, pay, and crew provisions were all regulated by the Seaman's Act. Remnants of this Act can still be found aboard merchant ships on the Station Bill, a posted document that lists many of the rights and responsibilities of each seaman.

The Merchant Marine Act of 1920, better known as the Jones Act, deals with shipping regulations between American ports. It requires all cargo carried between American ports to be carried on American flagged ships that are built in American shipyards and crewed by American seamen.

The idea behind the Jones Act is to insure that there is always an American Merchant Marine; that it is in the national interest for America to be able to transport goods around the world on her own ships. The Jones Act assumes that to remain a great nation, America needs to be able to project force around the world and must use that power wisely. According to the Jones Act, it would be difficult to supply our armies throughout the world if we had to rely solely on third-party contractors.

Not everyone agrees. In 2010 John McCain did his best to "fully repeal" the Jones Act and destroy the American Merchant Marine when he introduced legislation called the "Open America's Water Act." He argued that getting rid of the American Merchant Marine would reduce costs for consumers, although the same argument has denuded this country of its manufacturing base. (That argument might also increase profits for certain Chinese shipping companies that may or may not have contributed to Sen. McCain's various campaigns.) But I don't think that Sen. McCain's dislike of the American Merchant Marine is based on legalized corruption. He is a Navy man who amply demonstrated his admirable courage while held captive in Hanoi. His father was also a naval hero who played a considerable role in the defeat of the Japanese in WWII.

I believe I understand Sen McCain's feelings because my father, also a WWII naval hero, used to not have much use for the American Merchant

Marine—though I've been grinding him down over the last 35 years or so. I remember Dad telling me how merchant mariners demanded overtime before they would offload desperately needed supplies to the embattled Marines on Guadalcanal during WWII. How cargo operations were secured from Saturday afternoon until Monday as food, ammunition, and medical supplies ran low only a few miles away. Anyway, that's how the Navy tells the story (it isn't true) and I don't think Captain McCain would mind very much if the American Merchant Marine simply disappeared.

I mention this only because Merchant Shipping is an intensely political industry. If a federal law or two is changed, the entire industry might go the way of American textile mills or American consumer electronics manufacturers. If you think Corporate America should have no restrictions on whom they hire, what working conditions they offer, and unlimited profits without regard to environmental concerns, then the American Merchant Marine is not for you. You'd fit in about as well as a misogynist at a NOW convention.

To understand the importance of the labor unions in the American Merchant Marine, we must examine the 1934 West Coast Waterfront Strike, which culminated on "Bloody Thursday" when three apparently unarmed strikers were shot down by the police—two of them, Nick Bordoise and Howard Sperry, dying of their wounds.

The strike began on May 9, 1934 when all West Coast longshoremen walked off the job. They were joined by sailors several days later, tying up ships all over the West Coast. Strikebreakers were hired and attacked by strikers. Private security guards then shot and killed some of the strikers.

Employers tried to force open the port of San Francisco on July 3, triggering fighting between the police and the strikers. After a quiet Fourth of July the employers again tried to force open the port with tear gas and mounted police charges against the picket line. The strikers responded by throwing the tear gas canisters and rocks back at the police. By the end of the day two men were dead and both sides soberly took stock.

The strike was eventually settled, with seamen getting a guaranteed pay scale of $62.50 a month, overtime pay, and, most importantly, control of their hiring halls.

Though times and conditions have changed drastically, the shadow of "Bloody Thursday" still lingers over the Merchant Marine, possibly to its detriment, perhaps even contributing to its eventual demise. But it remains a powerful symbol that must be acknowledged.

Choosing Between Union and Non-Union

This brings us to an important choice facing you: going union or non-union. My advice is to keep an open mind. I've run into closed-minded seamen on both sides; it depends on your upbringing and experience which side of the fence you wind up on. Find a circumstance that works best for you and run with it.

I've been on all sides of the issue. I was a member of a union I hated, happily worked non-union for years, and presently I belong to a union that I'm thrilled with. Right up front, some unions are great, others are not so good. My thought presently is a good union is better than no union, but no union is better than a bad union. Like people, some unions are corrupt and others are not.

A number of years ago a good friend of mine took a job as an assistant patrolman of a union local that is now defunct, absorbed into another stronger union. In just over a year he took in over $85,000 in bribes from union members seeking to improve their job prospects by jumping the line. He decided he didn't want to live a life of a crook and quit the position and went back to sea and an honorable life.

Having said that, I believe most unions aren't corrupt, and some are quite admirable. If you join a union that turns out to be crooked, I would advise you to leave as soon as possible and find an honest union—they *are* out there.

I worked for many years for non-union companies, with mixed results. Some treated their employees with great respect, even gratitude. Others lied, cheated, stole, discriminated, and worse. In the end I wound up working for a great union—Masters, Mates, and Pilots—that trains, insures, protects and even provides an excellent retirement for its members. It provides me with a better deal than any of the non-union companies I worked for ever did, which is why I remain a member in good standing.

Non-union companies all have different benefit packages. I worked for one non-union tug company whose benefits package ended with the free hat and coffee mug they gave me on joining the company. I didn't stay very long.

So let's go over the possible benefits.

1. Vacation: for every day that you work, how much vacation do you accrue? Do you get paid on your time off or do you just get the time off?

2. Medical: By federal law if you are working on a vessel and you are hurt, the company must pay for your medical care. Are you provided with medical insurance when you're not on the ship? Is your family provided with medical insurance at any time? Is dental or eye care included?

3. Retirement: Is there one? Is it a 401-K plan? With matching funds? Is it a defined benefits plan?

4. Training: Is it provided at any level? What are the costs and restrictions?

5. Transportation: How much is provided? How often?

All maritime unions provide all of these benefits to one degree or another. I've worked for bottom feeder, non-union companies that provide none of these benefits, but only briefly. Sometimes these crummy non-union companies have their place, if only to obtain sea time and experience. They may not be a bad place to start, but they're a terrible place to wind up. Some of the top non-union companies, such as the oil companies, offer benefit packages and opportunities on par with the better unions. Keep your eyes open, don't believe everything you hear during the hiring process, and if someone offers you a better deal, think very seriously about taking it. Some non-union and union companies offer such miserable deals I'm baffled as to how they keep their vessels crewed.

American Seamen's Unions

Here's a list of the American Seamen's Unions.

1. **Seaman's Union of the Pacific (SUP)** provides unlicensed deck seamen's jobs. All of the hiring halls are on the West Coast. It's a great place to start if they are accepting applicants. They provide Able Bodied Seamen, the journeyman seaman position; Bosuns who supervise the deck seamen; and Ordinary Seamen, an entry level seaman's job that has nearly been phased out. They have a very generous contract that my union often benefits from through our me-too clauses. If contractually the sailors must be fed prime rib once a week, it's pretty hard not to feed the rest of the crew the same, even if it's not in their contract. Thanks, guys.

2. **Marine Fireman, Oilers and Wipers (MFOW)** provides unlicensed engine room employment. Possibly the most militant of the maritime unions, I sometimes wonder if they noticed the 'thirties are over, and the Pinkertons aren't shooting down union members in the streets anymore. But boy, do they have a good contract once you're in. Maybe there is a connection. MFOW members work as Jr. Engineers, Reefer Engineers, Electricians, and Wipers. They seem to have more jobs than members at the higher levels.

3. **Marine Engineers Beneficial Association (MEBA)** is the premiere marine engineers union; it's the oldest maritime trade union in the U.S. Its members work both the oceans and the Great Lakes on all types of vessels, but won't benefit you because they only represent licensed officers. They have a few deck officer jobs, but not very many.

4. **Masters, Mates and Pilots (MMP)**, my union. We like to believe we're the most talented and highly paid deck officers in the world. Perhaps we're right. In any event, after many years working for many different companies on many different types of floating platforms, this seems the best place for me. I don't know of any corruption within the union; I just wish they would write all of their convoluted work rules down in one place so I could stop fouling up the shipping rules. MM&P doesn't take any entry level personnel because you must have a Coast Guard deck license to join.

5. **Seaman's International Union (SIU)** is the biggest maritime union. This may be the best union for a novice to join as they have jobs all over the industry on every type of union ship. They have a very good school that provides free training for their members. They even have a program that trains their members for Coast Guard licenses, even though SIU has no licensed jobs; it's an impressive service for its members.

6. **American Marine Officers (AMO)** have a lot of jobs that don't pay as well as other similar unions and their union presidents seem to wind up in prison with remarkable consistency. They have a wide variety of jobs all around the country and are very aggressive in scooping up contracts from other unions by offering to accept less money for the same work.

7. **Inland Boatman's Union of the Pacific (IBU)** keeps regional hiring halls on the West Coast, Alaska, and Hawaii. They have some entry level jobs, but most require a level of experience. But they do sponsor the free training program at Tongue Point Jobs Corps Center in Oregon, which we will discuss in detail later on.

8. **MM&P United Inland Membership Group** is the fastest growing MM&P membership group, with jobs in three different geographical regions of the U. S.:

> • The Pacific Maritime Region (PMR) represents mariners working passenger ferries and tugs on the West Coast.
> • The Great Lakes and Rivers Region (GL&R) represents mariners working on "Lakers" and tugs working the Great Lakes and Inland Rivers.
> • The Atlantic and Gulf Region provides jobs on tugs running between Puerto Rico and the U.S.

As an entry level union seaman, then, you have five choices: SUP, MFOW, IBU, SIU and MMP Inland. The other unions don't take unlicensed applicants, so forget about them for now. We'll go over what you need to know about each entry level union to begin shipping. That's the simple half of the equation, since there are an unlimited number of non-union companies to look at here in the U.S. We'll break down the non-union jobs into two more categories: government and private. Appendix 2 gives the list of the various union contact numbers.

There are a surprising number of government organizations that hire seamen. The biggest is Military Sealift Command (MSC). But there is also NOAA and the Army Corps of Engineers.

I wish unions were a clearer choice. They should be the vastly superior system, giving the individual worker a bit of leverage in his dealings with his employer, who has vastly more resources. But real job security today depends on the employee making money for the employer, not the threat of a job action. Employers have many more options than in the past: moving enterprises overseas, bribing congress to change work rules, getting competing unions to bid against each other, going out of business, reorganizing under different rules.

In my naiveté I wish unions would concentrate on providing the very best labor possible through training, encouragement, and discipline. Cull the weak, stupid, and lazy. Make it obvious that there is no other equivalent pool of talent available. Offer the best available people for a premium price. Now, that would be a union I would value.

Many unions try, to a certain extent, but like parents who can never accept that their child is in the wrong, unions undermine their value by not working with their customers to provide the best available labor. Organizations that do not concentrate on providing the best possible product do not thrive when other options become available. Maximum job security is achieved by being better than anyone else. Selfishly I wish unions demanded excellence, if not competency.

Joining Seaman's International Union (SIU)

There are number of unions you can join with little or no maritime experience. Let's run through them in order of practicality.

Most seamen begin their career with SIU, because it is the biggest American maritime union, with entry level jobs in all three departments. Its school is called The Seafarers Harry Lundeberg School of Seamanship located on the campus of the Paul Hall Center for Maritime Training and Education, or more commonly, Piney Point. The school has an excellent beginner's program tailored to candidates with little or no practical maritime experience, called the Unlicensed Apprentice Program. It's not the only entry level union program, but it's a really good one.

Piney Point is a vocational school that has been training students for work at sea since 1967. One of its most attractive features is the advancement classes that continue after you graduate from the apprentice program, eventually qualifying you to sit for an Unlimited Third's license.

Think about it: the union provides free education to qualify you for a journeyman's level of employment and then provides more free training to move beyond the scope of jobs supplied by SIU. That's pretty generous, and they are to be commended. They even guarantee initial employment for all of their graduates.

There are eligibility requirements for both the Unlicensed Apprentice Program and the upgrade classes. It's a selective process and the Admissions committee is looking for candidates who they think will be successful working at sea. The candidates must show they have the discipline, ability, and fitness level to work on a ship. As with any union, it helps if you have a family member already in good standing in the union. Applicants are accepted throughout the year. The process is competitive; the best candidates are selected, and not everyone will make the cut. A few years back everyone who applied was accepted but candidates had to wait between three and four years before they could enter the program. Now, if you make the cut, it only takes a few months after acceptance to begin the program. About half of the instruction takes place on a working merchant ship and students are paid pretty well while aboard ship, so you can see why this is such a popular program. The program usually has between 15 and 20 students enrolled at any one time.

Here are the posted admission requirements:

- Must be 18 or older.
- Must be eligible to work in the U.S.
- Must be able to qualify for a MMC.
- Must be able to qualify for a TWIC.
- Cannot be on any type of probation or parole.
- Must have blood pressure normal for their age.
- Must have good teeth (see dental requirements).
- Must have good vision (or be restricted to the steward's department).

Deck department applicants must have a minimum of 20/200 in each eye, corrected to a minimum of 20/40 in each eye.

Engine department applicants must have a minimum of 20/200 in each eye, corrected to a minimum of 20/50 in each eye.

Applicants who wear glasses or contacts must possess 2 pairs of glasses or a pair of glasses and a pair of contacts.

The year-long Unlicensed Apprentice Program is the largest entry level seaman's training program in the United States and is offered on the campus of the Paul Hall Center for Maritime Training and Education in Piney Point, Maryland, about 60 miles from Washington D.C..

There is no charge for room and board or tuition but there are some other expenses, such as uniforms, a physical exam, drug test, benzene test, and application fees for the usual MMC, TWIC, and a passport. Starting to sound familiar, isn't it?

The fees all together are around $1,500, not too bad. The student is also responsible for the transportation costs to the campus.

Don't show up fat and out of shape. Working on a ship can be tough: there are long hours and occasionally physically demanding work. The physical exam will assess your ability to climb ladders and stairs (lots and lots of stairs); your agility and balance; your ability to lift 40 pounds; your ability to crouch, kneel, and crawl. Are you able to stand for long periods of time? Are you able to use the survival equipment? If you can't do these things you can't work on a ship and you will be sent home to work on your fitness. Get yourself in shape before you arrive and save yourself some embarrassment. While at the school you'll be required to participate in regular fitness training.

This is a serious program that has been developed to meet all the Coast Guard requirements. The school tries to approximate the routine of working on a ship in its training program. I've copied a typical day right from the SIU website, for an Unlicensed Apprentice (UA) during the first phase of the program:

0400 – wake-up
0415 – prepare dorm for morning inspection
0430 – breakfast
0445 – report to work in the Galley
0730 – mustering for morning colors
0800 – march to class
0800 – 1100 class
1100 – march to lunch
1130 – report to galley for lunch detail
1300 – march to class
1300 – 1600 afternoon class
1600 – return from class and march to evening meal
1630 – report to galley for evening meal duty
1630 – 1930 – galley duty
2000 – lights out

Training covers the skills, duties, and responsibilities required in all three departments through a course of study that includes classroom study and practical hands-on training. All students study firefighting, water survival, first aid, CPR, industrial relations, and social responsibility. Students will also learn about the shipping industry in general, the economics of marine transportation, and the effects of government policies and regulations.

Kind of sounds like this book, doesn't it?

Obviously this is a serious and demanding program, designed to mimic the regimented life aboard ship. In a fashion similar to the four-year maritime academies, the students are required to wear uniforms and march to and from class. The UA must follow strict grooming habits, and no jewelry or makeup is allowed. Student's cars are not allowed on campus; drugs and alcohol will get you kicked out. At the end of each course you must pass a test to pass the section. If you fail, you get to retest and if you fail again you'll have to visit the Review Board, which may or may not allow you to continue.

The SIU Unlicensed Apprentice Program application process is as follows:

Step #1

1. Please read all information about the Unlicensed Apprentice Program in its entirety prior to filling out the application. Fill out the electronic application online at www.seafarers.org/jobs/ua.html.

2. On a separate paper write an essay, of no less than 400 words, about "Why I want to be a Merchant Mariner." The essay may be handwritten or typed on a computer. **At the end of the essay, you must include the following statement: "I hereby affirm that this essay was written by me, and no one else." After this statement, sign your name.** Please mail this to the Admissions Office along with other required paperwork.

3. Provide three (3) non-family character references to be mailed into the Admissions Office by the person writing the reference. Please be sure they include your full name and mail to SHLSS Admissions, PO Box 75, Piney Point, Maryland 20674.

4. Provide high school and/or college transcripts (if applicable).

5. If prior military, provide a copy of your DD-214 long form. If your discharge from the military was anything other than honorable please provide information about discharge as well.

6. Send six passport size photos (no hats, head covers or sunglasses unless hat or head covering is worn for religious reasons.)

7. Please mail all necessary paperwork to the Admissions Office, Attn: UA Program, PO Box 75, Piney Point, Maryland 20674. Physical address is 45353 St. George's Ave., Piney Point, Maryland 20674. You have 30 days after an electronic application has been received to submit the remainder of the necessary paperwork or your application will be VOID. Once all the above information is received you will be contacted by mail to schedule a reading and math test at one of the SIU's local Union Halls. You must contact the Hall prior to arriving to set up the test and you must take your letter with you in order to be permitted to test.

8. Upon completion of Step #1, including testing, your application will be submitted to the selection committee. The committee meets once a month to pick applicants to move onto Step #2. You will be contacted by mail or email within 60 days after completing Step #1 if you have been selected to move onto Step #2. Due to the economy and other conditions, the need for apprentices fluctuates throughout the year therefore the class sizes will fluctuate depending on the amount of mariners needed. At any time the school reserves the right to not hold a selection committee.

Step #2

You will be notified by mail or email whether you are to continue on to Step #2 of the application process. If you are selected to continue to Step #2, you will be sent a set of Rules and Regulations for the UA Program. At this time you must provide copies of the following documents within 90 days or your application will be VOID. If you are unable to obtain the following documents within the allotted time frame it is the applicant's responsibility to advise the Admissions Office of any issues.

1. Transportation Workers Identification Credential (TWIC.) TWIC centers and appointment scheduling can be done on-

line at www.tsa.gov/twic or by calling 1-866-347-8942.

2. Merchant Mariners Credential (MMC) from the USCG. You must apply for your TWIC before you can apply for a MMC. Contact your local USCG Regional Exam Center for information and an application for a MMC, or go online to www.uscg.mil/nmc/ for further information.

3. Valid Passport

4. All applicants must have a complete dental examination administered by his/her private dentist. A dental letter must be sent to the Admissions Office, on your dentist's letterhead and must specifically state that the applicant does not have any cavities, pyorrhea, or periodontal disease and currently needs no work to be done. The letter must contain a current date.

5. Sign the UA Program Rules and Regulations and return them to the Admissions Office along with the other necessary documentation to complete Step #2.

6. All official government documents (TWIC, MMC, passport) should be copied and mailed to the Admissions Office, please do not send originals. Please be sure to send the original dental letter and a signed original of the UA Rules and Regulations.

7. Once an applicant has a completed file they will be advised approximately three months prior to their report date that they have been selected for class. The applicant will need to contact their local SIU Hall to set up their trainee physical, drug test and benzene test. This is a conditional acceptance letter and all medical exams must be completed on time and passed before an applicant can report for school. Students will be scheduled for classes on as needed basis again depending on industry needs.

If you have any questions about the application process please contact the Admissions Office at 301-944-0010, Ex. 2 or email Admissions@ seafarers.org.

Joining Seaman's Union of the Pacific (SUP)

The SUP is a much smaller union than the SIU, with hiring halls only on the West Coast. Its website, <www. Sailors.org>, isn't nearly as nice as the SIU website and they don't have an apprentice program like the SIU. They're not interested in talking to you until you have your paperwork, but will register you on presentation of an MMC, STCW (or BST certificate), recent drug screening, passport, and a $100.00 registration fee. On their website is a membership form that can be downloaded, filled out, and sent in to the union, along with copies of the above documents, to: Sailor's Union of the Pacific, 450 Harrison St., San Francisco, CA 94105.

The sticky wicket is the $100.00 fee. All it does is allow you to sit in the hiring hall as a class D for three months and hope a job comes up that no one else wants. If you luck into a job of at least 30 days, congratulations: your status will be upgraded to Class C and you now have infinitely more seniority than your Class D buddies. With a year of seatime you become a Class B and shipping gets easier. After six years of seatime (this is six years on a ship, not six years as a member of the union) you achieve Class A status and life is good. You only work on your favorite ships—ships where the chief mate isn't quite as irritating as usual, you can take every Christmas off, and you know all the good bars around the world.

But back to the sticky wicket. You may very well pay your $100.00 and not even sniff a job. It happens all the time. My brother spent an entire summer sitting in the San Francisco SUP union hall and never got close. So why would anyone bother with SUP when the SIU program is live greased rails in comparison? Only one reason: money. Many SUP jobs pay a lot better than equivalent SIU jobs. It's a deferred gratification deal; struggle through the early years and it should pay off once you reach Class B status, assuming SUP doesn't lose any more companies—they only have two main ones left, Matson and APL. But I want to be fair about this, I've seen the pay stubs of an SUP Able Bodied Seaman; on a full pay ship they make around $10,000 per month worked, counting both pay on the ship and vacation pay. Some SIU members say they do nearly as well. So check it out, and if you can make that much money at SIU then there may not be any reason to leave. Fair enough?

Remember the name, Sailors Union of the Pacific; the hiring halls are all on the West Coast and Hawai'i. They will only ship you out if you are at the hall and win the job, no exceptions. So SUP isn't always geographically desirable. It only fills deck jobs; if you're interested in the steward's department or the engine department you'll have to look elsewhere.

So, if you're a left-coasty potential deck seaman, should you bite the bullet, pay your money, and wait in the hall hoping for a lucky break? I'll give you the same answers I give most questions: Well . . . . It depends . . . . If you think you might sail on deck for the next 20 or 30 years in an unlicensed capacity, then it may make sense to fight your way into the SUP. But if you're just looking for quick seatime so you can upgrade into a licensed position, or you don't want to live on the West Coast, then join the SIU, it's easier.

Don't get me wrong, I like the SUP, most of the time; I just wish they had more jobs and their contract wasn't so painfully convoluted—it's like playing bourré and takes years to learn. The SUP deck department has been beating me senseless with their contract for years but they do take great pride in being the best American seamen available.

Joining Pacific Coast Marine Fireman, Oilers, Watertenders and Wipers Association (MFOW)

I should warn you that although the SUP website says they represent stewards and unlicensed engineers, I've never seen any. Oh, they probably have a couple of those jobs somewhere, but really they're an unlicensed deck seaman's union. The reason SUP engine department sailors are so scarce and possibly even mythical is because the SUP is affiliated with the MFOW, which stands for the Pacific Coast Marine Fireman, Oilers, Watertenders and Wipers Association. On a ship where the SUP fills the unlicensed deck jobs, the MFOW fills the unlicensed engineering jobs. These are always good paying jobs. In the higher reaches, such as reefer engineers and electricians, they don't have enough qualified members to fill all of the jobs.

The MFOW entry level jobs are as wipers, which then work into QMEDs or Junior Engineers jobs. The problem is there just aren't many wiper jobs out there. Most ships don't carry them anymore except under special circumstances such as preparing for a big inspection or if the ship is leaving the shipyard after a refit, which may only happen every five years or so. This may be a circumstance that is actually changing for the better (a rare occurrence in the Merchants.) Port State Inspections are up all around the world; they're inspections by the host country that determines if the ship is safe to allow entry into the port. These inspections can be tough, particularly if one of the host countries' ships is being detained in America for being unsafe—then a little payback may be chugging down the track. The inspectors will search and search until they find something. Ships are huge, like a village, and eventually something will be found. But we do our best, and still a "dirty" engine room can tie a ship up until it is cleaned to the satisfaction of the Port State Inspector. At some point it becomes cheaper to hire a wiper who spends his day cleaning the engine room. I've seen more wipers than ever lately, for that very reason.

MFOW is a hard-ass union: they flat out don't play. Take a look at their website at www.mfow.org. The biggest section of their website is a record of all their strikes dating back to 1886. It's a fascinating history, and although they're a very confrontational union, I have a sneaking respect for them. Particularly since once, when I had a serious problem with one of their members, I spoke with some of the MFOW senior union management and found them to be both thoughtful and helpful. Much of the living condition improvements aboard ship have come about at the MFOW's insistence, to the benefit of everyone else on board.

They make good wages—really good wages, the best unlicensed wages in the American Merchant Marine. The wiper and QMED jobs aren't particularly difficult; the wipers clean, and the QMEDs make rounds and take readings, sound tanks, and work under the direction of the first engineer—not too tough. It's a different story for the reefer engineers and electricians. The reefer may have three or four hundred refrigerated containers, each with its own refrigeration equipment, to keep humming. Or he may only have three, it varies. He spends most of his time in port unplugging and plugging in reefer boxes. When any of these boxes fail, he fixes them; when he can't, he tells the first engineer and they work on the problem together. A reefer engineer probably makes nearly $500 a day if you add everything up.

The other big MFOW job is Chief Electrician. It pays well, too; the numbers are laid out on the website. However, this is a very difficult job since one day he's working in the engine room repairing controllers, the next day he's troubleshooting a lighting circuit and trying to fix the elevator, the day after he's lamping up the cargo holds or fixing an electrical motor. A really good electrician is like gold and is treated accordingly. The MFOW has had trouble finding enough of them to fill all of the berths. You just can't learn enough to be successful in a couple of weeks of union school. But if you are a retired United States Navy or Coast Guard Electrician's Mate, have I got a job for you! You'll need the usual paperwork: MMC with the proper endorsements, STCW-95 with Rating Forming Part of an Engineering Watch (RFPEW), TWIC, passport, recent drug screen, and lastly and most importantly, electrical and electrical troubleshooting skills.

The Navy and the Coast Guard turn out the best chief electricians and there are never enough to go around. MFOW also accepts applications for other ratings, but they sure could use a few more electricians.

Joining the Inland Boatman's Union

This union supplies crew members to smaller vessels such as tug boats, research vessels, and ferry boats up and down the West Coast, Alaska, and Hawai'i. The union's name is a little confusing because they crew vessels working both inland waters and offshore waters. The offshore jobs tend to pay a little better than the inland jobs. On many of their vessels they have a vertical contract, which means they represent everyone on board, rather than just a single department. Sometimes the captain is a company manager and not a union member.

The contracts vary a little from company to company, but I'll give you a couple of examples just to give you an idea of what's out there.

> **Tidewater** runs tug and barges up and down the Columbia River and pays their ABs about $400 per 12-hour day. But the work schedule is two weeks on and two weeks off and the crew member isn't paid during his off time. On the other hand, a $5,600 monthly salary with 2 weeks off each month isn't a bad deal at all. The Columbia River is a nice place to work, as well.

> Another example, **Sause Brothers,** is a deep sea tug company that pays its ABs $18 an hour for a 12-hour day. It also uses a two-week-on, two-week-off system, but you get paid the same $216 a day on your time off as you do while working. That is a pretty good deal, since it works out to $432 per day worked. Tasty.

So how do you get started? The Jobs Corps School at Tongue Point is run by the IBU, so no wonder the school has pretty nearly a 100 percent job placement rate. You could enroll at Tongue Point for a 18 to 24 months, pay nothing, even receive a small stipend, then roll into one of these listed jobs with an AB's ticket and/or QMED's papers. The program accommodates 60 students, so with an 18-month minimum requirement, there are only about 40 spots for new students available each year. This sounds to me like a good deal. If you're interested, the information is in the Training and How to Get It section, under Maritime Schools. IBU also has a few entry level jobs you can sit in the hall and wait for . . . figure on about a year of waiting, though.

Forget that. Get yourself a deckhand job on one of the small passenger ships and start earning AB time; the under-100-ton sea time is applicable toward the smaller, more limited AB tickets, such as fishing boat or supply boat. They only require six months of sea time, so in under a year you'll have a restricted AB's ticket. The offshore tug boats require two-thirds of the crew have all of the paperwork; a lot of the IBU sailors don't have everything, so these jobs can be had if you complete your paperwork. Take advantage of the situation to advance your career quickly. These are good jobs and just the first step up the ladder.

If you have reservations about working inland waters rather than deep sea, don't. You won't see a lot of foreign ports with these jobs, but working tugs is fun, especially if you bond with the skipper and he starts training you to handle a boat. Tugboats are fun to drive. Pulling a log raft down a river beats the heck out of any office job I've ever heard of. I have friends who sail tugs and big ships; they seem to prefer driving tug boats, particularly since an awful lot of them go on to become harbor pilots, which is pretty much the top of the industry.

Joining MM&P United Inland Membership Group

Joining the United Inland Group (UIG) isn't much different from finding a non-union job. You have to hire on with one of their covered companies and then you have 30 days to join the union. It seems a little backwards to me, but nevertheless, that's how they do it. They do have a few top-to-bottom contracts where they represent both the licensed and unlicensed crew, but usually they represent only the licensed deck officers and the IBU represents the unlicensed crew. In Appendix 2 is a list of all the MMP Inland offices and in Appendix 1 is a list of all the companies they contract with. Just remember, MMP Inland and the United Inland Group (UIG) are the same organization—confusing, perhaps, but true.

Which Department Should You Choose?

- ## Steward's Department

    ### Steward Utility
    ### Chief Cook
    ### Chief Steward

- ## Engine Department

    ### Wiper
    ### Oiler
    ### Qualified Member of the Engine Department
    ### Junior Engineer
    ### Pumpman
    ### Reefer Engineer
    ### Electrician
    ### Third Assistant Engineer
    ### Second Assistant Engineer
    ### First Assistant Engineer
    ### Chief Engineer

- ## Deck Department

    ### Ordinary Seaman
    ### Able-Bodied Seaman
    ### Bosun
    ### Third Mate
    ### Second Mate
    ### Chief Mate

Which Department is Right For You?

Let's return to the question of which department is right for you. There is a school of thought that advocates applying to all and accepting the first firm offer. That's not a bad way to get your feet wet; just keep in mind that you haven't made up your mind as to which route to take. I've worked for a surprising number of captains who started out in the steward's department washing dishes; they just didn't stay there very long.

Here's the way the steward's department is structured. Let's begin our discussion at the bottom rung of the ladder and work our way up.

Steward's Department
| Chief Steward |
| Chief Cook |
| Steward Utility |

Steward Utility

There aren't many prerequisites for an entry-level steward's department job beyond a willingness to work long hours and do a considerable amount of government-required paperwork (that we will walk you through soon enough). Most ships are cafeteria style and no longer carry messmen who serve as waiters. Instead they carry steward utilities that have a number of responsibilities, including setting up the crew and officers' mess rooms, washing dishes, cleaning the rooms, and making the beds of the officers. They work at the direction of the chief steward, who may direct them to dump trash, load stores, or continue cleaning another interior space.

I've noticed a lot of foreign nationals working as steward utilities, particularly Filipino and Yemenis, for some reason. The wages at one time were so poor for a steward utility that it was customary for the ship's officers to tip their room steward when they got off. The wages have improved over the years and the custom is fading, unless the room steward does an exceptional job or if you want him to keep his mouth shut.

> Years ago a salty old chief mate told me, "You only have to get along with the captain, chief mate, chief cook, and room steward. Tell everyone else to kiss your ass."

If it's a union ship, the steward utility job will be filled by SIU. The next step up the ladder after steward utility is chief cook.

Chief Cook

If you plan on moving up to chief cook, do us both a favor and learn how to cook well. SIU has a school that will teach you the trade. They turn out some really good cooks; however, they also crank out chief cooks who "cook to the contract" without any passion. If you truly don't care about cooking for your shipmates, don't go this route; your crew will be miserable and they will make you miserable as well. But if you really enjoy cooking and making people happy, the industry needs you—badly.

Chief Steward

This is the top rung of the stewards department ladder. The chief steward runs the stewards department, which feeds the crew and keeps the ship livable. He orders the steward stores and supervises the rest of the steward's department. On some smaller vessels, such as a tugboat, the steward's department consists of only the cook, but other large government ships carry more than the typical three-man steward department.

Engine Department

Chief Engineer
First Assistant Engineer
Second Assistant Engineer
Third Assistant Engineer
Reefer Engineer or Electrician
QMED
Wiper

Wiper

The entry level position for the engine department is wiper. That's not a bad job description, because the wiper cleans and wipes. He follows the instructions of the first engineer and does what is asked, which may also include stowing supplies, assisting with fueling, cleaning the berthing areas of the unlicensed engine department, and anything else the first engineer needs done.

The trickiest aspect of this job is finding one. Many ships no longer carry wipers, but without sea time wipers cannot become oilers or qualified members of the engine department or junior engineers, the next steps up the ladder. The jobs are out there; they're just hard to get.

Ironically, once you get past the entry and midlevel positions, the unions are unable to find enough qualified personnel to fill all of their more specialized and higher paying positions, specifically electrician and reefer engineer. The money is fabulous, up to $500 a day, and they can't find takers—at least, competent takers.

But understand these aren't jobs you can fake. If you take a job as a reefer engineer on a container ship you had better be prepared to manage hundreds of refrigerated containers. You can't lose track of any of them; one alone can be worth over a million dollars lost if the reefer gets thawed. If the refrigeration unit fails, the reefer engineer had better take notice and see about fixing it. If the reefer can't fix the warming container, the first and chief engineer will assist, but they hate having to take over for an incompetent reefer engineer. The flip side is that if you're good, you'll be respected and very well treated.

The electrician isn't responsible for millions and millions of dollars of cargo, but he gets to work on all kinds of electrical problems. If the cargo lights burn out, call the electrician; if the mooring winches won't start, find the electrician; if an elevator is stuck, where's the electrician? Few electricians can fix everything, but they should be able to fix some of the things.

If you can do this kind of work, these are well-paying jobs. If you can't do this kind of work but would like to learn, there are ways. The union schools will teach you much of what you need to know. But you will probably have to really apply yourself. I'll give you an example.

I was working on a less-than-high-paying container ship when the reefer engineer quit. Actually, he faked an injury to get off the vessel when the chief engineer caught him cheating on his overtime.

The union sent out a replacement reefer on his first job. He reported aboard in the middle of the offload at a very busy time, so I gave him a quick orientation and sent him out on deck to take some temperature readings. Fifteen minutes later he was back in my office.

"Some of the refrigerated containers don't have numbers."

"Let's go take a look. Yeah, there they are. Instead of being vertical on both sides, they're horizontal, top and bottom. I've got to get back to ballasting."

Ten minutes later he was back in my office. "How do I

switch from Centigrade to Fahrenheit on the reefers?"

"Let's go look. See that little button with the F/C? Try that."

The chief engineer fired the new reefer engineer in the next port.

I'm not picking on reefers and electricians here—they have bailed me out of serious trouble many more times than I care to recollect—but if you can't find the container numbers when they're offset and you can't find the F/C button on your own, you're not worth $500 a day, no matter how many union classes you've taken. These are serious jobs, worthy of serious people, paying serious money.

Pumpman is another non-entry level unlicensed engine department rating. The pumpman's job is to keep the liquid cargo transfer system working. This usually involves maintaining and repairing pumps, valves, and other specialized equipment on a tanker. Though he's a member of the engine department, he's also the chief mate's right-hand man and must be able to repair and rebuild all of the tanker's cargo equipment.

After three years of sea time as a member of the black gang, or engine room department, the crew member is eligible to sit for his Third Engineers License and work his way up to first engineer and the big money.

Oiler

We should probably discuss what oilers, junior engineers and QMEDs do. They all have similar jobs. It used to be that when the wiper walked around the engine room wiping up spills and cleaning, the oiler made rounds checking on the engine's temperatures and lubrication—a higher calling. Now, with most ships sailing without a wiper, the oiler does both jobs plus whatever else his supervisor orders.

Qualified Members

Junior engineers and Qualified Members of the Engine Department fill the same position. They are a step up from oiler and must pass a QMED general knowledge exam and at least one other ratings exam such as: oiler, deck engineer, pumpman, electrician, or refrigeration engineer. A QMED spends his time lubricating, maintaining, and repairing equipment in the engine room. He may also be used to sound the various engine room tanks and to clean and re-stow tools. Since this is not an entry-level rating, junior engineers and QMEDs are expected to know how to react in an emergency and be familiar with industry standards and company policies.

Today most—but not all—ships run an automated engine room. This means the engineers normally are day workers, rather than watch-standers. They work from eight in the morning until five in the afternoon, seven days a week, and whenever else they are needed.

Ships are always understaffed and the work is never finished, so the overtime is usually considerable. On some ships the engine department is expected to work around four hours a day of overtime, just to keep the vessel running. Here's a tip, though: a First Engineer doesn't like to waste overtime, so if some members of his department think they're not getting enough overtime, it's probably because the First doesn't think he's getting enough work out of the disgruntled crewmember.

Boost your productivity through effort and knowledge and the First Engineer will probably try to work you too much. But if he has to show you how to do every task, he might as well do it himself and save the overtime for some of his more productive crew.

On union ships there are rules forbidding working the productive crewmembers while sitting the non-productive crewmembers. This is to prevent supervisors from favoring their friends at everyone else's expense. But the law of unintended consequences has taken over this situation. Ships' crews have been so drastically pared back over the years that there are rarely enough man hours available to accomplish everything that needs to be done in any of the departments. Now if someone isn't pulling their weight, either they must continue to be paid for doing very little or the entire department will see their overtime limited. Neither situation benefits the ship.

If it's a union ship, these unlicensed engine department jobs will be filled by either Seafarers International Union or Marine Fireman, Oilers, Wipers Union.

Assistant Engineers

The first assistant engineer runs the black gang, assigning work and stepping in when needed. He's usually a very smart man with grease under his fingernails. On an automated ship all of the assistant engineers are day workers, with the first assistant engineer being the busiest of the engineers, keeping track of the priorities and doing most of the more difficult work.

The second assistant engineer works under the direction of the first engineer and is usually responsible for the boilers and fuel. He is usually in charge of bunkering, though sometimes the chief engineer runs the bunkering.

The third assistant engineer is the junior licensed engineer. He is normally responsible for the sewage treatment system, bilge, and oily water separator systems. Of course the first engineer can assign him to any task that needs attention.

As a service to every third engineer in the fleet, let me now add a caution. The ship's sewage treatment plant is usually very temperamental. Most ships use a particularly flimsy type of toilet paper that can be easily digested by the treatment plant, which can digest that type of paper and whatever comes out of the crew members, and nothing else. Dental floss can jam up the system and certain feminine products are guaranteed to completely muck it up. So, particularly if you are the only woman on board, be very, very careful what you flush down the head, for the evidence can be damming.

Chief Engineer

The chief engineer is the senior engineer on board the vessel. He functions as a sort of captain of the engine room. Every chief runs his department a little differently. Some chiefs spend most of their time on paperwork, others with tools in their hands—whatever it takes to keep the engine running. It's always a good idea to get along with the chief engineer, just in case your head stops up, or the heat in your room stops working. On board a vessel the "chief" is always the chief engineer, never the chief mate or the chief cook: avoid that mistake if you can.

Deck Department

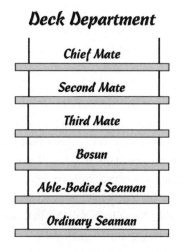

Chief Mate

Second Mate

Third Mate

Bosun

Able-Bodied Seaman

Ordinary Seaman

Ordinary Seaman

On to the deck department, where the entry-level position is ordinary seaman. As with the engine department, entry-level positions are hard to come by. Ships' crews are much smaller than they were even thirty years ago when a typical ship's deck gang ran to nine people or more. Each of the three watches (4 to 8, 8 to 12, and 12 to 4) carried two able-bodied seamen and an ordinary seaman. Today the average ship's unlicensed deck department has shrunk to five able-bodied seamen and a bosun, while most of the ordinary seamen's berths have been eliminated. But don't worry: we'll go over how to work around this problem.

But let me throw out a quick piece of advice. There are a few ordinary seaman's jobs around. If you need the sea time and manage to land one of these jobs, don't leave until ordered from the ship. If the company or union will allow you to stay for an extended period of time, suck it up and get the sea time; you need a year to qualify for a limited able-bodied seaman's ticket. It seems obvious, I know, but a surprising number of times I've seen a newbie leave early. Probably, being new to the industry, they're not prepared to leave their family and friends for an extended period of time. So get your head right, talk to your family, and go get your sea time: you can rest when you're dead.

An ordinary seaman can be either a watch-stander or a day worker or a combination of the two. I'll explain. A watch-stander in the deck department stands his watch on the bridge while the ship is under way. In port he may have to stand a deck watch or he may be off duty, it depends on the contract and the port. Different unions and companies handle in-port deck watches differently.

At sea, watch-standing able-bodied seamen and ordinary seamen have about the same job description; they are mostly lookouts. They watch for approaching watercraft, land, and changing weather conditions, and they keep an eye on the compass and steering. About the only difference between the two jobs is that an ordinary seaman cannot be required to hand steer the ship. Hand steering takes some practice, so a smart ordinary seaman will occasionally use his time on the bridge to practice his steering and achieve competency, because once he sails as able-bodied seaman, he must be able to hand steer the ship or he's going to get fired.

But the ordinary seaman's main responsibility is serving as a lookout. It's very easy to miss a small boat in a choppy sea, even with properly tuned radar, but careers and lives depend on that small boat being spotted and avoided. A good deck watch is one where the licensed deck officer and his unlicensed watch-stander partners work together to keep the ship safe and out of harm's way; they support each other and back each other up, insuring nothing gets missed. Everything else can be learned quickly: launching a lifeboat, shifting steering motors, even steering. But an attentive, professional lookout is a valuable addition to the ship's crew.

Able-Bodied Seaman

A day-working able-bodied seaman (usually shortened to dayman) is a completely different animal. He works from eight until five, similar to the day-working engineers. He'll be doing a lot of deck maintenance: chipping rust, painting decks, greasing deck machinery, slushing wires, and so on. He'll also prepare the ship for arrival in port and secure the ship for sea. A Dayman never runs out of work.

Bosun

The senior member of the unlicensed deck department, also known as the deck gang, is the bosun. The chief mate tells the bosun what needs to be done and the bosun uses the rest of the deck gang to see that it gets done. The bosun may be unlicensed, but he is still one of the key members of the ship's crew. A good bosun is a gift from God, usually able to accomplish nearly anything.

Third Mate

The third mate is the junior licensed deck officer and stands the 8 to 12 watch, which makes it easier for the captain to keep an eye on him. The third mate is the vessel safety officer, responsible for the condition of the lifeboats, firefighting, and oil clean up equipment.

Second Mate

The second mate is the vessel's primary navigator. He keeps the charts and navigation publications up to date and the bridge equipment in good order. He stands the mid watch, the 12 to 4 watch.

Chief Mate

In the deck department the chief mate is senior to all but the captain. He runs the deck department and manages the deck crew. Cargo operations and vessel stability are his concern. He's responsible for training the crew in firefighting, pirate attacks, abandoning ship, oil spill response, and other emergencies. He's usually the 4-to-8 watch-stander and running a couple of days behind.

I'll do a quick rundown of the licensed positions, just so you know who you need to listen to and who you don't.

We'll start at the top with the chief engineer and captain. They're roughly equivalent, though as in George Orwell's book *Animal Farm*, where some pigs are more equal than others, so is the captain a little more equal than the chief engineer. Most captains and chiefs work at presenting a common front to the crew, the company, and the rest of the world. Both hold positions of great responsibility, worthy of respect. A vessel gifted with superior senior management is a delight; one with poor senior management is hell.

Never forget that captains and chief engineers have much more authority and responsibility than equivalent managers do ashore. It's been like that for a very long time. The captain is responsible for the entire vessel, from the food the cook serves to seeing that the proper fire and lifeboat drills are carried out. The one exception is the engine room, where the chief engineer rules.

Many of the larger ships carry cadets, both deck and engine, from the various maritime academies. They are considered officers in training, but not yet officers. Some are in their first year and know very little; other senior cadets are quite skilled and a considerable help to the vessel. Most are from the federal Merchant Marine Academy at Kings Point, New York, which doesn't have its own training ship but sends its students out into the merchant fleet to acquire sea time. The state maritime academies use a different system that we will discuss later on.

So, to recap all the positions we've talked about, here they are again, listed within each department from the top down.

Deck Department, Licensed:
- **Master (Captain):** Senior officer aboard.
Responsible for all ship operations, keeps records and books.

Takes command of vessel in emergencies and in restricted waters. Receives and carries out instructions from home office.
- **First Officer (Chief Mate):** Stands the 4 x 8 watch.

Responsible for all deck operations such as cargo, deck maintenance, training and deck supplies.
- **Second Mate:** Stands the 12 to 4 watch.

Navigational officer, lays out appropriate charts and publications.
- **Third Mate:** Stands the 8 x 12 watch.

Junior deck officer on board, monitors safety equipment.
- **Radio Operator:** Very nearly an extinct position done in by technology. They attempted to make a transition from Radio Operator to Electronics Officer, mostly unsuccessfully.

Deck Department, Unlicensed
- **Boatswain (Bosun)**

Supervises the rest of the deck gang to carry out the orders of the chief mate.
- **Able Seaman (AB)**

Might be a watch-stander or a day worker involved with the day-to-day deckside maintenance of the vessel. As a watch stander he steers the vessel, keeps look out, makes rounds of the vessel, and assists the watch officer in any way needed.
- **Ordinary Seaman (OS)**

An apprentice seaman with the same duties as an AB but can't be required to steer or work aloft.

Engine Department, Licensed
- **Chief Engineer:** Head of engineer department, works closely with the captain. Responsible for all the mechanical equipment on board and water and fuel requirements. Coordinates shoreside repairs with port engineer.
- **First Engineer:** Directs the rest of the engine department's day work, does much of the more difficult hands-on engineering. Consults with the chief engineer regarding work priorities.
- **Second Engineer:** On steam vessels has responsibility for boilers, on diesel vessels for the evaporators and auxiliary equipment. Often does the bunkering.
- **Third Engineer:** Junior engineer on board; as such, responsible for the sewage treatment machinery.

Engine Department, Unlicensed

- **Qualified Member of the Engine Department (QMED)** - Can be a day worker or a watch stander if on a ship that still stands engine room watches. Has training in all crafts of engine maintenance such as welding, pumping and gauging fuel tanks and reading engine gauges.
- **Pumpman:** Operates pumps on tankers, assists the chief mate with all cargo equipment maintenance and monitoring.
- **Reefer Engineer:** Responsible for all refrigerated containers; loading, unloading, repairs, and monitoring. Also works on the ship's AC system.
- **Electrician**: Keeps all of the electrical equipment on board working, from changing light bulbs to troubleshooting balky electrical motors: a very demanding job.
- **Wiper:** Apprentice QMED. Cleans engine room, assists anyone in the engine room needing help.

Steward Department

- **Chief Steward:** Head of department, orders food and makes out menu. Does some of the cooking, often breakfast.
- **Chief Cook:** Cooks.
- **Steward Utility:** Cleans galley and living quarters, sets tables, prepares salads.

Training and How to Get It

- *The Two Different Training Paths*

- *Able Bodied Seaman*

- *Qualified Member of the Engine Department*

- *Maritime Schools*

- *Community College Programs*

- *Academies*

- *Hawsepipers*

- *Stewards Department Training*

The Two Different Training Paths

Before you begin your training program it is time to decide which department to pursue. If you decide to work in the steward's department, there isn't much more training that you need as far as the Coast Guard is concerned. Your union or company will probably expect you to complete some classes or certifications as you move up the ladder in the steward's department, but all in all it is far less involved than in either the deck or engine department.

All seamen in all three departments need to complete basic safety training (BST), but then the training diverges. All deck seamen need to learn and be tested on the same deck seamanship principles—watch standing requirements, knots, rigging, pollution prevention, even some simple rules of the road—to earn their papers. In the engine department the path is more complicated, with a number of different unlicensed ratings to be earned. Each of these ratings requires a separate test to be completed. We will soon get into these ratings in more detail, but for now let's start with deck department training.

Able Bodied Seaman

In the deck department, able bodied seaman is the next step up from ordinary seaman. The different types are: Unlimited, Limited, Special, Sail, Fishing and AB (Offshore Supply Vessel).

ABs are usually concerned with standing a bridge watch while under the supervision of the watch officer, working at the deck maintenance that keeps the vessel able to operate, and a plethora of additional tasks that come up daily, including pulling the lines prior to arrival, securing the decks after departure, standing anchor and launch watches, chipping vast amounts of rust and paint application, cleaning cargo holds on both dry cargo ships and tankers, hooking up tanker hoses, cargo lifts, and anything else that needs to be done on deck.

An AB's job varies considerably, depending on the nature of the vessel. An AB's job on a super tanker is considerably different from an AB's job on a supply boat. Which is better, depends on your personal preference.

To get an able bodied seaman's ticket you'll need a lifeboatman's endorsement, which requires a four-day class and costs from $500 to $900. The class will teach you everything you want to know about lifeboats and more: how to lower them, how to raise them, how to row them, how to navigate them—which was quite useful a couple of hundred years ago.

But it doesn't matter. You'll have to take a 75-question Coast Guard test and get at least 70 of the questions right. You will also have to demonstrate your ability with oars in an actual boat.

There are a number of schools offering these types of courses around the country. Type Maritime Schools into your search engine and you'll get all the information you need. At the end of the QMED section on page 114 there is a listing of different types of maritime training schools with a short description and contact information. These schools also train ABs, so check them out.

The school you choose should also offer an able bodied seaman class, which can run from a few days to a few weeks. Pay attention. Quite a few subjects will be covered, such as marlinspike seamanship, shipboard terminology, rules of the road, firefighting, towing, watchstanding, and helmsman duties, to name a few. The class usually runs about six days and costs between $700 and $1,000. Again, you'll have to pass a written test and tie ten different knots and a splice. Both the lifeboatman and ratings forming part of an able bodied seaman certificates have a one-year shelf life; the Coast Guard will accept them for up to a year after they've been earned.

Now let's talk about the different types of able bodied seamen's documents. They vary mostly by the type of sea service they require. There are three very restricted AB documents that are only good for employment on a particular type of vessel. They are AB (Offshore Supply Vessel), AB (Fishing), and AB (Sail). All three only require six months of sea time and may be the ticket if you only want to work on a vessel covered by one of the three categories.

Take particular care with your sea time letters, because these vessels are often run by companies that can be a little lackadaisical on the paperwork. The letter should also mention any special aspects of the vessel—for instance, if sails were involved, that would be a special aspect you'd want to document.

A special able bodied seaman's ticket takes 360 days of sea time on any waters. So after a year's sea time as an ordinary seaman you can get an AB's Special ticket. You'll then get a raise. You may get another raise as you earn bigger AB's tickets or you may not, depending on the company—some pay all the able bodied seamen the same, which is a good reason to get your AB's ticket as soon as you are eligible.

A limited able bodied seaman's ticket takes 540 days of sea time, or 18 months. If the vessels are over 99 gross tons, the sea time counts on all of the

AB tickets; if under, it counts on some of the AB tickets. This time doesn't have to be deep sea, either; rivers and lakes count as well. You will need BST, Lifeboatman and Ratings Forming Part of a Navigational Watch (RFPNW).

An Unlimited AB's ticket requires three years of sea service on Oceans or Great Lakes, the same as for a third mate's license; the time counts for either or both. As you work the sea time for your unlimited AB's ticket you can be taking the classes needed for a Third Mates License while on your vacation, perhaps even doing a little studying aboard ship. If you handle yourself correctly some of the deck officers will probably answer a few questions for you if you need help. If you apply yourself you could earn a license in about the same amount of time attending a Maritime Academy (4 years) would take. But you would be earning while you were learning and you wouldn't have to learn to salute or spit shine shoes—not a bad way to go.

For Able Body Seaman Unlimited you will need BST, Lifeboatman, and Ratings Forming Part of a Navigational Watch (RFPNW). Your 1080 days of sea time must be at least half on vessels of 1,600 gross tons, with none of it on vessels of less than 100 GT. Again, the three years of seatime required for an Unlimited AB's ticket also qualifies you to sit for an Unlimited Third Mates license test.

Qualified Member of the Engine Department (QMED)

A QMED is the engine department's equivalent to an AB. However, there are eight different QMED ratings:

1. Oiler
2. Refrigerating Engineer
3. Deck Engineer
4. Fireman/Watertender
5. Junior Engineer
6. Electrician
7. Machinist
8. Pumpman

Although their title refers to Engineer, Refrigerating and Junior Engineers are not licensed. They are, however, among the highest paid unlicensed crewmembers on the ship. Depending on your career goals and expertise you can apply for any or all of the ratings. Each has a different exam. Your QMED Endorsement on your MMC will also endorse your STCW as Rating Forming Part of an Engineering Watch (RFPEAW)— QMED. The other requirements are: At least 180 days of engineering department seatime in any capacity on vessels of over 750 kw/1000 hp, Basic Safety Training and Life Boatman.

There are two ways to earn a QMED endorsement:

1. Sit for the exam at a USCG regional exam center.
2. Attend a United States Coast Guard approved school.

Both have their advantages, depending on your situation. If you land an entry level engine department job and put in six months of sea service it might be simplest to buy a study guide (usually a CD of USCG test questions), study up—hopefully while still aboard ship—and take the USCG test. This is the cheapest, simplest way to go, but not necessarily the easiest.

Which brings us to our second strategy: if you are struggling for sea time or not that confident in your test-taking abilities, go to school. Get on the NMC website, look up approved courses, and find a school nearby that fits your needs and budget. There are a lot of them to choose from.

They usually take about a month, provide about half of your required seatime (3 months), and cost between $1,500 and $6,000. They usually brag of well over a 90 percent success rate, for what that's worth.

Stick with an approved course, and the certificate you earn on completion will serve as the Coast Guard exam as well as half of your seatime. No wonder they charge so much.

There are a lot of schools providing QMED training advertising on the Internet; stick with the ones listed on the Coast Guard website. QMED training tends to be more expensive than AB training, so be careful.

I can't recommend any of the private maritime training schools, as I'm not familiar enough with them all. However, there is a lot of competition out there and I know some of them are quite good, dedicated to providing the best possible professional training for the most reasonable price. If you can get a word-of-mouth recommendation and the school appears to be the best fit for you, then it might very well be your best option.

There is a page on the Coast Guard's National Maritime Center website where they list every school they have accredited in the country. I would encourage you to confirm that any school you may be thinking of attending is on that list. Trust, but verify.

Appendix 3 describes in greater detail most of the community colleges with a maritime program scattered around the country, as well as providing contact information for the seven four-year maritime academies. Information on other maritime-themed schools and maritime industry-themed schools is also provided. Unfortunately I can't tell you which program is best for you, since there are just too many variables. How well did you do in high school? Will your parents help support you through college? Do you or your family have the means to bribe a congressman? (It takes a congressional letter of recommendation to get into King's Point), do you want to be an officer or an unlicensed crewmember? Which department aboard ship are you interested in working in? Is a college degree important to either you or your mother?

I wish I were smart enough to write a program where you would answer a bunch of questions and out would pop up the name of the best training program for you. But I can't—all I can do is provide you with a list of options, highlighting some of the advantages and disadvantages that they all have and hope for the best. The more research you do the better. Call up the schools; get updated information on costs and availability. Grill them on how many of their graduates find jobs right out of the gate; so how much do they make? You get the idea.

I would suggest you start with the nearest school and keep moving your geographical limits outward until you find a program that meets your needs. On the bright side, all of the programs I talked to sounded pretty good. They all seem to understand how important it is to control costs, and how important it is to get a job quickly upon graduation. Let me know how things work out at your chosen training provider and I'll give them a kiss on the cheek or a kick in the pants on thebigbucksguide.com website, as needed.

Let's run through an assortment of different possibilities to give you an idea of what's available, in no particular order:

> **TRI Training Resources LTD. Inc.** of San Diego, CA offers a one month (159 hours) QMED—FOWT program for around $2,800. It covers half of your seatime, so you only have to come up with 90 days more. Days required for RFPEW is reduced from 180 to 60. Their website can be found at www.maritimetrainingschool.com.

Great Lakes Maritime Academy, part of Northwest Michigan college, is located in Traverse City, Michigan. Once a year it offers an 11 day QMED—FOWT program that costs $1,675 including housing. The endorsement is good for all waters even though the school is on the Great Lakes. They can be reached at www.mnc.edu or (877) 824-7447.

SeaSchool of Bayou La Batre, Alabama provides QMED training specifically for offshore supply boats. It's very reasonable at $995 for an eight-day class, including room and board. The problem is the rating is only good for offshore supply boats, so don't do it unless you're sure that's where you want to work. They can be reached at www.seaschool.com or (800) 247-3080.

Seattle Maritime Academy is a part of Seattle Central Community College and has a program that covers all of the seatime requirements through classes, a training vessel, and internships, including RFPEW. Graduates receive ratings for Oiler, Junior Engineer, Electrician, Refrigeration Engineer and Pumpman. In-state tuition is around $7,000, out-of-state tuition is around $18,000, and the program takes nine months to complete. It's expensive, but 95 percent of their students graduate and they all find work in the maritime industry. That's right, a 100 percent placement rate. That's what I'm talking about. They can be reached at www.seattlecentral.edu/maritime or (800) 906-7829.

Maritime Schools

There are a lot of really good opportunities out there. Tongue Point and the United States Merchant Marine Academy are free—hard to beat that. Other programs, depending on your needs, are just as good or maybe even better.

Some of the community colleges located on the nation's coasts offer all kinds of creative programs that solve all kinds of different problems. The department heads of these programs all seem to have good relationships with the local maritime companies and customize their programs to meet local needs. Some offer programs for high school juniors and seniors that provide seatime so that upon high school graduation they are within a few months of qualifying for an able seaman ticket. Others offer a one year program that results in an AB's ticket or a two year program that allows you to sit for a limited license.

They are all different, so spend a little time on the websites of the schools that interest you. I should warn you that some of these websites are hard to navigate to the maritime department section. I had to call a couple of them for hints, so if you get stuck call the school and ask for help. If I've listed it below it has a program somewhere. If you run across another community college with a maritime program, let me know and I'll include it in the next edition.

The Workboat Academy is a two-year program specifically designed for an entry-level person interested in becoming an officer. It consists of 32 weeks of classroom/simulator training and a minimum of 52 weeks of onboard training. It has relationships with many local companies who accept their cadets aboard their vessels who earn seatime as they learn their craft, not to mention a $900 a month stipend.

The Workboat Academy has campuses on both the East and West Coast. On the West Coast it is part of The Pacific Maritime Institute in Seattle; on the East Coast it's part of Marine Institute of Technology and Graduate Studies near Baltimore. *Full Disclosure: I'm a member of MM&P, which is affiliated with both institutions.*

This is an interesting program that splits the difference between a four-year academy and working your way up the hausepipe on your own. First the bad news: in 2012 the tuition for the two-year program is $32,750. That's a lot of money, but think about it for a minute. You'll get out of school with a license two years earlier than with a typical academy, with a starting income of at least $50,000 a year, which might be a better deal than attending the United States Merchant Marine Academy for free. It's starting to sound better, isn't it?

Before you are accepted into the program you have to pass two interviews; the expected one with the school and an additional interview with the company you've already selected to do your training with. Local companies agree to sponsor and provide training for a given number of students. Nothing is promised, but the hope is that the students continue on with their sponsoring companies after graduation and become valued employees. Handle your business, learn your trade, and on graduation you roll right into a good job that you've been well prepared for. That strikes me as a good deal.

On completion of the program and testing with the U.S. Coast Guard the trainee will receive:

- Rating Forming Part of a Navigation Watch
- Able Seaman, Limited
- Mate 500 GT Ocean
- Mate 1600 GT Near Coastal
- Mate Towing Endorsement
- SCCW95 Certificate OICNW on Vessels 200 GT (500 GT) or more
- One year of sea service credit for following an approved program of training.

The programs start once or twice a year. A Gulf Coast branch will be opening in 2012 or 2013 in New Orleans. Presently there are between 60 and 100 students in the program, between the two schools. The class sizes vary according to the employment needs of the sponsoring companies. The email address is www.workboatacademy.com.

Here's a last little kiss: the Mate 500 GT Ocean license test is similar to the Unlimited Third Mates test, so if you can get the unlimited seatime the Coast Guard will upgrade your 500 GT license to an Unlimited Third Mate's License.

You're welcome.

Tongue Point Jobs Corps Center is a really interesting operation. Job Corps is a training program that includes technical skills training as well as the opportunity to earn a GED or high school diploma, a driver's license, and employability skills necessary to land and keep a job. It's funded by the taxpayers through the Department of Labor—maybe the best use of tax dollars around. The curriculum is designed by the Department of Labor, while the Inland Boatman's Union provides the instructors, all with maritime experience and credentials. There are 125 Job Corps training sites throughout the country, but this is the only one with a Maritime Department/Seamanship program. TPJCC accepts candidates for this program from throughout the country because it's the only such program in

Job Corps. At this writing, TPJCC is rated to have 413 students, with 60 of them in the Seamanship program. Because of the sea-time requirements for the various credentials, the program takes a minimum of 18 months. Job Corps has a 24 month maximum time allowed. Once enrollment paperwork is complete, expect a wait of between 2 to 12 months for a spot to open up.

The Job Corps offers free education and career technical training. The Inland Boatman's Union tie-in is valuable because it provides hands-on, practical training as well as a clear path into the union on graduation. This training covers the deck side, engine side, and even training in galley cooking for all of their students, all of whom receive both an AB's and a QMED's ticket as well as a firm grasp of how to flip pancakes and scramble eggs on rocking and pitching vessels. In addition, training includes an internship. Towards the end of their Job Corps career, students are placed aboard working vessels from, among others, NOAA, Alaska Marine Highway, Army Corps of Engineers, Foss Maritime, Sause Brothers, and so forth. Those who do well are usually offered a job by the company they completed their internship with. I've talked to some of the graduates. They have really liked their instructors, who they said really seemed to care about the success of their students.

Job Corps provides room and board, trade clothing, and even a small stipend paid semi-monthly, as well as a lump sum when you complete the program (that's right; rather than your paying them for your education, they pay you to get it). Upon graduation the students are snapped up by the IBU and other maritime employers and are quickly working on the water making $25 an hour or more. There aren't any employment guarantees, but everyone who wants work quickly finds it.

The thing I like the most about this program is it's a second chance program. If you have some issues or just didn't win the lucky sperm lottery, this program can square you away for the rest of your life. While anyone would be well served in attending, Job Corps specializes in helping young men and women (age 16 to 24) who have had trouble with the traditional educational programs. They'll help you get a GED and then a real high school diploma. Tongue Point offers training in 16 trades, but we'll stick to the maritime program to preserve my focus. If you don't speak English very well, or have been socially promoted in school for years and only read at a fifth grade level or so, TPJCC is set up to help you succeed. If behavioral issues have held you back in the past, Tongue Point might be your ticket it you are serious about getting your stuff together.

The vast majority of their students (maybe 98 percent) are dead serious about taking advantage of this last opportunity; the other 2 percent knuckleheads either straighten out or are sent on their way. Once you enter the program they don't give up on you—only poor personal behavior can derail you. Drinking on campus, drugging, fighting, skipping classes are the types of behavior you need to avoid and you'll make it through.

I love this program; it's the only one of its type in the country that I've run across. If you're serious about getting your life together this is a great place to start: repair your education and train for a solid middle-class career. If you're not serious, though, pass; these spots are too valuable to waste.

What are the eligibility requirements? First, you have to be at least 17½ years old. Second, you have to be economically challenged, below the poverty level. This level varies around the country. In Seattle, to pick a city at random, the one-person household limit is $10,090, the four-person household limit is $28,429. The family income is measured, unless the candidate is 19 years or older or has a documented disability diagnosis; then only the candidate's income is considered. Just like public school systems, the Department of Labor uses the term "disability" in the broad sense. Third, you must obtain a referral from the IBU before you apply for enrollment and get a TWIC which shows you can pass the governmental screening. Even the cost of the TWIC is reimbursed after you've successfully completed a certain portion of the curriculum. Finally, a word of warning: just as with any employer, there's an entrance drug screening. Any seamanship candidate who fails that first screening on entry date is automatically barred from the program. A positive drug test at any time thereafter means automatic dismissal from the seamanship program.

This is the type of government program I believe in: grant a little luck to someone who hasn't been real fortunate. Train her up, work her hard, challenge her to graduate, help her find a good job, and then tax the beejesus out of her (like the rest of us) to pay for the next guy in the program. Let's stuff this campus with students so Job Corps has to build more of them. They can be reached at (503) 338-5036 or you can contact a Job Corps admissions counselor in your area.

Community College Programs

Community colleges offer more than their unlicensed maritime programs. A number of these schools offer two-year programs that result in a limited license. Some of these schools have been at it for years, while others are just getting started. These programs tend to be very practical courses of study that have been constructed in consultation with the local maritime companies, which makes their graduates very employable. Community Colleges traditionally provide some of the most cost effective education available.

Are they worth it? It depends on your goals. If you are looking to work in a part of the industry where a smaller license is sufficient, such as tugboats or supply boats, then absolutely it's worth it. You'll have a license in half of the time it takes to graduate from a four-year maritime academy, allowing you to begin working two years sooner. That's good for an extra $100,000 or $200,000. You feel me now? These community colleges ring the country with a fair bit of space among them, and they all have considerable populations to draw from. Check out your local program first; if you don't have to move and you can eat at home, it makes things a lot more affordable.

If you yearn to sail big ships across the seven seas, or become an admiralty lawyer eventually, then maybe the two-year programs aren't for you. It is possible to increase the size of your license down the road, with seatime of the correct tonnage or horsepower. I suspect most two-year graduates who find a berth with a good tugboat company have no desire to increase the size of their license to cover big ships. The money, living conditions, and vacation time are often as good on the smaller vessels as on the unlimited ships.

These community college programs all seem to cater to the local maritime community, often meeting with local companies to insure their graduates meet the local needs. Every educator running these programs that I talked to regards finding employment for their graduates as their highest duty. They get it.

All of the programs are set up a little differently, so do some investigating: in particular, find out where the graduates find work. Talk to the human resources department of the company—it's not a bad idea to start a dialog with your dream company early; they love that. If everything sounds satisfactory, go for it. If you do it right, you can almost find a job before you start school. Talk about taking the pressure off! To help you in your search, I've included a list of community colleges in Appendix 3.

One final word of warning: I love the community college programs. They're a fantastic way to get a bit of college and prepare you for a great career without acquiring a large student loan. But their websites tend to suck. Sometimes you have to learn the magic word before you can find the link to the maritime program. Don't give up, though, because if the college is listed in Appendix 3, the program actually exists. You may have to call the college, get a phone number for someone in the maritime program, and ask them for the secret word that opens up the maritime department web page. If I sound bitter it's because I've spent the last week cracking my head against these websites. Of course, you may be far more adept at navigating the web than I . . . .

Academies

Graduating from a Maritime Academy is another way of becoming a professional seaman we should discuss. There are seven Maritime Academies located around the U.S.: California Maritime Academy, Great Lakes Maritime Academy, Maine Maritime Academy, Massachusetts Maritime Academy, Texas A&M, SUNY Maritime Academy, and The United States Merchant Marine Academy.

One of the real joys of becoming a licensed Merchant Mariner officer is insulting and degrading the abilities, training, and prospects of anyone who attended a different academy. If the selected victim didn't happen to attend a maritime academy, but through hard work, initiative and discipline managed to earn a license on his own, well, that's even better because then all the academy boys and girls can jump on him, bringing the rest of the crew together. I know it sounds cruel and inhumane, but it does pass the time.

> Maritime academies are very different from most universities. They're still mostly male, quite regimented, and offer up a fair bit of adventure. When former academy classmates get together, the conversation often turns to school ship cruises and the madness that transpired. On my second cruise the seniors in my division decided to rent a school bus, load it with beer, food, around fifty midshipmen, and head for the hills for our cruise party. As we were in Fiji at the time, we didn't get very far until we came to the end of the road.
>
> We unloaded our gear and carried it to a nearby village, where our division commander informed the startled chief that we had come from a long way to party with his village, which was apparently cool with him. I'm a little hazy on the rest of the day; I do remember drinking a funky white liquid called Kava that we didn't bring. I remember the entire village turning out for the hot dog and hamburger feast, a lot of beer, and dancing Fijian dances with Fijian girls.

> Then we had to leave because our drunken division commander got himself in a coconut climbing contest that he lost. Then he decided to slide down it like a fireman's pole, peeling himself. He lost significant quantities of skin from his arms, chest, and thighs. I thought we should have stayed, but cooler heads prevailed and we took our fearless leader back to the ship for medical attention.

I don't actually think it much matters if an officer graduated from a particular academy or worked his way up through the ranks. He either checks the container lashings as ordered or he gun decks it. He either keeps the ship and crew safe while on watch or the rest of us are all in danger. What school you attended doesn't matter to me at all. Learn your job, do it with pride and diligence, and I'll be happy to sail with you any day.

If your goal is to sail some day as a licensed officer, in either the deck or engine department, there are good arguments to be made for attending an Academy and also for hiring on as an entry level seaman and working your way up, so let's discuss both.

Enrolling at an academy reminds me of a baby bird sitting in a nest. Whenever a parent lands on the nest the baby bird opens his mouth wide to receive a nice juicy worm. The academies know exactly what they're doing; just open your mouth and they'll keep jamming what you need to learn down your throat. You won't have to worry about acquiring the right amount of sea time or studying the right subjects or registering for Coast Guard tests: the schools take care of all that, it's a done deal. Just learn the rules, pass the classes, shine your shoes, make your bed, and pass your tests and in about four years you'll have an unlimited third engineers or mates license, a bachelor of science degree, and possibly a commission in the United States Navy.

If you want a college degree and have four years, this may be the best way to go. Some of the academies will validate general education classes if you have previous college experience and allow you to graduate in three years. So keep that in mind if you're considering attending an academy.

There are a couple of issues I should caution you about. You must be able to do math, at least through calculus, on either the deck or engine side. If you can't, you ain't going to graduate. If you are still in high school, study up. If you can get through high school calculus, you should do fine at the academy.

The other question to ask yourself is can you accept authority? I know this seems like a silly thing, but I went to school, briefly, with a number of guys who worked hard for months or years before their inability to deal with authority got them kicked out. I remember a heart-to-heart conversation with my dad my first week at the academy when I found out I had to shave off my moustache (it was a different day). I was considering quitting (it was a beautiful moustache). They are going to try and break you down. Expect it, deal with it, get over it; life gets worse, trust me.

The United States Merchant Marine Academy in Kings Point, New York is a federal service academy similar to the Naval or Coast Guard Academy. As such, it's free, though it does require some service commitments after graduation. Its students are even paid while training as cadets aboard merchant ships—not a lot, but something.

I've worked with a bunch of King's Point cadets aboard ship and found many of them to be young, hardworking, and capable. Some are there only because they've found a back door into Naval Flight School, but most have designs on working in some capacity in the transportation industry, either aboard ship or ashore.

The other six maritime academies are state schools affiliated with their state university systems. The state academies all operate their own training ships, rather than sending their cadets out on merchant ships to garner sea time. After the state school students have done three school cruises together, they have formed some extremely close bonds but they still don't have any practical merchant ship experience.

The federal cadets do have quite a bit of practical experience, because they ship out on merchant ships for a year but they usually go out as a pair with a single deck and engine cadet. Their sea project is extensive, but it's self-directed and not as demanding as the state academies.

Which is better? Well I like the state academies, but if I attended King's Point I might feel different. If you think you might be happy in a military school environment, the federal academy might be the way to go.

The other difference between the state schools and the federal school is the cost: the state schools aren't free. They're subsidized, but not free.

If you decide to attend a state academy, play the in-state tuition game. Many of the states extend their in-state tuition rates to other nearby states; the New York Maritime Academy, for instance, extends its in-state tuition rates all the way south to Alabama. Start investigating a year early, master the residency requirements for the school that seems to fit best, and move there. Once you achieve residency, you'll save 50 to 70 percent on tuition. This should drop your total costs to about $20,000 a year, much of which will be covered by the federal government if you qualify for a naval reserve commission. There you go—nearly free college.

These maritime academies are universities with real college degrees, so it's a bit of a two-for-one: a license and a B.S. degree. I've seen them all praised in catalogs of affordable colleges regularly; they're not a bad way to earn a college degree.

What's the catch? Accept a naval reserve commission and a year later you're fighting it out with Mujahedeen on top of a frozen mountain in Afghanistan, right?

Well, no. First of all, that's the SEALs and they're really hard to get into. It doesn't happen by accident. Your reserve commission will be in the inactive reserves and is actually a really nice thing to have, to my way of thinking. First of all, part of our nation's problem is we've turned into a country of takers with hardly anyone willing to do much beyond consume. If the nation is willing to provide you with a mostly free college education, accepting a Reserve Commission strikes me a fair exchange, and one that I agreed to myself. If you accept the $32,000 in MARAD money you will be obligated to remain in the Naval Reserves for four years and maintain your Coast Guard license for at least six years. These are very easy obligations to meet, right up there with continuing to breathe, so don't sweat it.

The commission is a nice thing to have for practical as well as patriotic reasons. As you sail, you'll be asked to go active duty for two weeks of the year, but you won't have to quit a job to make your two weeks, so if you miss a year or three no one cares. You get to request your duty station and there are some real interesting ones, so the two weeks of active duty usually turn out to be a heck of a lot of fun.

The Navy realizes that there are some things civilian mariners do better than naval officers and tend to treat us very well during our two weeks of active duty. If the job market ever really tanks (the various maritime academies claim a 95 percent job placement rate) you can count on two weeks of employment a year or even shifting to active duty status—not a bad thing to have in your back pocket in these uncertain times. But I have to tell you that it feels good when I'm filling out a form asking about military service and I can check off Retired Navy rather than None.

Appendix 3 has a list of contact information for the seven four-year maritime academies. There are many other maritime programs offered in various middle and high schools around the country. These programs provide rigorous academic programs with a focus on maritime studies, science, and technology. They also provide studies and opportunity to enter maritime careers upon graduation or to pursue further advanced maritime education at a vocational school, community college, service academy, or maritime academy.

A list of high schools or associations with a maritime-oriented program is available on line at www.madra.dot.gov. Once there, click on the "Education" heading. Numerous other schools around the country provide maritime training for new and experienced mariners that we haven't discussed. The Coast Guard lists almost 2,000 Coast Guard-approved courses offered by almost 250 training providers.

Before you select any maritime training school always be sure to check that it is on the current list online at the USCG Website: www.uscg.mil/nmc/mmc appcourses.asp. Additional schools are listed on the "Careers Afloat" Website at www.marad.dot.gov. Click on the "Education" heading.

Hawsepipers

I have sailed with the offspring of ship's masters who have chosen to attend maritime academies, usually King's Point, because it's free, or one of the state academies if they are unable to face the dreary military aspects of a semi-military academy. The state academies also feature some military customs, though less than King's Point. Other ship's master's offspring choose another route. After high school they join a top notch unlicensed union or private company and start working. Landing the first job is usually hard, but so is Hell Week at an academy. They continue sailing and accruing seatime until they have enough to sit for their license. All the while they're earning a mid-five-figure income and generating no student loan debt. After five or six years they'll have enough time to sit for a license—not a bad way to go if college doesn't have an appeal.

Climbing the hausepipe is the term used to describe starting out in a shipboard entry level position and advancing to a licensed officer position. It isn't as common as it once was, but it is still quite doable. There are a lot of classes you'll have to pay for if you can't find a company or a union to pay them for you. Hawsepipers usually have a better understanding of deck seamanship than academy grads, especially if they sailed as bosuns.

Hawsepipe engineers are rare. It's possible to teach yourself celestial navigation out of a book, but I'm not so sure about thermodynamics. I'm going to get killed for saying this, but engineering is harder than the deck side. There is just so much to learn: electronics, turbines, boilers, controllers, evaporators, purifiers, pumps, refrigeration . . . the list is endless and you have to know it all. The MEBA union school and perhaps the Navy or Coast Guard are just as good as the academies, but it would take an extraordinary person to teach himself engineering. If you want to have a successful career as a licensed marine engineer you will need to go to school, for a long time. Not just a license preparatory school; there is just too much to learn.

I don't want to give the impression that you need a license to have a successful mariner career; any more than you have to be an officer to have a successful military career. Both institutions depend on trained, dedicated, senior non-commissioned officers to survive and thrive. The bosuns and reefer engineers are the non-commissioned officers of the Merchant Marine and are vital to the successful operation of the vessel. They are paid nearly as well as the junior officers and are at least as important. If you never get a Coast Guard license but work your way into a senior unlicensed position on a ship, your impact will be considerable and you will be greatly respected.

Stewards Department Training

I don't have much information on moving up in the stewards department. Once you garner the entry level stewards department rating on your MMD, you're done with the Coast Guard. You will need the same basic safety training as everyone else, though, if you sail internationally. Promotions to chief cook or chief steward are not Coast Guard ratings, and are just between you and your company or union. The best training available is through Seafarers International Union and their school at Piney Point.

But please—and I realize I'm repeating myself here—don't take a chief cook or chief steward's job until you know how to cook. It's possible to sit through any union school class and learn nothing if you don't apply yourself, but don't do it. Treat the job with the respect it deserves and you'll be well respected by the entire crew. Put out the bare minimum effort and you'll quickly gain a reputation as a "belly robber," and going to sea won't be much fun anymore.

Do more than expected and few things can improve the morale of a ship faster than a good stewards department.

Government Paperwork

- Entry Level Qualifications
- Getting Started
- TWIC
- Drug Test
- Physicals
- Application
- Fees
- Passport Photo/Fingerprints
- Passport
- Additional Hints
- Standards in Training and Certification of Watchkeeping (STCW)
- Resume and Cover Letter
- Seatime
- Restricted Seatime
- Time and One-Half Service
- Using Military Time as Sea Service Time
- Creative Ways to Earn Sea Time
- Recency
- Renewals
- The Next Step
- Code of Federal Regulations

Entry Level Qualifications

You need to be in good health, with good vision and color perception. Good physical condition is also required because there is plenty of heavy lifting to be done. You must have some toughness because temperatures can vary from one extreme to another, sometimes during the same voyage. Near the Equator the engine room temperature can exceed 140 degrees; standing bow lookout while entering Dutch Harbor can be colder than you can imagine. You must be able to stand for hours at a time and climb all manner of steel ladders. You'll need the dexterity to slide through tight quarters and good balance to keep on your feet on a wet, heaving deck.

If you plan to earn yourself a Coast Guard license and an officer's position, you'll need some math skills to pass the examinations on either the deck or engine side. If you're still in school, hit the math hard now; it will come in handy.

Getting Started

To be successful in a maritime career, you need to be flexible. You don't have to decide which department you want to spend the rest of your seagoing career in just yet. For your first contract, grab the first job offered, make some money, gain some experience, and you'll be able to make a more informed decision at the end of your first contract.

The Coast Guard will even let you use three months of sea time in the deck department for engine room time and vice versa. I think this is prudent as it allows you to try different departments to find the one that fits you best, without penalty.

To be as employable as possible, you're going to need as many endorsements and classes and ratings as possible. For instance, your initial Merchant Mariners Credential (MMC) should list entry level ratings in all three departments. Then as you become eligible or have the time and money, continue acquiring merit badges—they will only make you more employable. It took me over twenty years to gather most of the various licenses and classes required to keep working, and I still have to renew some of the classes periodically and sit through the new ones that continue to be dreamed up. You never really finish taking new classes and training, or updating your old ones, until you retire.

Title 46 CFR 10.215(d)(2) requires that a mariner applying for a Steward's Department Food Handler rating must provide a statement from a licensed physician, physician assistant, or nurse practitioner attesting that they are free of communicable diseases. Applications for any/all entry level ratings that contain the doctor's letter will get an endorsement that includes Steward's Department (F.H.), but without the letter and without a request for a food handler endorsement, you will get only Ordinary Seaman, Wiper, and Stewards Department. That's not good. Most entry level Steward Department jobs include working in the galley as well as a whole bunch of cleaning; without the Food Handler endorsement you'll miss out on a lot of Steward's Department jobs. So get the letter as cheaply as you can and send it along with your application package. If you ask for a Food Handler endorsement and don't include the letter stating you are free of communicable diseases, the package will sit at the Regional Exam Center for two months, waiting for the additional paperwork, and then it will be sent back.

This is an easy detail to miss, so I'm going to repeat myself:

If you are applying for entry level ratings and wish to have food handler included on your Merchant Mariner's Credential (MMC), be sure to apply for *"Ordinary Seamen, Wiper, Steward's Department (F.H.)* AND be sure to include the statement from your physician attesting that you are free of communicable diseases. This statement can be written on the CG Form 719K, CG Form 719K/E or be provided separately.

Got it? The Coast Guard is considering adding the statement to the next revision of both forms because the present system is causing a lot of problems.

Now why do I keep raving about sea time? Why is it so important to the beginning mariner? Can't you just make a living, see the world, and enjoy yourself? No, you can't. I insist that you keep careful track of your sea time even if you think this is a one-time lark, never to be repeated. Nobody knows what tomorrow holds. Maybe you will never have cause to use documented sea time. Maybe your plan is to return to college and graduate to a desk job with a particularly attractive personal assistant. And maybe things don't quite work out the way you hope, you start thinking about the money you made aboard ship and how much you enjoyed a day off in Hong Kong, then next thing you know you start looking for a ship, planning your new career, and pining for your undocumented sea time. So do me a favor: keep track of all your accrued sea time from the beginning and just file it away. Thanks, you just might owe me a beer someday.

In the coming battle you will be dealing with the following governmental bureaucracies: The Transportation Security Administration (TSA), the United States Coast Guard (USCG), and the National Maritime Center (NMC, USCG). Gird your loins and good luck.

A word of hopefully unnecessary advice: be nice. The customer service reps on the other end of the phone are there to help you and had no hand in constructing the labyrinth you are entering. Respect them and they will help you make it through, assuming you didn't do something irretrievably stupid previously in your life—but we'll get into that shortly.

To work as a seaman you will need a Merchant Mariners Document (MMC); its source is the USCG. The Coast Guard will require the following before issuing an MMC:

1. TWIC Card
2. Drug Test
3. Physical
4. Application for Merchant Mariner
5. Fees
6. Passport photos/Fingerprints
7. Passport or Identification

TWIC

A good place to start is by applying for a Transportation Worker Identification Credential (TWIC). Its purpose is to supply the worker with a biometric credential that allows only properly vetted workers unescorted access to port facilities and ships. Many different occupations are required to obtain the cards, including seamen, longshoremen, truck drivers, taxi drivers, ship repair contractors, and port facility workers. If you want to go to sea you will have to get a TWIC card.

It normally costs $132.50 for your first card, with the price reduced to $105.25 if you already have a Merchant Mariners Credential or certain other documents listed on the website: www.twicinformation.tsa.dhs.gov. The card is good for five years and then you have to buy another one for the same price. If you lose your card it will cost $60.00 for a replacement. You can pay with a money order, certified/cashier's check, corporate check, or credit card. Checks must be made out to Lockheed Martin. (See what I mean about this being a good business for corporate America?)

Acquiring a TWIC card is a four-step process: optional pre-enrollment, in-person enrollment, security threat assessment, notification of results, and card pick-up. It is best to visit the website and use the optional pre-enrollment form to start the process rolling by listing your biographical information, selecting the most convenient enrollment center, and making an appointment for your in-person enrollment. There are about 168 enrollment centers to choose from, but if there is none nearby, you are going to have to travel, because you must enroll in person. It usually takes about 10 or 15 minutes to provide any more required information, provide required identification, fill out forms, get fingerprinted, pay the fee, and take a picture. For a list of acceptable identification papers go to www.tsa.gov/twic. Click on the listing of acceptable documents for U.S. citizens or click on the listing of acceptable documents for non-U.S. citizens. Citizens of Puerto Rico applying for a TWIC have their own place to click on the same website.

It usually takes six to eight weeks after enrollment before the TWIC is ready. Various problems may extend the wait. You'll be notified by phone when your card is ready, and you'll have to pick it up in person at a specified enrollment center. If you have further questions about the TWIC, check the website or call (866) 347-8942 for recorded information.

The original TWIC program consisted of two parts. The first part was an extremely difficult-to-counterfeit card that indicated the holder had been vetted and was found to be worthy of admittance to port facilities around the world. The second aspect of the plan was for a secure card reader located at the entrance of each facility, to insure only holders of valid TWICs were admitted. However, while over 1.8 million cards have been bought by waterfront workers at considerable difficulty, the card readers have never arrived. Apparently the technological problems have yet to be solved, though my bank has a machine that gives me cash whenever I insert my card in the reader. It makes me wonder if all the TWIC stakeholders are as committed as mariners are forced to be.

Drug Test

There is a very precise method for taking a drug test; no variation is permitted. For instance, if you must take a pre-employment drug test, it is unlikely the test will satisfy the Coast Guard as well, unless it is exactly the type called for. However, as in Option 3 shown below, you can take a pre-employment drug test and ask the company to write on company letterhead that you passed a pre-employment drug test, and the Coast Guard will accept that. The test procedures must be followed exactly or the test will not be accepted. The correct exam centers and laboratories must be used, as well. Don't take any short cuts; educate yourself in advance and you'll do fine.

If you're not sure if you can pass a drug test, wait. It usually takes a month or so for pot to leave your system, cocaine only a few days. I actually knew someone stupid enough to flunk a pre-hire drug test because of cocaine (the brother-in-law of the Human Resources Manager). We speculated he must have been doing lines on the way to the testing facility, so I suppose it can happen.

If you can't get clean for a test, this is not the right industry for you. Whenever something bad happens on a ship—a grounding, collision, injury, or other disaster—the law requires that everyone who may have had a hand in the situation be drug tested. In practicality everyone gets tested. If you come up positive, your life takes an immediate and dramatic turn for the worse. You won't work in the industry again for a long time and the USCG will have you under its thumb with a considerable list of hoops to jump through before you can return to work. Chances are your seagoing career will come to an end. If you can't get clean, give it up; you're just wasting your time and everyone else's.

I first left the industry in the late '80s to go commercial fishing. At the time, going to sea was a constant battle with drunks, particularly leaving port, but drug testing was just coming into practice. The saying was, "If we're in port for over 24 hours, a drunk will be fired." When I returned to merchant shipping about 10 years later, just about the entire navy of cartoon drunks was gone.

"Where did all the drunks go?" I asked. "Not that I'm complaining."

"Drug tests got 'em."

> "But getting stoned wasn't the problem; I could have used a few more mellow pot heads, but the drunks were killing me."
>
> "Well, as it turned out, most of the raving alcoholics also did a little of this and that on the side, got caught by the drug tests, and are now out of the industry."

I'm not sure that is true, but it's as good an explanation as any. It's a different industry today—the drunk or stoner is a rare exception, rather than the expectation. Good thing, too, as the crews are smaller and the lifestyle more stressed. However, it has diminished the quality of the sea stories dramatically. Consequently, if you have substance abuse issues this is not the industry for you—just a quiet little word to the wise.

Before the USCG will issue you an MMC you must prove you are drug free. You have three options to do so.

Option 1: Take a USCG drug test within the last 185 days using a DOT 5 Panel (SAMHSA 5 Panel) test for opiates, marijuana, cocaine, phencyclidine and amphetamines. The test must be taken at an approved clinic and evaluated at an approved lab. The list for both can be found at the Coast Guard website at http://uscg.mil/STCW/ Merchant Mariner Licensing and Documentation. Click on "DRUG TEST INFO." It goes over the same information as discussed here.

Option 2: Reference 46 CFR 16.220(c)(2) states an ORIGINAL DATED letter on marine employer of drug test consortium stationery or for military members, an ORIGINAL DATED letter from your command on command letterhead attesting to participation in random drug testing programs. The following examples must be followed word for word, with no variation.

EXAMPLE 1 (From Marine Employers or Drug Test Consortium): APPLICANT'S NAME and either SOCIAL SECURITY NUMBER or MARINER'S REFERENCE NUMBER has been subject to a random testing program meeting the criteria of Title 46 CFR 16.230 for at least 60 days during the previous

185 days and has not failed nor refused to participate in a chemical test for dangerous drugs.

EXAMPLE 2 (Active Duty Military, Reserve, or recently retired Military/Military Sealift Command/NOAA/Army Corps of Engineers): APPLICANT'S NAME and either SOCIAL SECURITY NUMBER or MARINER REFERENCE NUMBER has been subject to random testing program for at least 60 days during the previous 185 days and has not failed to participate in a chemical test for dangerous drugs.

EXAMPLE 3 (Active Duty Military): This is to certify that APPLICANT'S NAME and either SOCIAL SECURITY NUMBER or MARINER REFERENCE NUMBER has been subject to random drug testing while on active duty with the U.S. Armed Forces. This member has been on continuous active duty since DATE. This individual has not failed nor refused any drug test.

Option 3: In accordance with 46 CFR 16.220(c)(1), an ORIGINAL DATED letter on marine employer stationery signed by a company official, stating that you have passed a pre-employment or random chemical test for dangerous drugs within the past 185 days.

EXAMPLE: APPLICANT'S NAME and either SOCIAL SECURITY NUMBER or MARINER REFERENCE NUMBER passed a chemical test for dangerous drugs, required under Title 46 CFR 16.210 or 16.230. On DATE (note that date must not be more than six months previous to the date of letter) and APPLICANT'S NAME has had no subsequent positive drug test results since that date.

That's about it for the drug and alcohol testing, except I'll reiterate how dangerous drug and even alcohol issues can be to a present day mariner's career. Remember the Exxon Valdez oil spill? What was it caused by? Drunken captain, right?

Wrong.

The captain had left the bridge at the time of the grounding. He left the watch in the hands of a Coast Guard licensed third officer, who had also been tested and found competent to conn the ship through Prince Williams Sound (I also have been tested by the USCG and found competent to conn a ship through Prince William Sound, for what it's worth) by the same United States Coast Guard that later tried to crucify him. The third officer somehow managed to hit virtually the only shallow spot not next to the shore in the entire Sound.

As it turns out, the State of Alaska had received billions and billions of dollars in oil tax revenues, some of which were supposed to be spent in part on oil recovery equipment. They weren't. The various oil companies involved in the Alaska pipeline were supposed to have all sorts of oil contingency plans in place should the unthinkable occur. They didn't. The United States Coast Guard was supposed to have a system of pilotage and vessel traffic control in place that would guarantee an accident couldn't happen. It happened. They would all like you to believe it was all Captain Hazelwood's fault. It wasn't.

So, obviously they needed a scapegoat. Captain Hazelwood was it. He was alcohol tested 12 hours after the grounding and he came up with alcohol in his blood. The Coast Guard then announced the grounding was due to his drinking. Imagine if you were involved in a car accident, then the next morning the police came to your house, tested you for alcohol, and charged you with a DUI. They then announced to the media that you were driving drunk. It wouldn't be fair, and it wasn't fair to Captain Hazelwood, who sued the Coast Guard and won. The last I heard he was teaching at one of the state maritime academies. I wish him well.

The point is you can get in a whole lot of trouble with drugs or alcohol going to sea if something bad happens, even if you didn't screw up, particularly as you move up the ladder. The image of a drunken sailor isn't nearly as pervasive—or as tolerated—as it once was.

Physicals

This also can be very complicated if you don't do it exactly as set out on the Coast Guard website. The section on physicals was 75 pages plus appendixes last I looked. There is nothing in it except perhaps blindness that will automatically disqualify you from getting an MMC. Take a look at the physical ability guidelines on page 15 and medical conditions subject to additional review on page 20 to get an idea of what level of health and fitness the Coast Guard is looking for.

I've had to treat both stroke and heart attack victims aboard ship and so am quite happy there are health requirements to getting an MMC. The physical must be recorded on the proper Coast Guard form (which can be found at www.uscg.mil/STCW/) in the application packet, or it doesn't count. You can also visit your Regional Exam Center (listed in Appendix 4) and pick up a hard copy of the physical examination form (CG-719K).

Bottom line, your doctor must convince the Coast Guard you are fit for sea duty.

The physical has a one-year life span from the time the doctor dates it, but once on file with the Coasties it lives for another three years, meaning you will not have to redo it if you upgrade your Coast Guard documents within three years. Cool, huh?

Keep in mind if you belong to a union or many companies they will pay for both your drug tests and physicals, so ask. I'm determined to save you the price of this book and that might just do it. Obviously if you're just starting out, that doesn't apply, so we'll have to keep looking for savings.

The medical requirements are becoming more stringent over time. They can't be too tough yet, as I still see sailors in their eighties aboard ship, but the regulations are headed in that direction. A quite overweight friend of mine is a deck officer who tried to renew his license recently. He was told by the Coast Guard he needed to take a sleep apnea test to determine if he was able to get a good night's sleep. He eventually passed all of the tests and got his license renewed, but he was on the beach for six months before everything was completed.

Application

Again, you can pick up the entire application package, with all of the forms you need at a regional exam center, or you can call them and have them mailed to you, or you can download them from the USCG website. To download them go to www.uscg.mil/STCW/ and click on the "Merchant Mariner Info" tab. Now click on "application and forms download". You'll see a list of forms; click on form CG-719B. Work through the form patiently, fill it out completely, and sign it.

The application lays the groundwork for a background check. They are mainly looking for criminal convictions and substance abuse issues. There is a specific assessment period for each type of conviction. The assessment period is how long you have to wait to get a Merchant Mariners Credential after each conviction. You can, however, ask for a reconsideration request. For example: A larceny conviction means you can't get an MMC for 3 to 5 years. But say you're convicted of stealing a candy bar while you were a minor. You can ask for a reconsideration request and the Coast Guard may shorten the wait, or not, depends. Even a murder conviction generates only a twenty-year assessment period. So, just about the time you're getting out of the joint…

Be completely truthful on your application. Lying will get you turned down, while the truth will usually only add some complications. In this age of cross-referencing computer systems you aren't going to get away with too many lies. The application is a federal government document and it is a criminal offense to be untruthful on it. If you have questions about how your criminal convictions might affect your USCG paperwork, take a look at 46 CFR 10.201, which lays out rules for licensing former criminals.

The background check can be reused for a year. It is required for an original license or documents, also a renewal or an upgrade. It can take a remarkably long time—months, even. The Coast Guard can usually tell you how long the checks are running. Remember the background check you had to get for your TWIC card? The USCG knows nothing about it; it was done by the TSA and doesn't count for the Coast Guard. But they are allowed only three days to complete the check and it's usually done in a day because they use the FBI data base.

Fees

Everything costs. There is an evaluation fee, a testing fee, and an issuance fee. Refer to Appendix 6 for a complete explanation and table of USCG fees excerpted directly from the USCG Manual. During the application process, try to insure all of the required information is transferred to your new documents by discussing all of the endorsements you hope to acquire at the Regional Exam Center. If some are missed you'll have to send them back and you'll pay all over again. To protect yourself, know what endorsements you are entitled to and make sure you have all the proper documentation.

It's not that the examiners are incompetent; it's just so complicated, especially when you advance in your career and are entitled to a dozen different little merit badges, all of which are important. It becomes very easy to miss one or two and you'll have to start over and repay the fees. Know what you need, bring the proper documentation, and try to remain cheerful and polite, even when you get crushed. I know of what I speak.

Get yourself a 1-inch-thick three-ring binder with clear inserts and pockets. As you acquire documents, certifications, licenses, sea time letters, drug free letters, and so on and so on, place them all in the binder. Keep it organized and it will save you much heartache over time. Now all you have to do is not lose the binder and not forget to stow your documents and you're golden. This organization will help you with the Coast Guard, finding a job, clearing through the union hall, and signing on a ship.

> One time I left my papers on the roof of my car when I drove off. I was able to recover my dropped documents, but for years my license sported tire tracks across it, not a good look. Protect your documents.

Passport Photos/Fingerprints

I've got some good news. You will be fingerprinted and photographed for your TWIC card; those same prints and pictures are forwarded to the Coast Guard and used for your MMC. They do not have to be redone, a nice little bonus that didn't used to be true. As the old toast says, "God bless Samuel Plimsol and the United States Coast Guard." (Samuel Plimsol, an old dead Brit, is regarded as the father of the Plimsol mark, painted on every merchant ship in the world to reveal overloading.)

Passport

You don't actually need a passport to get an MMC, but this is a really good time to get one. You can use it as proof of identification for the Coast Guard and I'm going to keep beating you over the head with the idea that you need to acquire every little endorsement and advantage available to make yourself more attractive to prospective employers. For many ships a passport is a pre-employment condition and rush passports cost more. So why not get it now?

It's even possible to get a free work-only passport that is perfectly valid. But I think the idea is perfectly silly. If you want to work as a merchant mariner you're probably looking for adventure and excitement; world travel is something you're looking forward to. But a work-only passport isn't valid for personal travel. Crossing between Uganda to Rwanda in East Africa is going to be tough if you have to convince a border guard that you are traveling to Rwanda to catch a ship. Get a regular passport; you'll be glad you did.

Go to www.travel.state.gov to find how to get a passport efficiently. You'll need to:

1. Fill out Form DS-11
2. Submit Completed Form DS-11 in person
3. Submit evidence of U.S. citizenship
4. Present identification
5. Submit a photocopy of the identification document(s) presented (step 4)
6. Pay applicable fee
7. Provide one passport photo
8. The most difficult requirement is proof of U.S. citizenship if you don't have a certified birth certificate. The problem can be solved; it just takes time and money, so start now.

Identification and Proof of Citizenship

You'll need a couple of pieces of identification plus proof of citizenship or proof of resident alien status. Your passport will serve as identification and proof of citizenship. The Coast Guard website gives a list of acceptable forms of identification and proof of citizenship. You'll need at least one photo ID document. If you're planning on mailing your application package you can photocopy your identification and proof of citizenship.

Additional Hints

We are almost done, but let's go over a few more things that should help smooth the process a little bit. When you mail off your application package for a Merchant Mariners Credential you'll send it to the Regional Exam Center of your choice. There is a list of exam centers in Appendix 4. The

Regional Exam Center will take a look at your package, contact you if they spot any problems, and then send the final package to the National Maritime Center, where it will be evaluated again and acted on.

I suggest you patronize your closest REC, because there will be times when you'll need to visit in person. Even if you live hundreds of miles away from the closest REC I'd use it, or at least the one in the city you most enjoy visiting. Take notes when you talk on the phone, including names, dates and what was discussed.

It is a good idea to hand-deliver as much paperwork to the REC as possible. You can use the mail if you have to, but be aware you are taking a risk. If you do use the mail, follow up in a few days with a phone call to establish if the package arrived. Send your items registered mail to confirm delivery. Use an "ATT:" in the address to direct it to whomever you spoke to about mailing something.

Once you pick an REC, stick with it unless the center is so hopeless that you have to make a change. These centers are getting better so this shouldn't happen.

It wasn't that long ago that there was no such thing as the National Exam Center; you just went down to the local Coast Guard office with all of your paperwork in order, and your documents were produced within a day, usually less. If one office didn't accept your sea time you could sneak off to the next office and try again, often successfully. Bribery was also a real problem.

> Years ago I remember asking an able bodied seaman on a tanker to tie something off with a bowline; he looked at me as if I asked him to find the derivatives of a calculus equation, which struck me as odd at the time. A couple of years later some of the local Coast Guard examiners were indicted for selling seamen's papers and it all made sense. I think the NMC has alleviated many of those problems.

As I've said, once you pick a Regional Exam Center, stick with it. If you move your files around, bad things can happen— such as your files getting lost. Use the same REC and get your answers from the same REC, they'll be more consistent.

Remember I advised you to stay cool, no matter what? If you can pull that off, the people in your local REC will respond and go out of their way to help you. As you get to know them things will tend to go easier and smoother, just like in any other bureaucracy. If you have no choice you can legally move your file from one REC to another, just make sure it happens with confirmation phone calls or volunteer to transport the file yourself.

The next step, after you've picked an REC and demonstrated yourself to be a fine human being, is to establish a relationship with the people behind the desk at the center. There is usually a go-to person at each office who has been there for a while and has a really good understanding of the rules and regulations. That's who you want to get to know. Be pleasant, thoughtful and understanding—and try to get that person's email address. Then you'll be able to ask the right person the hard questions and get good information in writing. As your applications are evaluated, approval will be forthcoming by email, so keep the return address. It's the pipeline to the evaluators: how valuable is that?

Learn the system as quickly as you can. The USCG website has hours and hours of information on it. Read it, learn it, know it. The National Exam Center is staffed with really knowledgeable people; I've called a lot and never been disappointed. Their phone number is (888) 427-5662, their website is www.uscg.mil/nmc/

The following are the top ten reasons Coast Guard licensing and MMD Applications are delayed. I stole it right off of their website.

1. Medical Condition
Additional medical information is required whenever a medical condition is identified on the Merchant Marine Personnel Physical Examination Report.

2. Sea Service
Missing or conflicting information on the sea service letter (e.g., not including tonnage or horsepower, the position listed does not agree with other documents in the application package, or conflicting waters). Service should be documented with discharges, letters from marine employers, or small boat sea service forms. If a small boat service form is used, it must be certified and signed by the owner or proof of individual ownership is required.

3. Applications

If the application is not completed, it will be returned for correction. Three signatures are mandatory: Section III ("Have you ever... ?" questions), Section V (consent of National Driver Registry check), and Section VI (application certification). When the "Applying for:" block is left blank or is incomplete, the REC is left to guess what you want.

4. Copies of Required Certificates/Documents *Photocopies of essential documents must be provided. These may include Radar Observer Certificates, other course completion certificates, 1ˢᵗ Aid/CPR certificates, Towing Officer Assessment Records (TOARs), STCW assessments, citizenship documents when required, etc.*

5. Drug Screen

A drug screen is often rejected because it does not contain the Medical Review Officer's (MRO) signature or the Code of Federal Regulations, Title 46, Part 16, Section 220.

6. Current or Past License, Document, and/or SCTW

Owner of a certificate who does not indicate it in the history (Section II of the application) or does not include a copy of their credentials (front and back) with the application package. This especially applies for renewals and mariners with past transactions at other RECs.

7. Physical Exam

If the Merchant Marine Personnel Physical Examination/Certification Report is not complete, it will be returned for correction. Particular attention is paid to the "competent", "not competent", and "needs further review" boxes, which are frequently blank. Often the type of color vision exam given in Section IV is not indicated or mariners who wear glasses and/or contacts submit exams without their uncorrected vision listed in Section III.

8. Awaiting Information

NMC must verify your credentials. Often the Mariner forgets information or we need more information in order to evaluate your experience, medical history, drug testing, or approved courses. Please include all required information.

9. Training Certificate(s)

Please make sure that you include copies of all training certificates, approved courses, or any qualifying certificate to help support your claim for a rating or credential.

10. User Fees

No or incorrect payments are included with the application. Licensing user fees changed as of October 4, 1999. Current fees are published in the most recent Code of Federal Regulations, Title 46, Part 10, Section 109 and the web.

There it is; that's what you need to know to get your original MMC from the USCG. Hopefully I've overstated the difficulty and you'll have no problem getting what you need from the Coast Guard. Your Merchant Mariners Document used to be a driver's-license-sized card with your picture on the front and a list of your qualifications on the back; now it's a sticker that goes in your Merchant Mariners Credential Book (the little red book that looks like a passport).

Make sure to tell the USCG you want an entry level endorsement for each of the three departments: Ordinary Seaman, Wiper, and Steward/Foodhandler. Your plan may be to work your way up in the engine room, but you may still have to start off making beds and washing dishes. As I stated before, in order to get the Steward/Foodhandler endorsement you must include a letter from your doctor stating you are free from all communicable diseases as part of your physical, a requirement I most heartily endorse. The bad news is: You're on to the next piece of paper, the STCW.

Standards in Training and Certification of Watchkeeping (STCW)

The STCW certificate includes your picture and lists your endorsements. It is an 8½ by 11-inch sheet of paper with writing on both sides. It is as important to you as your MMC. Do not lose either one; they are both vital.

In 1991 the United States joined the International Maritime Organization (IMO), an arm of the United Nations (UN). The IMO was created to provide international regulations for ships, thereby providing some level of protection for both the vessel crews and the environment. Consequently, we must follow IMO regulations, the Standards in Training and Certification of Watchkeeping (STCW) being one such regulation. The IMO has a website detailing its history and purpose, if you're interested: www.imo.org.

The IMO creates regulations that all of its signatories are party to and must obey. Each signatory country then creates its own regulations that insure its flag ships are in compliance with the IMO regulations. The U.S. government does this by publishing regulations in the Code of Federal Regulations (CFR's); they are available online at www.uscode.house.gov/usc.htm. We will come back to the CFRs again and again. They're not much fun to read (actually they completely suck) but are invaluable because they contain all the rules that run our professional lives. If you plan to work as a licensed officer you will have to learn how to look up regulations in the CFRs; this skill is part of the Coast Guard licensing tests. In the meantime it will help you plan out your career by laying out the various requirements—not a bad thing to get comfortable with.

The United States Coast Guard enforces the rules promulgated in the CFRs, with help from the American Bureau of Shipping, an organization made up of professional seafarers. The average Coast Guard inspector spends a lot of time thumbing through his CFRs, so you don't have much chance of winning an argument with him without a passage in the CRFs to back you up.

Now that you know the players and the acronyms, let's return to the subject of this section. The STCW certificate came about after a series of environmentally disastrous groundings around the world indicated much more comprehensive training was required for the world's merchant mariners. Regulations were drawn up to improve vessel inspections, port control, communications, mariner training, mariner fitness, and certification. These regulations, which are the guts of STCW 95, went into effect in February of 2002.

Not every mariner needs an STCW certificate to work. If the vessel you're working on sails outside of U.S. waters (over 200 nautical miles offshore) you will need STCW 95. So if you get a job on a harbor tug you can be a thunderhead, continue to work, and not get an STCW. However, when the tug is transferred to Anchorage, Alaska and has to transit either international waters or the inside passage (Canadian Waters), you'll have to get off, aggravating your employer. Many companies require the STCW even if their vessels don't; some companies or unions will pay for the STCW training.

But don't wait: get the Basic Safety Training (BST) endorsement for your STCW as soon as you are able. It's a five-day course and you might even learn something useful— like how to save your own life. The course will cover firefighting and prevention, safe working practices, marine pollution prevention, shipboard communications, first aid, CPR, and emergency equipment such as life jackets, survival suits, life boats, and life rafts. The cost is usually just under $1,000, so try to find a company or union willing to pay for some or all of your professional training. If you can't, then pay for it yourself; you'll earn the money back in a week or two.

Again, you need to make yourself attractive to employers by acquiring certificates and endorsements. The STCW certificate opens up the world of international shipping, so it's the next milestone to achieve after your MMC.

Resume and Cover Letter

You don't need a resume and a cover letter to get your seaman's documents, but you may very well need them to get a job, once you get your documents. There are many Internet sources of instruction on writing a resume, and many lengthy books on the subject as well. I'll give you a short rundown so you can quickly write something that will get you hired. If this is your first job and you don't have a resume, you can whip one together yourself by bringing attention to your skills, despite your lack of on-the-job experience.

Instructions:

In a bold font, type your name, address, phone number, and e-mail address at the top of your resume. Center it at the top of the page.

List your skills in bullet points. Use the header "SKILLS:" If the bullet points are incomplete sentences, that is fine, but don't finish them with a period.

Next, list your achievements (ACHIEVEMENTS:), including any awards you've won. Use the same bullet point style as your skills.

List your work experience (WORK EXPERIENCE:), even if the position was part of your family duties, volunteer work or a part-time job you held while in school. Start with your most current position, specifying the start and end dates, followed by the company and location as a header. Finish up with the duties you performed.

Specify your education next (EDUCATION:), listing all of your education. For example, list your college even if you did not complete college with a degree. If you do have a high school diploma or a college degree, by all means include it. Also list any courses that might make your resume stand out among the others.

Name your interests (INTERESTS:), including those that may prove you physically fit.

Listing your physical statistics—height, weight, and birth date—is not required, but once again, may serve you well in showing you are physically fit for the job.

Final Tips

Be sure to include a well-written cover letter with your resume. I've enclosed a sample resume and cover letter that follow the above format. Make yourself clear; write a clear heading for each section of your resume. Use one, crisp font, such as Arial. Avoid using fancy fonts and italics. You want your resume and cover letter to scan easily, in case the reader wants to put your resume into a data base for future reference. Use consistent spacing format. Be direct and to the point. Avoid going over two pages on your resume. Your work should be easy to read and understand. For gosh sakes, use your spell check and ask an English major to review it!

John Wannabee
100000 Main Street
Driggs, ID 00000
Phone: 123-345-5678

February 28. 2012

Captain Tugaholic
Oregon Oceanographic
Back Breaker Lane
Never Ending Bay, OR 00000

Dear Captain Tugaholic:

I am very interested in working for you on the R/V Woopie. I have wanted to work aboard a boat for as long as I can remember, and I am doing everything I can possibly think of to land the job. I worked as a deckhand the last three summers on my uncle's salmon boat and learned that I want to make my career on the sea.

While I am lacking seagoing experience, I grew up on a dairy farm in Driggs, Idaho and I am accustomed to performing under extreme conditions: hard work and long hours, usually while cold, hungry, or both. I can fix just about any farming equipment that needs attention. During the off season, I worked for Grand Targhee Ski Resort as a short order cook in the Trap Bar and Grill. This required the ability to cook, so I have these skills to offer in the galley.

The most satisfying work I have done has been some of the toughest. I've gone deep sea fishing with my relatives on the Washington Coast many times so I know I have no seasickness problems. To sum things up, the good news is that you would not need to teach me how to work. My parents already did that for us. I would love to show you that my deal is to work harder than anyone else, that I am a quick learner, and I know how to follow directions under pressure. I'd love the opportunity to prove it.

I look forward to hearing from you soon.

Sincerely,

John Wannabee

John Wannabee
100000 Main Street
Driggs, ID 00000
Phone: 123-345-5678

SKILLS:
- Accomplished short order cook; Grand Targhee Resort, Trap Bar & Grill
- Great team player
- Able to work long hours, under extreme conditions, while maintaining quality
- Mechanically skilled
- Experienced with boats and navigation

ACHIEVEMENTS:
- Completely restored and rebuilt 1957 John Deere tractor
- Won "Best Barbeque" three years running, at Teton Valley County Fair
- Completed three salmon fishing Seasons: 2009-2011
- Took Pope and Young Archery record for elk: 2009
- Raised $4,300 in pledge monies for "Running Long for the Cure" 27-mile marathon: 2010

WORK EXPERIENCE:
2000 to Present: Wannabee Best Dairy Farm, Driggs, Idaho
I operated all milking and heavy equipment dairy farming equipment and implements. Learned all about diesel repair of all farming equipment. Assisted in calving in the spring, milking every morning.
2008 to Present: Grand Targhee Ski Resort Trap Bar and Grill
Worked with a team of restaurant and bar employees to prepare and serve high quality breakfast, lunch, and dinner during ski season.
Summers of 2011, 2010, 2009: The Ironhead
 Worked as a deckhand on this salmon boat during my last three summer breaks from school

EDUCATION:
High school diploma at Teton Valley High school, Driggs, ID in 2008

INTERESTS:
Cooking, skiing, snowboarding, mountain biking, big game hunting & fishing

PHYSICAL STATISTICS:
Height: 6' 2"   Weight: 200   Birth date: 11/30/1990

Sea Time

I've already touched on the importance of keeping track of your sea time; now I'm going to beat it to death. Why is sea time so important? Well, when you start out you may only make a couple of thousand dollars a month. Would you like to increase that by about 1,000 percent? You can, but it's going to take sea time.

To move up the ladder in the Merchant Marine takes endorsements and bigger and bigger licenses, which in turn require tests and sea time. You can only take a Coast Guard test after you have accrued a specified number of days at sea working in the correct department. At times this sea time is more valuable than money. I've taken pay cuts to earn required sea time. Sometimes it's the Coast Guard that requires a particular type of sea time, sometimes it's a union that wants the sea time.

It's a pain, it's part of life, but just don't ever waste sea time by failing to document earned sea time that you think you will never need. I know I'm being redundant all over again, but I really want to hammer home the value of sea time. Even on small vessels the sea time counts for something, so document any time that you can and just throw it in a file until you need it.

Often the Coast Guard will allow you to use partial sea time that doesn't really seem to fit the next license, such as using 3 months of engine time toward your deck license. Document it all and you may be pleasantly surprised. At the least, you'll never have to try and track down bankrupt companies or retired skippers to try to resurrect sea time.

The USCG offers a bewildering array of licenses, based on tonnage of the vessel, the department licensed, and the waters covered. The best way to evaluate available licenses in both deck and engine departments is to go to the USCG website at www.uscg.mil/nmc. Select the Applications button on the left side of the screen. Now select Check Lists, and then select a category.

You will have the following options: Deck Officers, Engineering Officers, or duplications, Entry Level, Radio Officer, Renewal and VSO. You will most likely be interested in the first two, Deck or Engineering Officer. There are 47 deck options and 18 engineering options on the respective drop down menus. Click on the title that seems appropriate and you will arrive at a list of all of the requirements for that particular license.

The general requirements are usually fairly similar. It is the sea service requirements that you need to pay attention to. It will be a few years before you can start actively stalking a license, but I've included the list so you can plan a strategy to sit for a license as you become eligible. I want you to start thinking about that massive pay raise; it makes it easier to study for your next test.

The easiest way to document sea time is with a USCG Certificate of Discharge (CG-718). Many—but not all—companies use the form. It's small, green, and includes all the information the USCG is looking for in a sea time letter. It contains the name, citizenship, Merchant Mariners Number and signature of the seaman, signature of the Master of the vessel, the seaman's rating, dates and ports of shipment and discharge, name, class and Official number of the vessel, name of employer, and nature of the voyage.

Keep these certificates of discharge. They are also used by companies and unions to document sea time for vacation pay and benefits eligibility. A sealed plastic pouch in that 3-ring binder we talked about is not a bad place to keep them.

If your company doesn't automatically provide a certificate of discharge, a letter on company letterhead will do the trick, with the following caveats:

1. It must be signed by the vessel master, owner or human resources manager, and must contain
2. name and official number of vessel;
3. vessel's gross tonnage;
4. dates of signing on and off of the vessel;
5. nature of voyage: Foreign, Coastwise, Inland, Western Rivers, Great Lakes;
6. description of duties, letter of watch standing; and
7. special characteristics of the vessel, such as sailing or towing.

Some smaller companies are hard to get letters of sea time out of; they either don't know how or just can't be bothered. In that case, write it yourself, type it on company letterhead, and have the appropriate person sign it.

Number 6 refers to a letter of watch standing. There are deck seaman jobs that do not include standing watch on the bridge, such as some dayman jobs. The Coast Guard wants to see that some of your sea time (usually six months) includes bridge watch duties. So you'll need a letter of watch standing. This is a fairly new requirement, so it may not be familiar to the vessel's captain or owner.

The Policy letter 01-02 states, "Applicants must present evidence of three years sea service which includes six months service performing bridge watchkeeping duties under the supervision of a qualified master or licensed officer."

Here's a sample of what the Coast Guard is looking for:

To Whom It May Concern:

AB Jackie Hardcharger (social security number) performed bridge watch standing duties as part of the bridge team under the master or licensed deck officer from (time aboard vessel) until (time off of the vessel) while working aboard the (vessel name).

Best Regards,

Vessel Master

Restricted Sea Time

This can be bad news. If you work on a ship that never or seldom leaves the dock, the USCG doesn't believe your sea time is as valuable as sea time earned on vessels actually sailing the seven seas. So they dock you; you may have to spend 3 days aboard ship for each day of sea time credit. That's the bad news.

The good news is that these types of vessels can be a great deal of fun. How cool would it be to work on a gambling ship that never lets her lines go? A lot, but you may not make much money or get much sea time.

A lot of these vessels that don't go anywhere don't pay very well, which means they have a lot of openings and you might very well start out on one. It's important to know what you're getting into, and the company certainly isn't going to tell you that the sea time on their vessel isn't worth a whole lot. As long as you know the details before signing on, you can make your own decision.

> I spent a few months on an Oil Response Vessel that stayed tied to the berth most of the time. I made very little money, didn't enjoy myself at all, but it tided me over until I could find a better job. You do what you have to do.

Here is the breakdown on evaluating sea time for ships that get under way very little or not at all. I'm going to copy the NMC Policy letter 09-01 so you get it right from the horse's mouth. You don't have to read this letter until you need to, when you're offered a job on a vessel that doesn't get under way very much.

1. *This policy letter sets forth the standards for crediting of sea service on vessels that may spend all or a significant amount of their time moored, such as casino vessels, oil spill response vessels (OSRV), liftboats, and vessels operating in a semi-operational or reduced operating status.*

2. *Reference (a) provides for the evaluation of service in a marine related area, other than at sea, or on unique vessels, for a determination of equivalence to traditional service. Actual underway service is essential to development of the skills, experience, and knowledge expected of a licensed merchant marine officer or qualified rating. Time while moored may provide some of the professional experience, but cannot substitute equally for actual underway experience.*

3. *Regional Examination Centers (REC) shall credit such time as follows:*

    a. Service On Vessels that Do Not Get Under Way: This includes vessels that are actually in operation but do not get under way (such as dock-side casino vessels), and whose service is mandated by the vessel's Certificate of Inspection (COI).

        (1) Engineering department: Dockside service may be credited day-for-day for renewals, upgrades, recency, and original license/Merchant Mariner Document (MMD).

        (2) Deck department: Dockside service may be credited as follows in accordance with reference (a):

            (a) Renewal: Service is credited as "closely related service" for renewal of licenses and MMDs. Mariners, who dem-

onstrate three years of service within the last five years, in any capacity in the deck department, will be eligible for renewal. In addition, deck officers will be required to successfully complete the Rules of the Road open-book exercise. When submit ted in combination with underway service, such service may be credited at the rate of three days of service equals one day of credit up to a maximum credit of 180 days.

(b) Raise In Grade/Upgrade of MMD Rating: Service may be credited for upgrade if it is similar in nature to the duties performed aboard an in-service, underway vessel. Such service may be credited for up to 180 days of the service required for an upgrade at the rate of three days of service equals one day of credit.

(c) Original License or MMD: Such service may be credited for up to one-half of the required service for the particular license or MMD ap plied for, but not more than 180 days of credit, at the rate of three days of service equals one day of credit.

b. *Service Aboard Commercial Vessels That Get Underway of Only Limited Periods:* This includes vessels that are actually in operation and occasionally get underway for short voyages. On any day that a vessel gets underway, service by deck and engineering crewmembers may be credited day for day, for renewals, upgrades, recency, and original license or MMD. This recognizes crew duties necessary for preparing the vessel before and after the voyage, as well as the duties associated with even a limited period of vessel operation, which fall into regu lar deck and engineering responsibilities for a vessel in traditional service. On days when these vessels do not get underway, service may be credited in accordance with paragraph 3.

c. <u>Service Aboard Commercial Vessels Operating in an Artificial Impoundment:</u> *Service by deck and engineering crewmembers on vessels that are in opera tion within an artificial impoundment, and whose service is mandated by the COI, will be credited in accordance with paragraph 3.a.*

d. <u>Service Aboard Liftboats:</u> *Service may be credited without restriction on days when the vessel is underway. When elevated and in operation under authority of the vessel's COI, service may be credited as follows:*

> **(1) Engineering Department:** *If the engineering plant is operational and engineering personnel are standing a regular watch, then service may be cred ited in accordance with paragraph 3.a.(1). If the en gineering plant is non-operational, service shall be credited in the same manner as deck department personnel described in paragraph 3.a.(2).*

> **(2) Deck Department:** *When elevated for extended periods service may be credited in accordance with 3.a.(a).*

e. <u>Service On Vessels In a Semi-Operational Status:</u> *This includes vessels such as oil spill response vessels, an chored (extended-period) pre-positioned ready reserve ves sels, and other vessels moored and in a semi-operational or "on-call" status, which are maintained, manned, and operated to facilitate a rapid deployment. Service may be credited with out restriction on days when the vessel is underway. Moored service may be credited as credited as follows (except as oth erwise provided for in reference (b) for Military Sealift Com mand (MSC) operational tempo (OPTEMPO) ships and other fast sealift ships):*

> **(1) Engineering Department:** *If the engineering plant is operational and engineering personnel are standing a regular watch or required to perform maintenance or repair, then service may be cred ited in accordance with paragraph 3.a.(1). If the en gineering plant is non-operational, service shall be*

credited in the same manner as deck department personnel described in paragraph 3.a.(2).

(2) Deck Department: Service shall be credited in accordance with paragraph 3.a.(2).

f. _Reduced Operating Service (ROS) Vessels:_ *There are a variety of vessels that spend the majority of their time moored, with reduced crews, and limited operating systems. Service may be credited without restriction on days when the vessel is underway. During all other times service shall be credited as follows:*

(1) **Engineering Department:** *Service shall be credited in accordance with reference (c).*

(2) **Deck Department:** *Service shall be credited in accordance with paragraph 3.a.(2).*

g. _Oil Spill Response Barges (OSRBs):_ *These vessels are non-self-propelled and spend significant time at anchor. They are not required to have licensed personnel onboard and do not have a pilothouse or engineering space. Service may be credited as follows.*

(1) *While engaged in spill response operations or exercises, regardless of underway, anchored, or moored status, service may be credited day-for-day toward deck department rating and renewals.*

(2) *While anchored or moored in a standby status, service may be credited at the rate of one day sea service credit for every four days worked towards deck department ratings and renewals for up to six months of the service required for any deck rating that requires 12 months or more of service, and not more than half of the service required for other deck ratings (i.e. AB-OSV & AB-Fish). Such service may also be credited as "closely related service" for the purpose of renewing a deck rating.*

(3) *While engaged in oil collection or transfer operations, service may be credited day-for-day toward qualification as Tankerman-PIC (Barge). While anchored or moored and in a standby status, such service may be*

> credited as meeting the requirements contained in 46
> CFR 13.303(a)(2).
> (4) Service on OSRBs will not be credited toward qualifi
> cation as Rating Forming Part of the Navigation Watch under
> reference (b).

Time and One-Half Service

Now we get to examine the other side of the coin: ships that provide more sea time than you would expect.

Traditionally, each day spent on a ship provides a day of sea service for the Coast Guard. Traditionally seamen work an eight-hour day with overtime tacked on as needed. However, some vessels today work six hours on and six hours off—usually smaller vessels that may only carry two deck licenses.

The Coast Guard agreed with the assumption that longer days should earn more sea time. They will assign 1.5 days of sea service for each 12-hour day. However, it must be a straight time day; in other words, if you work 8 hours of straight time and 4 hours of overtime you will not be eligible for time and a half service. I suspect this is because the Coast Guard isn't eager to examine overtime sheets to assign sea time. I can't say that I blame them.

The next problem is documentation; it's easy to claim twelve hour work days in a letter, but it's hard for the Coast Guard to verify the legitimacy of the letter. Particularly since most of these smaller vessels are classified as Uninspected Vessels which the USCG doesn't monitor nearly as closely as Inspected Vessels. The time and a half sea service letter should include all of the usual information plus "a comprehensive description of the vessel(s) operating schedule, watchstanding duties, percentage of underway service, and any other details that may support additional credit." I'm going to resume quoting Coast Guard Policy letter 09-01:

**Acceptance of Time-and-One-Half Service:** With the exception of vessels described in paragraphs 3.e and 3.f above, if a mariner works a twelve-hour day in a crew position on a vessel over 100 gross tons, and such a work schedule is legal, time-and-one-half credit should be given. The mariner must provide adequate documentation from the operating company that the 12-hour day was authorized and practiced. Twelve-hour days will normally consist of watchstanding, but could consist of day-work directly involved with the *operation and maintenance of the vessel when operating under the authority of the COI. Work hours for some vessels are specified in Title 46, United States Code 8104. Sea service letters indicating possible violation of regulation or law should be referred to a Coast Guard marine investigating officer.*

That last sentence refers to STCW rest requirements, which state a crewman must receive 11 hours rest in any 24- hour period. The hours of rest can't be divided into more than two periods, one of which must be at least 6 hours long. There are exceptions to this rule, but they just get more and more complicated and I feel like I'm starting to lose you already. Please don't document in your sea service letter that you violated the STCW rest requirements by working too many hours. Twelve-hour days should get you your time-and-a-half sea time rather than an investigation by a Coast Guard marine investigating officer. It can get a little tricky, can't it?

Using Military Time as Sea Service Time

I think it's safe to say only Navy or Coast Guard time will count as sea service time. However, if you served aboard ship in another branch of the service (such as the Marines) and think you should qualify for some sea service time, call the NEC and run it by them. I am impressed with everyone I've talked to at the National Exam Center. When I ask them an extremely convoluted and difficult question they always seem to take it as a challenge to give me the most accurate answer possible, rather than seeing my request as an imposition. I've had nothing but good luck with them.

The Coast Guard will only accept a Transcript of Military Service to document military sea time. It comes from the Department of Veterans Affairs (VA); they handle proofs of service for everyone, be they active duty, reserve, or retired.

There are several ways to obtain your Transcript of Military Service. The easiest way is to go to www.archives.gov and pull up Form 180, which is a request for a Transcript of Military Service. You can fill it out and submit it online, or you can fax it to (314) 871-9195, or you can mail it to the appropriate address on the bottom of form 180. It takes about 10 business days to receive your transcript after you've submitted Form 180.

Not all Navy or Coast Guard time counts as sea time. It must be either bridge- or engine-related. Check the USCG Marine Safety Manual for information on what each rating qualifies for. In the back there is an excerpt from the manual in Appendix 5. You will find that some rates qualify for sea time, some rates qualify for partial sea time and some rates don't qualify for anything.

Since many warships spend a lot of time tied up to the dock, the Coast Guard doesn't give day-for-day sea service credit for military sea time. The manual says they'll give 60 percent sea time, but the nice people at the NEC tell me that it's been changed—now they give 70 percent. Someone must have thrown quite a fit.

If you read the excerpt in the back you'll find that there are some exceptions to that rule if you have the proper documentation. I can see why deck time alongside a dock shouldn't count for much, but on the engineering side if the plant is running, why does being tied up matter? Doesn't seem fair, but when I asked my friends at the NEC about it they just told me that was the policy.

If you are presently in the military and are planning on a civilian career as a mariner, you can really help yourself by starting to prepare before you get out. If you wait too long it may be difficult to go back and dig up the documents you need. Get letters of watch standing from each ship you serve on, if you qualify (see page 149).

Bring a merchant marine physical form CG 719K to your final physical before you get out. You can get a copy of the form from the NEC or from their website. Once it's filled out it is good for a year. Save yourself some money.

Ask for a drug test letter from your command. They should write you a letter stating exactly what the Coast Guard wants to hear, that you've been subject to random drug testing (see page 132).

Keep all of your original training certificates and all of your PQS and official letters.

Be sure to take as much appropriate training as possible while still in the military. Some of the training may actually meet some of the requirements for a MMC or license. Check with the NMC if you think that might be possible.

A last thing to consider is completing your military retirement. If you've served a number of years in the military but are still short of your 20, you don't have to lose those years. If you take a job with NOAA, the Army

Corps of Engineers, or Military Sealift Command you can continue earning years on your governmental pension. Working for a private company, hired by MSC, won't do the trick; it will have to be with MSC proper.

It's really important to manage your retirement while you're still young. It will make an enormous difference in the quality of your life when you're old—take it from an old guy.

Creative Ways to Earn Sea Time

You don't have to be on a ship to get sea time. I don't want to spend a lot of time on this because the rules are tedious and they don't really come into play too much until you start gunning for a license or a license upgrade, although sea time can also be earned by wipers and ordinaries by going to school.

Schooling is the main way to rack up sea time ashore. The STCWs are international requirements that all signatory nations must follow. The U.S. imposes additional sea time requirements that we all must follow to upgrade; apparently this is completely legal. The STCW sea time requirements must be met by sea service. The additional U.S. requirements may be met by sea service or by approved education. The various Maritime Academies have their own system that they've hashed out: most of their sea time requirements are completed academically, though they do earn about a year of sea time, at sea, on a ship. We'll get into that a little further down the line.

Usually about one-third of the time required for an Able Bodied Seaman's ticket can be earned by taking an approved course. It only takes 180 days of service as a wiper before you can sit for Qualified Member of the Engine Department, so sea time isn't quite the hassle in the engine room as it is on deck.

As you move up the ladder, approved courses can earn you a month or two of sea service for your next license. Sometimes non-academy college courses will also be accepted in lieu of sea time—ask your REC. Serving as a port engineer or port captain earns limited sea time, as does teaching at an approved maritime industry school. So keep your mind open if you need the sea time and call the NMC or your REC if you have any questions. You may find a cozy little loophole.

Recency

This isn't a problem for the new mariner, but in time it can become one, so we'd better go over it. If you have an unlicensed ticket, either deck or engine or a license, either deck or engine, you need to sail on it for at least 360 days out of the last five years to avoid hassles when you renew your documents. If you don't have the sea time, you can still renew—you just have to take an open book test first.

> It happened to me. I had been running fishing boats in the Bering Sea for a number of years when I dropped in for a quick license renewal. I had an Unlimited Masters License, so I wasn't issuing myself sea time letters as the recency requirements had just been invented and I was clueless.
>
> I explained this to the person behind the counter, who said, "You'll have to take either a closed book test in our exam room, as we don't allow resource books in our exam room, or you can take it home, complete it, and return it tomorrow."
>
> The test wasn't that hard, just annoying. I took it, passed it and renewed my license all in an afternoon.

Keep your discharge slips and sea time letters even if you're not planning to upgrade. You'll need them to avoid a test on renewal of your papers.

Renewals

This is the one your mother warned you about. You have one year of grace period. If your license or document expires and you do not renew it within one year, you have to retest for the whole thing. Reread that last line. You lose it.

> I was talking to someone at the National Exam Center. "So if your documents expire and you don't start the renewal within the one year grace period you lose your documents?"
>
> "No, you don't lose them, you just have to retake the tests, and your sea time doesn't disappear."

Let me translate: if you have to retest, you lose your documents. That would just be awful. If you decide to put your documents aside for a few years and try something more sensible for a while, I understand, I'm good with that. Get a real job. Don't worry about Recency; it takes just a simple open book test at renewal to bring everything up to snuff. But don't let your stuff expire past the grace year. Not unless you're absolutely sure you never want to go to sea again, and even then I would say renew. Just in case . . .

One last thing on the whole document or license renewal: start early. Six months or so in advance is about right. A lot can go wrong, especially with medical or DUI issues. Give yourself time; you don't want to give up a good job because the wrong thing expires. Pay attention, start early, and you should be fine.

The Next Step

Keep your eye on the next rung of the ladder at all times. Know what the next raise in grade is, and what you need to do to accomplish it. It makes a big difference if you start working on the next set of requirements before you accrue the required seatime; why wait? As soon as you have enough documented sea service, send off your paperwork and you're on your way to the next level. With that in mind we'll discuss the second rung of the ladder in each of the departments. After that you're on your own, although *The New Hawsepipe* by Lenard Lambert is a useful book that will help you up the rest of the deck department ladder.

Code of Federal Regulations (CFRs)

We'd better discuss the Code of Federal Regulations (CFRs) again. They are a giant compilation of all the rules and regulations written at the behest of the American federal government, which makes them pretty close to infinite. Fortunately they're broken into sections, which makes them usable.

They are no fun to read—actually less fun to read than the phone book, which at least sports some entertaining names now and again. They are, however, very powerful. Once you learn to read them you no longer have to depend on someone else to explain things to you; you can look things up yourself, like a grown-up. I suggest you learn how to read them, if not enjoy them.

A good place to start is the section dealing with certification of seamen. The Coast Guard, to their credit, makes available those CFRs that the National Exam Center is concerned with, in a continuously updated version on their website. Go to USCG.mil/nms and click on the Rules and Codes tab. From there you can easily access CFR Title 46, parts 10 thru 15, which directly relates to the granting of various types of seamen's credentials.

The rules can and do change. If you're relying on even a year-old hardcopy of the CFRs, you could be in trouble. You can prevent that by confirming your understandings on this continuously updated page.

> Once upon a time I showed up at my local USCG regional exam center to take my Unlimited Masters License exam, only to be told that the Coast Guard had changed their mind and would not let me test.
>
> "Why is that" I asked.
>
> "Well, we sent our West Coast fishing industry seatime letters to Seattle, where most of the West Coast fishermen do their licensing. The evaluator there rejected your seatime because he thinks you haven't done enough stability or cargo handling on a fishing boat."
>
> "But that's just flat out wrong," I whined. "Nowhere in the CFRs do the sea service requirements ever mention any stability or cargo handling requirements, even if it is true, which it isn't. We struggle to keep the boat upright all the time."
>
> Obviously I'm still not completely over this miscarriage of justice by the USCG, particularly since I'd spent the previous month in a licensing test preparatory frenzy (I bet they never thought I'd write a book about them).
>
> Anyway, I lost the argument and gave up. What I should have done is looked up the appropriate passage in the CFRs, made an appointment to see as senior an examiner as soon as possible, and shown him in black and white just how far out of compliance they were on this issue.
>
> Several years later, due to a potential job opportunity, I asked my REC to take another look at my seatime, which was quickly accepted.
>
> I was told, "We were sued by someone when we

turned down his fishing vessel seatime. We lost, so now we accept the time." (Thanks for the lawsuit, whoever you are. Send me a note and I'll send you a free book or something.)

This is a really annoying story. I'm annoyed at the jackass who decided to make up his own licensing rules and I'm annoyed at myself for letting him get away with it for a few years. The CFRs are written down in black and white and are usually pretty clear; use them when you need to.

A Practical Exercise in Finding a Job

My son's best friend Billy just graduated from high school and by an odd co-incidence has asked me to help him find work as a merchant mariner. Why don't you all ride along as we find him useful employment on a ship? This should work out well for all of us. As Billy finds employment, you can watch how an organized job search happens and I get Billy the heck out of my basement.

First, a few details. Billy has worked on engines for years with his dad, who is a diesel mechanic, and already knows he wants to work in the engine room. Billy lives in Idaho and is a serious snow boarder and shoots an elk every year. He doesn't want to give that up, either, which rules out ferry work since there aren't any ferries in Idaho, and makes supply boats less attractive because he would have to pay for a long commute to the Gulf of Mexico every couple of weeks. He's looking for a job that runs 60 to 180 days in a row so he can make some significant bank between commutes.

The first step is to start on the paperwork, which can drag on and on. The TWIC is the first order of business, since it's a prerequisite for a MMC. We covered the process in depth in the last chapter, but a quick recap: www. twicprogram.tsa.dhs.gov/TWICWebApp/ is the relevant website. The card normally costs $132.50 and takes between 6 and 8 weeks to finish. The website gives a list of all the enrollment centers (most of them are on the coasts or the Great Lakes, but not all).

Billy's biggest problem, besides the $132.50, is there are no TWIC en-rollment centers in Idaho; he'll have to drive to Seattle, Washington twice. Sorry, but there is no other way to do it. It is recommended that you pre-enroll over the Internet, but you still have to stop by in person to submit your paperwork and return in person to pick up your TWIC. See page 131 to review the process.

He has all of the required identification and got a reservation at the TWIC office, so he's leaving tomorrow for Seattle. Good news, the trip went smoothly, except for the speeding ticket just outside of Dillon, Montana. While he waits for the TWIC to be completed, he has a number of other things he can work on. He can order a passport locally; see the www.travel. state.gov website for the nearest place to order one. They cost $110 and it is money well spent, as many jobs require one and Billy's planning a surfing vacation to Costa Rica should he find a real job. He's downloaded the MMC application package from www.uscg.mil/nmc/ and has started filling out the application. He's still covered by his parent's medical insurance so his physical is free, but he did have to pay $40 for a drug test.

Billy can't really start applying for work until he receives his MMC, because most companies require a copy up front with an application. But he can start planning his strategy. He's pretty much broke, so he's planning on taking the first job offered. Then, once he decides if he wants to stay in the industry, he can target a particular company or union. He won't apply for a yacht job because he has neither experience nor money, so he probably won't be able to land a paying job on a yacht.

Now is the time for him to write a good-looking resume. I've included a quick guide to writing a solid resume in the Government Paperwork chapter. He spent some time on it; he used expensive paper and a matching envelope; he used similar fonts on the resume, cover letter, and envelope. He was careful to not have any misspellings or misapplications of grammar.

The feel of a resume is particularly important if there aren't yet a lot of accomplishments to recount. It indicates a seriousness of purpose. Billy wrote it up and saved it electronically so he can update it easily. He'll most likely be revisiting it every year for the next decade, so he'll save the matching paper and envelopes as well.

Having done a little research, Billy finds that a MMC and TWIC are not required to work aboard some of the American non-union cruise ships since they are so small—under 100 GT. He's decided to apply for all of them even though he won't get as much credit for sea time on them, again because of their size.

These companies all have an employment section on their websites, which Billy fills out. He's applying for an entry level position in all three departments even though he prefers engineering. Right now, he just needs a job.

He finds it interesting how similar the general requirements are for all the non-union American cruise ships. They are as follows:

- You must be at least 18 years of age.
- You must have a high school diploma.
- The vessels are U.S. registered. Therefore, all shipboard employees must be able to legally work in the United States.
- All positions require pre-employment, random, and reason

able cause alcohol and drug testing, as per U.S. Coast Guard regulations.
- Physical Demands: All shipboard positions can be physically demanding. Repetitive motion, bending, climbing, and often heavy lifting are requirements of most positions. Every crew member works every day while on board.
- Uniform/Grooming Standards: It is important that your attire and personal grooming reflect a positive and professional image. The company has a uniform policy that all crewmembers need to adhere to.

Got it? Billy is going to have to lay off of the pot for a month or so, and that whole personal grooming deal will be a challenge, but you got to do what you got to do if you want a job.

He contacted the following companies through their websites:

> Lindblad Expeditions
> > lexjobs@expeditions.com
> Blount Small Ship Adventures
> > Personnel@blountsmallshipadventures.com
> American Cruise Lines
> > www.americancruiselines.com/employment.php
> American Safari Cruises/InnerSea Discoveries
> > careers@innerseadiscoveries.com

Coastal Marine runs some small breakbulk freighters from Seattle to Western Alaska. They don't require an MMC for the position of deckhand, wiper, or cook and they pay pretty well. Billy stopped by their office, dropped off an application and a resume, and showed his face around the office while he was in town. Billy isn't much of a cook, but he'd make a heck of a wiper or even a deckhand in a pinch. Maybe he'll get lucky and get a call back before all of his paperwork comes through. He'll check in with them periodically since this is his favorite opportunity so far.

Coastal Marine really liked his diesel repair and maintenance background, and Billy is intrigued by an opportunity to visit some of the small Alaskan coastal villages. Sailing on small vessels in Alaskan waters is rough in the winter, much worse than Billy can imagine. But he considers himself a "tough guy" so I just nod my head sagely and smirk internally. By the time he figures it out, it'll be too late and he'll either sink or swim. Actually, I think he'll do fine once he gets over the seasickness that most everyone suffers through in the Gulf of Alaska at first.

Billy is thinking he may really want to make going to sea his career, so he's looking into the Tongue Point Jobs Corps Center near Astoria, Oregon. He checked out their website at www.tonguepointjobcorps.gov, and gave them a call at (503) 325-2131. He found them to be very helpful and since he's 18, broke, and no longer listed as a dependent on his parent's tax return, he is eligible for the school. The only problem is he'll have to wait a year before a spot opens up.

So he signed up but is still looking for a job that will let him earn some money and also give him a chance to test-drive the industry, which is not a bad plan. He talked to some of the union officials at the IBU and they told him they had plenty of openings for ABs with all of the paperwork that we keep repeating ourselves about.

Billy got in contact with SIU through their website; he's applying for acceptance into their Unlicensed Apprentice program. He has applied for his TWIC, MMC, and passport and is waiting on all of them simultaneously. I had to loan him a little money to make it all happen. Well, actually it wasn't really a loan because my septic tank backed up and he had to dig it out and clear it—hey, better him than me.

Presently he's waiting to hear back from the small vessel companies that don't require an MMC. If they offer him a job before the USCG paperwork comes through, he'll take anything they offer. If SIU accepts him into their program, he'll happily enter their program. He signed up for Tongue Point and will grab a spot if he's available when one opens up.

Now he waits, checking in weekly with each potential company . . . . My guess is he'll have something within a month that will start earning him some type of seatime and generate some practical experience. This vital first step will help him decide if a seagoing career is really for him and if there is any truth to the fantastic sea stories I've been filling his head with.

Ruminations In Closing

- *Girlfriends, Boyfriends, and Relationships in General*

- *Random Tips in No Particular Order*

- *The Union Dilemma*

- *The Future*

Girlfriends, Boyfriends, and Relationships in General

Before you decide to take a run at a career at sea, I strongly urge you to discuss the idea exhaustively with your girlfriend, wife, or significant other. You must have their complete buy-in or it simply won't work. Without their full support, one of two things will happen: you will either lose him or her, or you'll put a ton of effort into establishing a career that you won't be able to pursue. Both of these outcomes are bad, usually.

Or, it can work for you. Got a wife or girlfriend you'd like to get rid of, but prefer that they believe it was their idea? This ought to do it.

It is, of course, possible to maintain a stable, caring relationship and go to sea; thousands of couples do it. But it isn't easy, and it takes a special woman, like my wife (love you baby), to pull it off. It helps if she is a low-maintenance partner, one who can kill her own snakes, a woman who is able to solve problems while you are on the other side of the world. Outside interests, a solid family, or close friend support system also help, greatly. Just remember to treat her really well when you're home, call from overseas when you can, and bring home presents and giant checks on your return, and you should do fine with the right partner.

But this is something you need to think about and discuss now, rather than when you come home and all of your gear is in boxes in the garage and the local pot dealer is happily ensconced in the master bedroom. Just giving you a heads-up: we've all been there.

Being separated from your family is by far the most difficult aspect of shipping out, in my opinion. Some men and women never adjust, others do and even thrive. I've been doing it for over thirty years and would put myself somewhere in the middle.

Frankly, my wife would have probably thrown me out years ago if she didn't catch a break from me periodically. We have a small honeymoon several times a year. But she also knows that there is no other way I can make this kind of money in this short a time, so she allows it. I'm able to provide my family with a solid, middleclass lifestyle while living in the middle of the Rocky Mountains, and still have six months a year off to annoy my family with my full attention. Some women think that is a fair tradeoff, others don't.

Sometimes it works best when you establish a maritime career first and then find a partner at ease with the situation. At least she knows what she's getting into from the beginning.

If you are still single but would like to be married and still ship out, I do have a couple of suggestions. Wait. Don't get married young. A seaman's second marriage usually works out better than his first marriage, because he, and usually his spouse as well, are older and more mature. So save yourself the aggravation and child support from the first marriage and skip it.

Marriage in general is difficult in the 21st century; marriage with long absences is even more difficult. The extra maturity will come in handy, I promise you. Just as it says in *Cosmo*, communication is the key.

Do not downplay the difficulty of a long-distance, interrupted relationship; once begun, there should be no surprises. Maybe a practice run, to see how much both parties like the situation, isn't a bad idea. I'm not advocating living in sin; I just hate seeing kids grow up without two parents, so figure it out before you have any children—so I guess I *am* suggesting you live in sin prior to Junior's conception.

I would estimate around half of all seamen remain single. The other half marry—sometimes repeatedly. Consider these issues seriously as you do your due diligence; it's one of the big ones.

I once shipped out with a guy who was the overtime king. He worked four to six hours extra every day until he decided to take a couple of months off. He surprised us by getting married on his vacation. I don't know if it was a sudden decision or if he just hadn't told us his plans. In any event, he came back to work energized and excited. His goal in life was to own his own delicatessen with his new, young, beautiful wife.

He continued to work as many hours as possible and sent home his entire check each month. After four months or so he decided to take another well- earned vacation and visit his new wife.

"Baby, how much do we have in the bank account now?" was one of the first things he asked her.

"What do you mean?"

"You know, how much have we saved for our delicatessen, out of all the money I've been sending home?"

Long story short, there was no money in the bank account. The wifey had been spending the checks as fast as they arrived. She was taking her friends out to lunch, paying their cover charges in the clubs. She was buying new clothes like never before—I remember his mentioning a couple of short leather dresses. She was living the lifestyle of the rich and famous.

He got up and walked out. Started divorce proceedings the next day.

This is what you want to avoid. Keep in mind this was as much his fault as hers. He should have made it clear what he expected, rather than assuming the love of his life would automatically "do the right thing."

It's all about communication. You can read about it in *Cosmo*.

My very first job, a long, long time ago, was on a small, grubby research vessel named the S.P. *Lee,* which was blessed with an outstanding crew that was not improved by my rookie presence. My watch partner was an old Fin by the name of Anchor Larson; he was old school—so old school that he had begun shipping on sailing ships, square riggers working the Baltic Sea.

We spoke very little outside of business, for ours was a formal relationship. But on the last day of the first contract I ever worked, Anchor shared some wisdom with me and I would be remiss if I did not pass it along.

"Mate," he advised me, "never go home without calling first. It saves embarrassment. But as soon as you do get home, you walk right into your house, past your girlfriend, and into the bathroom and see if the toilet seat is up."

It is advice I have followed faithfully for over thirty years now. It has always stood me in good stead and now I pass it along to you.

Random Tips In No Particular Order

Don't whistle on a ship.

It's bad luck going back to the days of sail when it might keep the watch from noting a change in the sound of the wind through the rigging. Today if you whistle, especially on the bridge, you will be accused of whistling up a storm—not something you want to do.

Don't bring your gear aboard in a suitcase.

That's what sea bags are for. Suitcases are thought to be bad luck, but more importantly, there isn't a lot of room to store them either.

Bring enough clothes.

My last ship, one of the new officers asked for some coveralls, which we didn't have in his size. He told me on his last ship they had supplied company coveralls to work in so he didn't bring any work clothes. So, bring some work clothes, just in case your new ship declines to dress you.

Make sure you have the right footwear.

If you slip on a wet deck and hurt yourself, the insurance investigator will be checking the condition of your shoes. If the soles are worn out, it won't go well for you.

Be very careful about sitting on the bridge.

For years no one sat on the bridge except the captain. It's different now, as some union contracts require a chair for the helmsman. But it can still be a little problematic if you sit in the captain's chair or if the cadet sits when the captain is standing. Different captains have different feelings on this issue, so feel it out.

Keep a positive attitude.

Avoid complaining, whining, or bringing your problems from ashore onto the ship. Man up; it's not easy for any of us, we all just deal with it. If you stay positive, it will be easier for you and for your shipmates as well.

Be considerate of your shipmates.

This is a big one. Remember, half of the job is getting along with the other people on the ship. Golden Rule, do more than your share, all of that good stuff. If you work at being a good shipmate it will eventually become second nature and you will have a much happier life, I promise.

Only flush down the head (toilet) what comes out of you and approved toilet paper.

The sewage system can be very delicate, prone to jam up if used improperly. Then the third engineer and engineering cadet will have a very bad day, made even worse when they find the tampon that caused the problem. I'm just trying to save you some embarrassment.

If you're a day worker in line to eat, let the watch-standers go ahead.

They have a limited amount of time to eat before they have to relieve someone. Don't get upset; it's the way it is done.

Lend a hand.

If you see someone struggling up the gangway with their bags, give them a hand, no matter what their position is on the ship. It's just good karma.

Always show up at a lifeboat drill with a hat, long pants, and long sleeves.

If you're in an open boat you'll need the protection from the sun. Most ships require a life jacket; some will allow you to bring your survival suit instead.

Always carry a pocket knife.

Someone on the ship can tell you what a seaman without a knife is like; I won't, because my kids might read this.

Learn your knots.

It's not that hard. Take three feet of line and practice for a few hours. Nothing makes you look like a donkey faster than a bowline that falls apart or a square knot that morphs into a granny knot.

Watch what you talk about.

Stay away from discussions about politics and religion, particularly at meal time or coffee time. Some people take these issues extremely seriously and you need to be able to live on the same ship with them. Do you really want to know that the guy in the next room listens to Rush Limbaugh or voted for Nancy Pelosi?

Be quiet in the berthing areas, even at mid-day.

Some watch-standers work the night shift and need to be able to sleep. Try to avoid slamming nearby doors or yelling greetings down the passageway.

If the ship sinks, don't forget to bring your overtime sheet.

There have been cases where seamen are plucked out of the sea only to be screwed out of their unpaid overtime by the company. I've heard of mariners who have learned the hard way to keep a copy of their current overtime next to their survival suit, something that I am admittedly too lazy to do.

If you stand a watch, always relieve a few minutes early.

You don't ever want to be late, but if some day you are unavoidably late, those many days of being a little early will mitigate the transgression.

Learn everything you can.

Ask questions, try not to make the same mistake too many times, and most people will show you much of what they know. You'll be surprised how often you'll learn something in the morning and use your new knowledge in the afternoon. If you're planning to advance in the industry, this may be the most important advice I can give you. Cadets are expected to come out after their "work hours" and trace systems or practice celestial navigation. If you do the same, you'll immediately get the reputation of someone who is serious about learning their trade.

The Union Dilemma

I'm a middle-of-the-road guy when it comes to unions. I know they're never the low cost provider of labor and they're often the creator of work rules that approach lunacy. But I'm also certain that without union influences the maritime industry would never have evolved into an organization to be proud of. It would never have provided wages and benefits geared solidly to the middle class; it wouldn't be an industry worthy of your time or mine. It is also a mistake to assume these gains are carved in stone, never to be taken away.

Today, probably the two biggest issues facing maritime labor are medical insurance and retirements—also possibly the two biggest issues facing America. They are both expensive to provide and offer fertile ground for ambitious unions to carve off expenses to undercut their rivals. Unscrupulous unions offer less and less to their members to acquire additional jobs, to win in a zero sum game. The members of these predatory unions are eligible for additional jobs but at reduced benefits.

Is this inevitable? A gift capitalism has given us or cursed us with? I don't know. I suppose it depends on our vision of the future.

The better maritime unions have given us excellent medical care for ourselves and our families. They often provide us with a generous defined benefits retirement plan as well, a service that is presently offered to well under 10 percent of workers in America.

Do we deserve it? Does any American worker deserve it? Again, that depends on our vision of the future. Most of America depends on a 401-k plan for their retirement. It's not a great system, with enormous uncertainties for the retirees built in. But it's much cheaper and is predictable for the employers. It is a benefit we may well lose as bottom feeder unions approach the shipping companies and offer to supply labor with a much cheaper retirement system.

If this strikes you as odd behavior for a labor union, it does me as well. Why would a labor union undercut what little leverage workers have left in this county? I thought good union members were not supposed to cross any picket line of another union, let alone resign another union's jobs at a lower cost. Why would they do this?

Perhaps for the same reason corporate managers steal from the company owners, the stockholders, through back-dating stock options and by appointing tame board members who then approve absurd compensation packages for the very same people who appointed them, in a display of greed and corruption. Will a particular union achieve more power, money and influence if it is able to cockroach jobs from other unions in a race to the bottom of the compensation pile? Of course, but who does it benefit other than union management or the companies who are able to play off one union against another to reduce labor costs? Not even the winning union members who are now locked into a cycle of declining wages and benefits.

We can't expect our government leaders to do anything; they've all been bought, apparently. Even our champions have proved time and again to be primarily interested in their own enrichment.

I see no integrity in Washington, none. The Republican's rail against the deficit-creating Democrats, ignoring the inconvenient fact those same Republicans fought two wars off of the books. They ignored the cost of those wars, yet expect us to regard them as the party of financial responsibility. Sorry, I can't do that. Why should the Republican Party improve if given a pass?

The Democrats squeal about the greedy Republicans, willing to destroy our great nation to facilitate their own enrichment. Yet Charlie Rangel, Maxine Waters, and Nancy Pelosi, to name a few senior Democratic congress members, are certainly as corrupt as any they decry. How can we rely on those who have proven themselves venal and dishonest, in either party, to save us?

We have to make the right choices. We have to do the honorable thing, surround ourselves with decent people, and work for ethical organizations. As I write this the American Maritime Organization has replaced another union's workers with its own on Liberty Marine ships. The president of MEBA, Mike Jewell, wrote an open letter to members of AMO in response, I've taken the liberty of transcribing it verbatim:

September 30, 2011

Dear AMO Members,

I am writing to you on behalf of my membership. They are hard-working maritime officers, just like you, with bills to pay and families to support. This letter is about Union Solidarity, the House of Labor, and our struggle to maintain basic working rights and fair contracts.

Liberty Maritime's actions in locking out the M.E.B.A. officers and entering into a contract with the AMO is neither fair nor respectful to the mariners who have given excellent service to the company since its inception. Liberty's actions are only meant to divide the labor movement at a time when working men and women are under attack on all fronts. Therefore, I am personally appealing to you to not cross our picket line that we have set up to protest Liberty's despicable actions.

For too long, maritime labor unions have been pitted against each other by the very companies that we produce profits for. These fights only serve to hurt our unity and decrease benefits for everyone involved. This battle has gone on for too long, now is the time to take a stand and stop it. Please stand with us in solidarity and support us as we make a statement not just for our own members, but for all union members —and not let Liberty play divide and conquer.

This fight is between the M.E.B.A. and the company, not between labor unions. Please stand with us during this struggle and support us. Your leadership may encourage you to cross our picket line. I ask you to hold firm with us in Union Solidarity.

The purpose of a labor union is to protect and advance the working conditions, rights, and standard of living for all working men and women. The strength and power of a union lies not in a single organization but the Labor Movement as a whole being unified. Please remember this even if you are encouraged by your own leadership to board a Liberty ship and take our jobs. I ask for you to stand with us and all labor and send a strong message on behalf of all working men and women.

In Unity and Friendship,
Mike Jewell
M.E.B.A National President

Interesting that Mr. Jewell refrained from criticizing the leadership of AMO, isn't it? He probably figured it's hard to influence someone's behavior by insulting the organization they work for. When an organization's lack of integrity allows it to do the wrong thing, we all suffer as it becomes easier and more accepted with each bad act. I have no respect for either political party, Wall Street, or the leadership of AMO. There is nothing I personally can do about their actions except hold them in contempt, and hope for a better day when a more ethical organization arises to take their place.

Am I making a mountain out of a molehill? Am I overstating the harm created by one union cockroaching the jobs from another union? I'm going to copy the opening paragraphs of the home page of the Seaman's Union of the Pacific webpage below:

> The origins of the Sailors' Union of the Pacific go back to March 6, 1885, when the Coast Seaman's Union was organized on the San Francisco waterfront by a group of three hundred sailors dissatisfied by the wages and conditions aboard ship that existed at that time.
>
> In 1886, the Steamship Sailors' Union was organized and in 1891 merged with the Coast Seaman's Union to form the Sailors' Union of the Pacific.
>
> The reasons for that merger are clearly stated in the preamble to the SUP Constitution. "... having been organized separately ... and having thoroughly learned the value of organization, and further, that two organizations of the same craft are not for the best interests of men working at the said craft, we have determined to form one Union ...."

Perhaps that's one of the reasons unions have fallen so out of favor with the American public: they sometimes place the interests of their leadership over the interests of American workers in general. It's hard to claim the moral high ground when the selfishness is so blatant.

So what can we do? Stand by and do nothing while waiting for the latest AMO president to be incarcerated?

Actually, there is one thing we all can do—the right thing. Our leaders have not set a very good example for the rest of us. But let's not allow the corruption at the top of our society to trickle down and infect the rest of us. A day's work for a day's pay matters; mastering your trade and showing up on time matters. So does training your subordinates and seeing that their needs are met and that they are treated fairly. If we don't hold ourselves to a higher standard than the cravens above us, we will surely perish.

Unions have worked themselves into the unfortunate position where much of their energy is directed at protecting the lazy and the unfit, and in the process they've lost some of their soul. There is a lot of power in a union; it is up to the membership and the leadership how it is to be used. Each time it is used to evade consequences of bad acts, it weakens the union a little bit. Each time it is used properly to improve the life of a valued union member or increases the quality of the contracted labor, it strengthens the union. I have seen companies take routes away from American-flag ships due to the actions of one serial incompetent and give that route to a foreign fleet. I've been gob-smacked by a union—a union that is now defunct—that provided space to personal injury lawyers in their hall to dig up business. We have met the enemy and he is some of us.

Earlier I wondered if the maritime union's bloody birth might end up resulting in their death. We can't battle the companies to a draw anymore. They are not the enemy anymore; the world has changed and labor needs these companies to prosper. The shipping companies have too many options, too many lawyers, too many and too much competition.

We have the power, however, to provide the best maritime labor available on earth, if we want to. Being better than anyone else is probably the best job security we will ever know. It is a new way of looking at things that has not been necessary in the past. Those days are gone.

Any union member who uses the union to protect himself from the consequences of his incompetency or sloth should be ashamed of himself, particularly if it becomes a life strategy. Any union member who strives to do his best to do his duty for his own benefit and the benefit of his union is truly my union brother, no matter what his affiliation, because he has done his part to improve or maintain the quality of American union labor.

The Future

Will a commitment to professionalism be enough to keep the American Merchant Marine afloat? I don't know, but it might. Some American LNG terminals are requiring a percentage of American crew, just because the operation is so potentially dangerous. All of these new regulations for vessels entering American ports may be difficult for the low-cost providers of labor to comply with. Continual increases in sophistication of the world's ships may also prove beneficial to the survival of First World mariners. We have all seen the environmental damage a maritime disaster can cause.

You get what you pay for. The safest, best trained seamen in the world are usually the most expensive. Using the cheapest seamen in the world takes a penny off the cost of every item in Wal-Mart and improves the employment figures in Sierra Leone. But maybe that's not the way to go. Maybe protecting our coast lines and providing good jobs to our own citizens is worth those extra pennies. But that is for the country to decide.

The Merchant Marine will continue to evolve and change. It will continue to add efficiency and reduce its deleterious effect on the environment. The ships will continue to grow and crews will continue to shrink slowly as technology continues to improve. But moving goods by water in enormous quantities is not likely to be replaced by a more efficient system in our lifetimes. If you consider the waterways in Asia, the maritime options in America have barely been scratched. As our roads fill up, our waterways become more viable for the transport of goods and people. I see more and more ferries and short haul coasters in our nation's future.

Presently, goods requiring transport from one American port to another for the most part go by truck. This isn't a good thing because each container requires its own internal combustion engine, polluting our air and crowding our highways. On some highways paralleling the coast line an entire lane is taken up with big trucks towing containers.

Loading hundreds or even thousands of these containers on a ship or barge for a trip up the coast might be the way to go. This plan is called the Domestic Short Sea Shipping industry and presently it doesn't exist, but it should. The problem is the harbor taxes a ship pays each time it enters port. It's enough so that it makes short sea shipping unfeasible. The industry is working to change the harbor tax structure, and if these efforts are successful, a new coastal shipping industry might be born with a lot of benefits for the industry and the country.

Water will be used more and more to transport goods and passengers as time goes on, for various reasons. Presently the New York waterfront is undergoing a renaissance. For hundreds of years the waterfront was used for manufacturing. Raw materials were barged in and finished products were shipped out all over the world, so it made sense to build factories next to the water.

Today everything is built in China and the waterfront factories in New York sit empty—at least until someone knocks them down and builds condos in their place. Who doesn't want to live on the water?

The problem is no subway stops to service these waterfront towers. The subway lines slip deeper underground to pass beneath the adjacent rivers, forcing them too deep to allow surface access and subway stations.

So how do you get to a subway stop if you live on the waterfront? By ferry. The New York waterfront is serviced by a network of ferry boats that give access to the rest of the public transportation system. This is a trend that will continue and expand throughout other American urban areas located on the water.

I think our military obligations overseas may well decline in the future as we reflect on their costs. This will reduce the need for MSC and military cargo on American ships, shrinking those fleets a bit, but I don't see them going away. We will no doubt remain the world's preeminent military power for the foreseeable future.

If you decide to pursue a maritime career, keep an eye on Alaska. The state has experienced three gold rushes already and there may be another on the way. The first gold rush, a real one, took place just before the birth of the twentieth century; the second one was actually a pipeline construction project that took place in the '70s. A tough young man with minimal skills could make his way north and quickly land a job that paid 3 or 4 times what he had been earning in the lower 48. That rush was quickly followed by a crab and seafood bonanza. New fishing boats were regularly paid for in their first season of work. Both the crew shares and the danger were fantastic.

A friend of mine dropped out of high school when his girl-friend was expecting. He quickly found work on a boat headed for the Alaskan crab grounds and made just over $100,000 (this was in the late '70s) his first season. He flew home, met his son;

bought a house, a car and a truck; bought clothes and a diamond ring for his fiancée.

Life was good until the IRS showed up with their hand out. Now, most crab boats don't withhold taxes; they just issue a 1099.

"Taxes?" My friend was shocked. "I have to share my earnings? I worked 22 hours a day, 7 days a week, freezing my ass off, and now I have to share what I made?"

Yep, he had to sell the house, the cars, and the ring to get the IRS off of his back. He just about broke even.

The following season he was back on the foredeck of an Alaskan crabber with a much improved understanding of the American tax system.

That, my friends is a gold rush. I'm sniffing another one, one that I'm probably too old to participate in. No one's talking about it too much yet, but the signs are there: drilling leases opening up, high end location specific simulators being built, and rigs starting to move. They are coming to the Bering and Chuckchi Sea in a big way.

If the North Sea, located between Scotland and Norway, is any guide, jobs on both the rigs and the support vessels will pay well, really well. It's going to be rough—the Bering and Chuckchi Sea are no joke about nine months out of the year—but "bank" will be made by those who can handle the conditions. Boats will be lost, perhaps even rigs. But it's coming, if you're interested. Or, I could be completely wrong.

Another interesting Alaskan rumor is that the USCG expects the Northwest Passage (above North America) to be open most of the year by 2040. Ships sailing between Europe and Asia will save around a million dollars per voyage in today's dollars crossing north of Alaska and Canada, particularly since the tariff for a round trip through the Suez Canal is about $300,000 for an average container ship. The new route will have the additional benefits of avoiding two of the most annoying groups of people on earth, Somali pirates and Suez Canal pilots.

What other effects global warming will have on the American Merchant Marine I don't know yet, but I'm sure there will be more.

Much of the world has cargo preference laws where a certain percentage of its imports and exports must be carried on ships flying its flag. We have a few minimal laws requiring government cargo or give-away agriculture products to be carried on American ships, but very, very little of American imports or exports are carried on our ships. It may be time for a cargo preference bill.

We've lost most of our manufacturing base overseas. Unfortunately, our manufacturing jobs may never come back; the factories are closed or gone, the workers moved on to greener pastures. With the right-sized cargo preference bill, the American Merchant Marine could be whatever size we want it to be. Pass one law and the ships will come out of mothballs to carry the cargo until new ships could be built to fill the demand efficiently. I may live to see it, I may not. But it would be one hell of a way to add a lot of jobs to our economy quickly, and every one of you men and women would have amazing opportunities to advance yourself to your full potential.

Let me leave you with a bit of good news. As I've described earlier, maritime wages have been declining for over thirty years. That, I believe, is about to change. The maritime industry is about to be rescued by the offshore oil drilling industry.

America has radically shifted its sources of energy over the last few years. Over the next five or ten years we look to become energy independent, possibly even energy exporting. All sorts of new technologies are coming on line, such as shale oil, tar sands, fracking, and deep water drilling. These new energy sources have arisen out of the high cost of crude oil; at nearly $100 per barrel they make sense. It turns out that the Gulf of Mexico covers a huge pool of crude oil, one of the biggest pools on earth. The only problem is that oil is deep, deep, deep underwater and difficult to extract.

However we are going to get it, the offshore oil industry is exploding to meet America's energy needs. It remains one of the healthiest sectors of the economy and a key component of America's recovery. I haven't discussed the offshore drilling industry at length in this book, but I will in the next one, The Big Bucks Guide to Working on an Offshore Oil Rig. Sorry—I just don't know the industry well enough yet, although my brother, David, does. We'll get back to you on this industry as soon as we are able.

Back to the good news (sorry about the digression): the offshore oil industry is paying incredible wages, nearly twice typical seagoing wages. $90-a-barrel crude oil will do that to an industry. Many professional seamen are migrating from tankers, ferries, container ships, and research ships to the offshore drilling industry in search of higher wages. I read one internal document where the president of a bottom-feeder labor organization was complaining about his members deserting his organization in droves for much higher paying jobs on drill ships. He dismissed these new jobs as not worth having because "they are dependent on the price of gasoline." Anyone else think we'll be returning to cheap oil anytime soon?

But what do I know? It seems to me if a union leader is complaining about his members leaving his organization for better jobs, more money, and improved working conditions maybe the problem isn't with the seamen. Just sayin' . . . . Clearly the organization isn't adding much value to its members' professional lives if they can do better on their own. There is always a lot of truth involved when people vote with their feet.

I think the offshore drilling industry is here to stay and that it will eventually have a significant impact on wages throughout the maritime industry because it will be hard to retain valuable, trained workers when they can vastly increase their income by quitting. I believe the days of salary cuts are over; we may even see the first significant wage increases in a very long time. God knows, we deserve it.

Appendices

- *Appendix 1: Ships and Shipping
                Company Information*
- *Appendix 2: Unions*
- *Appendix 3: Training*
- *Appendix 4: Paperwork*
- *Appendix 5: Excerpt
                USCG Equivalent Service
                for Licenses*
- *Appendix 6: Excerpt
                USCG Mariner's Fees*

Appendix 1: Ships and Shipping Company Information

MMP Inland Contracted Companies

Alaska Marine Highway System
7559 North Tongass Highway
Ketchikan, Alaska 99901-9101
Telephone: (907) 465-3941 Fax: (907) 465-8824
Website: http://dot.alaska.gov/amhs/Sailing/Employment/index.html

AMNAV Maritime Services
Bay Area Headquarters
AMNAV Maritime Services
201 Burma Road
Oakland, CA 94607 USA
Telephone: (510) 834-8847 Fax: (510) 834-8873

> Southern California Office
> AMNAV Maritime Services
> 110 Pine Avenue, Suite 804
> Long Beach, CA 90802
> Telephone: (310) 901-3383 Fax: (562) 435-8131
> Website: www.amnav.com/html/about_amnav.html

Bay Delta Maritime
P O Box 2088
San Francisco, CA 94126
Office: Pier 17 The Embarcadero
San Francisco, CA 94111
Telephone: (415) 693-5800 Fax: (415) 781-2344
Website: www.baydeltamaritime.com

Black Ball Transport
Victoria, British Columbia, Canada
430 Belleville Street
Victoria, BC V8V 1W9
Telephone: (250) 386-2202 Fax: (250) 386-2207
    Port Angeles, Washington, USA
    101 E. Railroad Avenue
    Port Angeles, WA, 98362
    Telephone: (360) 457-4491 Fax: (360) 457-4493
    Website: www.cohoferry.com/main/

Blue and Gold Fleet
Pier 39 San Francisco, CA
Telephone: (415) 705-8200 Fax: (415) 705-5429
Email: info@blueandgoldfleet.com
Website: www.blueandgoldfleet.com

Brusco Towing
801 Levee Street
Hoquiam, WA 98550
Telephone: (360) 532-3352
Website: www.bruscotug.com/dredging.html

Cetacean Marine Inc.
611 Phippen-Waiters Road, Suite 108
Dania Beach, FL 33004
Telephone: (954) 922-5494 Fax: (954) 922-4399
email: quarterdeck@cetaceanmarine.com
Website: www.cetaceanmarine.com/

City of Chicago Marine Pilot Engineers
Careers Center, City Hall, Room 100
121 North LaSalle Street
Telephone: (312) 744-9567 9:00 am to 5:00 pm
Visit our Online Service Page to Apply for City of Chicago Jobs Online
Website: www.cityofchicago.org/city/en.html

Connolly Pacific Company
Connolly-Pacific Co.
1925 Pier D Street
Long Beach, CA 90802
Telephone: (562) 437-2831   Fax: (562) 435-2035

Catalina Island Quarry
P.O. Box 276
901 Pebbly Beach Road
Avalon, CA 90704
Telephone: (310) 510-0626   Fax: (310) 510-1099
Website: www.connollypacific.com

Crowley Marine Services
9487 Regency Square Blvd.
Jacksonville, FL 32225
Telephone: (800) 276-9539 or (904) 727-2200
Website: www.crowley.com

Dunlap Towing Co.
Attn: Erik Hansen
2702 Federal Ave
Everett, WA 98201
Telephone: (425) 388-0549 Fax: (425) 259-6305
e-mail: erikh@dunlaptowing.com   Website: www.dunlaptowing.com

Erie Sand and Gravel
2 East Bay Drive
Erie, PA 16507
Telephone: (814) 453-6721 Fax: (814) 453-5138
Website: www.eriesandandgravel.com

Foss International Corporate Headquarters
1151 Fairview Ave. N.
Seattle, WA 98109
Telephone: (206) 281-3800 or (800) 426-2885
e-mail: info@foss.com   Website: www.Foss.com

Great Lakes Towing
The Great Lakes Group
4500 Division Avenue
Cleveland, Ohio 44102-2228
Attn: Operations Department
Telephone: (216) 621-4854
e-mail: info@foss.com   Website: www.thegreatlakesgroup.com

Ketchikan Gateway Borough
1900 First Avenue, Suite 210
Ketchikan, Alaska 99901
Telephone: (907) 228-6625 New Fax: (907) 228-6684
Website: www.borough.ketchikan.ak.us/airport/airport_ferry.htm

Kindra Lakes Towing
9864 Avenue N
Chicago, IL 60617
Telephone: (773) 721-1180 Fax: (773) 721-4138
Website: www.kindralake.com

King County
516 Third Avenue Room 1200
Seattle WA 98104
Telephone: (206) 296-1020
Website: www.kingcountyferries.org/default.aspx

Knutsen Towboat
PO Box 908
Coos Bay, OR 97420-0908
Telephone: (541) 267-3195 Fax: (541) 267-5675
Website: www.knutsontowboat.com

McAllister Brothers, Inc.
To apply online for a position please go to Website for further information
about employmentat McAllister or to email your resume contact.
NO PHONE CALLS PLEASE
Website: www.mcallistertowing.com

Oscar Niemeth Towing
PO Box 24848
Oakland, CA 94623
Telephone: (925) 237-1139 Fax: (510) 234-3212
e-mail: greg@oscartugs.com   Website: www.oscartugs.com

Ross Island Sand and Gravel
4315 SE McLoughlin Blvd
Portland, OR,97202-5055
Telephone: (503) 239-5504 Fax: (503) 235-1350

Shaver Transportation
4900 N.W. Front Avenue
Portland, Oregon 97210-1104
Telephone: (503) 228-8850 Fax (503) 274-7098
Website: www.shavertransportation.com

Wahkiakum County Ferries
Mailing: P.O. Box 97, Cathlamet, WA 98612
Street Address: 64 Main Street, Cathlamet, WA 98612
Telephone: (360) 795-3301 Fax: (360) 795-0342
email: pedersenp@co.wahkiakum.wa.us   Office hours: 8:00 am to 5:00 pm
Website: www.co.wahkiakum.wa..us/depts/pw/index.htm

Washington State Ferries
2901 Third Avenue Suite 500
Seattle WA98121-3014
Telephone: (206) 515-3400
Website: www.wadot.wa.gov/ferries/index.cfm

Westar Marine
Pier 50 Bldg. C
San Francisco, CA 94158
Telephone: (415) 495-3191 Fax: (415) 495-0683
Website: www.westarmarineservices.com

Whatcom County Ferries, Whatcom County Courthouse
311 Grand Ave
Bellingham, WA 98225
Website: www.whatcomcounty.us/as/hr/jobs/open_jobs.jsp

Offshore Supply Boats

Aries Marine Corporation
Attn: Personnel Dept.
PO Drawer 51789
Lafayette, LA 70505
Website: www.ariesmarine.com
   Aries Marine employs 300 persons on 16 lift boats and 14 supply boats.

BywaterMarine
PO Box 10182
Bainbridge Island, WA 70345
Telephone: (206) 855-9335
Email: info@bywatermarine.com
   Bywater has 3 supply boats.

C&E Boat Rentals, LLC
16009 E Main St.
Cut Off, LA 70345
Telephone: (985) 632-6166
Email: careers@ceboatrental.com
   C&E operate 6 dynamic positioning mini-supply boats.

C&G Boats, Inc.
1216 South Bayou Drive
Golden Meadow, La 70357
Telephone: (800) 259-5155
Website: www.cgboats.com
   C&G have a diversified fleet of 32 vessels consisting of crew boats, utility
   boats and supply boats.

Coastal Crewboats
PO Box 2418
Rockport, TX 78381-2418
Email: info@coastalcrewboats.com
   Coastal Crewboats are always taking applications for licensed captains
   and deckhands. Coastal Crewboats specializes in support for production
   operations in the Gulf of Mexico and inland waters. The boats operate
   along the Gulf Coast from Port Mansfield, TX to Venice, LA and range in
   size from 77 feet to 14 feet. Crewboats start at 42 feet.

Edison Chouest Offshore
16201 East Main
Galliano, LA 70354
Telephone: (985) 601-4444   Website: www.chouest.com
  Edison has 8000 employees and 200 vessels up to 400 feet in length. They
  design, build and operate their own fleet of anchor handling tugs, supply
  boats, crewboats, and assist tugs.

Fleet Operators
PO Box 350
Morgan City, LA 70381
Telephone: (985) 384-4866   Website: info@fleetoperators.com
  Fleet Operators run 5 utility boats.

Fourchon Launch Services, LLC
EPS Logistics Dock
1 Norman Docet Dr
Golden Meadow, LA 70357
Telephone: (985) 396-3960
Website: info@Fourchonlaunch.com
  Fourchon's 110-foot crewboat, *Capt. Cody*, runs every day to nearby
  anchored tankers.

Freedom Marine Services
111 Evergreen Drive
Houma, LA 70364
Telephone: (985) 872-9511
Website: info@freedom-marine.com
  Freedom operates 3 supply vessels.

Graham Gulf, Inc.
PO Box 158
6590 Half Mile Road
Irvington, Alabama 36544
Telephone: (251) 957-1012
Website: www.grahamgulf.com
  The Graham Gulf fleet consists of 5 fast supply vessels and 9 crew boats.

Gulfmark Offshore, Inc.

10111 Richmond Ave, Ste 340
Houston, TX 77042
Telephone: (713) 963-9522
Website: www.gulfmark.com

Gulfmark runs a fleet of 89 vessels around the world, based out of the North Sea, Southeast Asia and the Americas. Some of these vessels are American flag, many are not.

Gulf Offshore Logistics

120 White Rose Dr.
Raceland, LA 70394
Telephone: (866) 532-1060
Email: hr@gulf-log.com
Gulf Offshore owns and operates eleven deepwater service vessels and charters a number of others as well.

Hornbeck Offshore Services

103 Northpark Blvd., Ste 300
Covington, LA 70433
Telephone: (985) 727-2000
Website: www.hornbeckoffshore.com

Hornbeck owns and operates a fleet of offshore supply vessels, multi-purpose supply vessels, tugs, anchor handling/towing-supply vessels, and specialty vessels.

Iberia Marine Service, LLC

3015 Gene Flash Road
New Iberia, LA 70560
Telephone: (337) 365-3784
Website: www.iberiamarineservice.com

Iberia operates 10 fast crew boats throughout the Gulf of Mexico.

Kevin Gros Consulting & Marine Services, Inc.

13080 West Main Street
PO Box 1412
Larose, LA 70373
Telephone: (985) 798-7607
Website: www.kgoffshore.com

Kevin Gros Consulting & Marine Services own and operate a fleet of 14 offshore service vessels ranging from a 140' utility vessel to a 240' AHTS vessel.

Labonde Marine
1661 Hwy 182
PO Box 2945
Morgan City, LA 70381
Telephone: (985) 399-9066
Website: www.labondemarine.com
    Labonde operates 15 crew boats and 5 supply boats.

Muchowich Offshore Oil Services
1608 Old Angleton Road
Clute, TX 77531
Telephone: (800) 622-1851
Website: www.offshoreoil.com
    Muchowich runs 8 crew boats in the Gulf of Mexico ranging in size from
    110 feet to 162 feet.

Odyssea Marine, Inc.
2250 River Road
PO Box 758
Berwick, LA 70342
Telephone: (866) 693-5707
Website: www.odysseamarine.com
    Odyssea runs a fleet of about 35 anchor handling/towing vessels and
    offshore supply vessels.

Ryan Marine Services, Inc.
At Colombia Harbor
7500 Harborside Drive
Galveston, TX 77554
Website: www.ryanmarine.com
    Ryan Marine operates 17 vessels ranging from a 177 foot 4 point anchor
    vessel to 5 crew boats and 11 utility/supply vessels.

Seacor Marine LLC
7910 Main Street, 2nd Floor
Houma, LA 70360
Telephone: (866) 468-6732
Website: www.seacormarine.com
    Seacor runs anchor handling towing supply vessels, platform supply
    vessels, mini supply vessels, crew/fast supply vessels, standby safety
    vessels, towing supply vessels, and specialty vessels.

SoCal Ship Services
971 S. Seaside Ave.
Terminal Island, CA 90731
Website: www.ship-services.com
SoCal operates two 100-foot offshore supply boats and eight 100-foot crew boats off of Southern California.

St. Mary Marine LLC
PO Box 5724
Slidell, LA 70469
Telephone: (985) 290-9343
Website: www.stmarymarine.com

Tidewater Marine
2000 West Sam Houston Pkway South
Ste 1280
Houston, TX 77042
Telephone: (713) 470-5300
Website: www.tdw.com
Tidewater Marine is the largest fleet in the world, serving the offshore energy industry around the world with over 350 vessels. They have boats working out of North and South America, Europe, Asia, Africa, and Australia.

Ferries

Alaska Marine Highway System
(covers coastal Alaska, British Columbia and Washington)
www.dot.ak.us/amhs/
Anderson Ferry
(crosses the Ohio River near Cincinnati)
www.andersonferry.org
Arkansas Highway and Transportation Department
(a single ferry crosses Bull Shoals Lake)
www.arkansasroadstories.com/peel.html
Blue and Gold Fleet
(San Francisco Bay)
www.blueandgoldfleet.com/

BillyBey Ferry Company
    (Weehawken, New Jersey)
Black Ball Transport
    (Olympic Peninsula to Vancouver Island)
Casco Bay Lines
    (Portland, Maine to Casco Bay Islands)
Cape May-Lewes Ferry
    (runs between Cape May County, New Jersey and Lewes, Delaware)
Canby Ferry
    (cable-pulled ferry runs across the Willamette River in Clackamas County)
Fire Island Ferries
    (service between Bay Shore, NY and Fire Island, NY)
Golden Gate Transit Ferries
    (Crosses the San Francisco Bay)
Governors Island Alliance
    (New York City)
Harris County, Texas
    (crosses the Buffalo Bayou near the San Jacinto Monument)
Inter-Island Ferry Authority
    (Southeast Alaska)
Jet Express
    (American Lake Erie Islands)
Kelley's Island Ferry
    (Lake Erie to Kelley's Island, Ohio)
Lake Champlain Transportation Company
    (runs between Vermont and New York)
Lake Express
    (Lake Michigan)
Liberty Water Taxi
    (Jersey City, NJ and Manhattan, NY)
Louisiana Department of Transportation and Development Ferries
    (all over Louisiana)
Massachusetts Bay Transportation Authority
    (Boston Harbor)
Miller Boat Line
    (American Lake Erie Islands)
Millersburg Ferry
    (runs between Millersburg, PA and Liverpool, PA)

New York Waterway
   (several ferry systems running around Manhattan)
Oxford-Bellevue Ferry
   (Talbot County, Maryland)
RiverLink Ferry
   (runs between Philadelphia and Camden)
Staten Island Ferry
   (runs between Staten Island and Manhattan)
Texas Department of Transportation
   (operates ferries in Galveston and Port Aransas)
The Steamship Authority
   (Nantucket Sound, Massachusetts)
Valley View Ferry
   (crosses the Kentucky River at Lexington KY)

Tankers

Alaskan Explorer

Year Built:	2005
Licensed Engineering Officers Union:	MEBA
Licensed Deck Officer Union:	non-union
Unlicensed Union:	SIU
Operator:	Alaska Tanker Company
DWT:	193,049

Alaskan Frontier

Year Built:	2004
Licensed Engineering Officers Union:	MEBA
Licensed Deck Officer Union:	non-union
Unlicensed Union:	SIU
Operator:	Alaska Tanker Company
DWT:	193,049

Alaskan Legend

Year Built:	2006
Licensed Engineering Officers Union:	MEBA
Licensed Deck Officer Union:	non-union
Unlicensed Union:	SIU
Operator:	Alaska Tanker Company

DWT: 193,049

Alaskan Navigator
Year Built: 2005
Licensed Engineering Officers Union: MEBA
Licensed Deck Officer Union: non-union
Unlicensed Union: SIU
Operator: Alaska Tanker Company
DWT: 193,049

Blue Ridge
Year Built: 1981
Licensed Engineering Officers Union: AMO
Licensed Deck Officer Union: D & E
Unlicensed Union: SIU
Operator: Crowley Petroleum Transport
DWT: 40,631

California Voyager
Year Built: 1999
Licensed Engineering Officers Union: non-union
Licensed Deck Officer Union: non-union
Unlicensed Union: non-union
Operator: Chevron USA
DWT: 45,656

Charleston
Year Built: 1983
Licensed Engineering Officers Union: AMO
Licensed Deck Officer Union: D & E
Unlicensed Union: SIU
Operator: USS Vessel Management LLC
DWT: 48,844

Chemical Pioneer
Year Built: 1968
Licensed Engineering Officers Union: AMO
Licensed Deck Officer Union: D & E
Unlicensed Union: SIU
Operator: USS Vessel Management LLC

DWT: 34,930

Coast Range
Year Built: 1981
Licensed Engineering Officers Union: AMO
Licensed Deck Officer Union: D & E
Unlicensed Union: SIU
Operator: Crowley Petroleum Transport
DWT: 40,631

Colorado Voyager
Year Built: 1976
Licensed Engineering Officers Union: non-union
Licensed Deck Officer Union: non-union
Unlicensed Union: non-union
Operator: Chevron USA
DWT: 39,842

Golden State
Year Built: 2009
Licensed Engineering Officers Union: AMO
Licensed Deck Officer Union: D & E
Unlicensed Union: SIU
Operator: Crowley Maritime Corporation
DWT: 48,632

Kodiak
Year Built: 1978
Licensed Engineering Officers Union: non-union
Licensed Deck Officer Union: non-union
Unlicensed Union: non-union
Operator: Sea River Maritime (EXXON)
DWT: 124,644

Mississippi Voyager
Year Built: 1998
Licensed Engineering Officers Union: non-union
Licensed Deck Officer Union: non-union
Unlicensed Union: non-union
Operator: Chevron USA Inc.
DWT: 46,094

Overseas Anacortes

Year Built:	2010
Licensed Engineering Officers Union:	MEBA
Licensed Deck Officer Union:	non-union
Unlicensed Union:	SIU
Operator:	OSG Ship Management
DWT:	46,656

Overseas Boston

Year Built:	2009
Licensed Engineering Officers Union:	MEBA
Licensed Deck Officer Union:	non-union
Unlicensed Union:	SIU
Operator:	OSG Ship Management
DWT:	46,815

Overseas Cascade

Year Built:	2009
Licensed Engineering Officers Union:	MEBA
Licensed Deck Officer Union:	non-union
Unlicensed Union:	SIU
Operator:	OSG Ship Management
DWT:	46,815

Overseas Chinook

Year Built:	2010
Licensed Engineering Officers Union:	MEBA
Licensed Deck Officer Union:	non-union
Unlicensed Union:	SIU
Operator:	OSG Ship Management
DWT:	46,815

Overseas Houston

Year Built:	2007
Licensed Engineering Officers Union:	MEBA
Licensed Deck Officer Union:	non-union
Unlicensed Union:	SIU
Operator:	OSG Ship Management
DWT:	46,815

Overseas Long Beach
Year Built:	2007
Licensed Engineering Officers Union:	MEBA
Licensed Deck Officer Union:	non-union
Unlicensed Union:	SIU
Operator:	OSG Ship Management
DWT:	46,815

Overseas Los Angeles
Year Built:	2007
Licensed Engineering Officers Union:	MEBA
Licensed Deck Officer Union:	non-union
Unlicensed Union:	SIU
Operator:	OSG Ship Management
DWT:	46,815

Overseas Martinez
Year Built:	2007
Licensed Engineering Officers Union:	MEBA
Licensed Deck Officer Union:	non-union
Unlicensed Union:	SIU
Operator:	OSG Ship Management
DWT:	46,815

Overseas New York
Year Built:	2010
Licensed Engineering Officers Union:	MEBA
Licensed Deck Officer Union:	non-union
Unlicensed Union:	SIU
Operator:	OSG Ship Management
DWT:	46,815

Overseas Nikiski
Year Built:	2009
Licensed Engineering Officers Union:	MEBA
Licensed Deck Officer Union:	non-union
Unlicensed Union:	SIU
Operator:	OSG Ship Management
DWT:	46,815

Overseas Tampa

Year Built:	2011
Licensed Engineering Officers Union:	MEBA
Licensed Deck Officer Union:	non-union
Unlicensed Union:	SIU
Operator:	OSG Ship Management
DWT:	46,815

Overseas Texas City

Year Built:	2008
Licensed Engineering Officers Union:	MEBA
Licensed Deck Officer Union:	non-union
Unlicensed Union:	SIU
Operator:	OSG Ship Management
DWT:	46,815

Pelican State

Year Built:	2009
Licensed Engineering Officers Union:	AMO
Licensed Deck Officer Union:	D & E
Unlicensed Union:	SIU
Operator:	Crowley Maritime Corporation
DWT:	48,598

Polar Adventure

Year Built:	2004
Licensed Engineering Officers Union:	non-union
Licensed Deck Officer Union:	non-union
Unlicensed Union:	non-union
Operator:	Polar Tankers Inc.
DWT:	141,740

Polar Discovery

Year Built:	2003
Licensed Engineering Officers Union:	non-union
Licensed Deck Officer Union:	non-union
Unlicensed Union:	non-union
Operator:	Polar Tankers Inc.
DWT:	141,740

Polar Endeavor

Year Built:	2001
Licensed Engineering Officers Union:	non-union
Licensed Deck Officer Union:	non-union
Unlicensed Union:	non-union
Operator:	Polar Tankers Inc.
DWT:	141,740

Polar Enterprise

Year Built:	2006
Licensed Engineering Officers Union:	non-union
Licensed Deck Officer Union:	non-union
Unlicensed Union:	non-union
Operator:	Polar Tankers Inc.
DWT:	141,740

Polar Resolution

Year Built:	2002
Licensed Engineering Officers Union:	non-union
Licensed Deck Officer Union:	non-union
Unlicensed Union:	non-union
Operator:	Polar Tankers Inc.
DWT:	141,740

S/R American Progress

Year Built:	1997
Licensed Engineering Officers Union:	non-union
Licensed Deck Officer Union:	non-union
Unlicensed Union:	non-union
Operator:	Sea River Maritime (Exxon)
DWT:	46,103

S/R Baytown

Year Built:	1984
Licensed Engineering Officers Union:	non-union
Licensed Deck Officer Union:	non-union
Unlicensed Union:	non-union
Operator:	Sea River Maritime (Exxon)
DWT:	58,646

S/R *Long Beach*

Year Built:	1987
Licensed Engineering Officers Union:	non-union
Licensed Deck Officer Union:	non-union
Unlicensed Union:	non-union
Operator:	Sea River Maritime (Exxon)
DWT:	214,862

S/R *Wilmington*

Year Built:	1984
Licensed Engineering Officers Union:	non-union
Licensed Deck Officer Union:	non-union
Unlicensed Union:	non-union
Operator:	Sea River Maritime (Exxon)
DWT:	48,846

Seabulk America

Year Built:	1975
Licensed Engineering Officers Union:	AMO
Licensed Deck Officer Union:	D & E
Unlicensed Union:	SIU
Operator:	Seabulk Tankers Inc.
DWT:	46,312

SeabulkArctic

Year Built:	1998
Licensed Engineering Officers Union:	AMO
Licensed Deck Officer Union:	D & E
Unlicensed Union:	SIU
Operator:	Seabulk Tankers Inc.
DWT:	46,103

Seabulk Challenge

Year Built:	1981
Licensed Engineering Officers Union:	AMO
Licensed Deck Officer Union:	D & E
Unlicensed Union:	SIU
Operator:	Seabulk Tankers Inc.
DWT:	49,636

Seabulk Energy

Year Built:	1999
Licensed Engineering Officers Union:	AMO
Licensed Deck Officer Union:	D & E
Unlicensed Union:	SIU
Operator:	Seabulk Tankers Inc.
DWT:	45,671

Seabulk Pride

Year Built:	1998
Licensed Engineering Officers Union:	AMO
Licensed Deck Officer Union:	D & E
Unlicensed Union:	SIU
Operator:	Seabulk Tankers Inc.
DWT:	46,094

Seabulk Trader

Year Built:	1981
Licensed Engineering Officers Union:	AMO
Licensed Deck Officer Union:	D & E
Unlicensed Union:	SIU
Operator:	Seabulk Tankers Inc.
DWT:	49,568

Sierra

Year Built:	1979
Licensed Engineering Officers Union:	non-union
Licensed Deck Officer Union:	non-union
Unlicensed Union:	non-union
Operator:	Sea River Maritime (Exxon)
DWT:	125,133

Sulpher Enterprise

Year Built:	1994
Licensed Engineering Officers Union:	MEBA
Licensed Deck Officer Union:	MMP
Unlicensed Union:	SIU
Operator:	LMS Ships Management
DWT:	21,649

Sunshine State

Year Built:	2009
Licensed Engineering Officers Union:	AMO
Licensed Deck Officer Union:	D & E
Unlicensed Union:	SIU
Operator:	Crowley Maritime Corporation
DWT:	48,633

Washington Voyager

Year Built:	1976
Licensed Engineering Officers Union:	non-union
Licensed Deck Officer Union:	non-union
Unlicensed Union:	non-union
Operator:	Chevron USA
DWT:	39,795

Foreign Trade International

US-Flag Oceangoing Privately Owned
Foreign Trade Fleet over 10,000 DWT

Maersk Michigan

Year Built:	2003
Licensed Engineering Officers Union:	AMO
Licensed Deck Officer Union:	D & E
Unlicensed Union:	SIU
Operator:	Maersk Line Ltd
DWT:	47,047

Maersk Rhode Island

Year Built:	2002
Licensed Engineering Officers Union:	AMO
Licensed Deck Officer Union:	D & E
Unlicensed Union:	SIU
Operator:	Maersk Line Ltd
DWT:	34,801

Overseas Luxmar

Year Built:	1998
Licensed Engineering Officers Union:	MEBA
Licensed Deck Officer Union:	non-union
Unlicensed Union:	SIU
Operator:	OSG Ship Management
DWT:	45,999

Overseas Maremar

Year Built:	1998
Licensed Engineering Officers Union:	MEBA
Licensed Deck Officer Union:	non-union
Unlicensed Union:	SIU
Operator:	OSG Ship Management
DWT:	47,225

Non-Union Companies

Alaska Tanker Company

15400 NW Greenbrier Pkwy
Parkside Bldg Suite A400
Beaverton, Or 97006
Phone: 503-207-0075
Email: art.balfe@aktanker.com
Website: www.aktanker.com

Chevron USA

www.chevron.com
Apply via "Jobs" on Website

Exxon (Sea River Maritime)

www.exxon.com
Apply via "Careers" on Website
Note: You will need to complete the E-Verify process and review the Right
to Work notice before you can proceed with completing and submitting
your job application.

OSG Ship Management
www.osg.com
Access "Contact Us", next "Career Opportunities" and finally "Careers at Sea"

Polar Tankers Inc. (Subsidiary of Conoco Phillips)
300 Oceangate
Long Beach, CA 90802-6801
Telephone: (562) 388-1400

Research Vessels, Global

Operating Institution:	Scripps Institution of Oceanography
Ship:	*Melville*
Ship Website:	www.shipsked.ucsd.edu/ships/melville/
Marine Personnel Manager:	Ms. Mary Maldonado
Email:	mmaldonado@ucsd.edu
Telephone:	(858) 534-1633

Operating Institution:	Woods Hole Oceanographic Institution
Ship:	*Knorr*
Ship Website:	www.whoi.edu/page.do?pid=8157
JOBS button:	Employment Page; Current Openings, Job Applications, Employment Policies
Telephone:	(508) 289-2253 to speak with one of our Employment Services Specialists

Operating Institution:	University of Washington
Ship:	*Thomas G Thompson*
Ship Website:	www.ocean.washington.edu/vessels/ TGT/tgt.html
VESSELS button:	Employment Opportunities
Operating Institution:	Scripps Institution of Oceanography
Ship:	*Roger Revelle*
Ship Website:	www.shipsked.ucsd.edu/ships/Roger_ Revelle/
Marine Personnel Manager:	Ms. Mary Maldonado
Email:	mmaldonado@ucsd.edu
Telephone:	(858)-534-1633

Operating Institution: Woods Hole Oceanographic Institution
Ship: ***Atlantis***
Ship Website: http://www.whoi.edu/page.do?pid=8143
JOBS button: Employment Page; Current Openings, Job
Applications, Employment Policies
Telephone: (508) 289-2253 to speak with one of our
Employment Services Specialists

Operating Institution: Lamont-Doherty Earth Observatory
Ship: ***Marcus Langseth***
Ship Website: www.ldeo.columbia.edu/research/office-
of-marine-operations
Recruitment and Staffing: Virginia A. Beck
Email: ginnyb@ldeo.columbia.edu
Telephone: (845) 365-8846

Ocean/Intermediate

Operating Institution: University of Hawaii
Ship: ***Kilo Moana***
Ship Website: www.soest.hawaii.edu/UMC/KiloMoana.
htm
Telephone: (808) 842-9813
Fax: (808) 842-9833
Toll Free: (888) 800-0460

Operating Institution: Oregon State University
Ship: ***Wecoma***
Ship Website: www.shipops.oregonstate.edu/ops/
wecoma/
Employment Contact: Monita Cheever
Email: hantzecm@onid.orst.edu
Telephone: (541) 867-0295

Operating Institution:	University of Rhode Island
Ship:	*Endeavor*
Ship Website:	www.gso.uri.edu/node/26
Director of Marine Operations:	Tom Glennon
Email:	marsup@gso.uri.edu
Telephone:	(401) 874-6556
Fax	(401) 874-6574

Operating Institution:	Woods Hole Oceanographic Institution
Ship:	*Oceanus*
Ship Website:	www.whoi.edu/page.do?pid=8158
JOBS button:	Employment Page; Current Openings, Job Applications, Employment Policies
Telephone:	(508) 289-2253 to speak with one of our Employment Services Specialists

Operating Institution:	Scripps Institution of Oceanography
Ship:	*New Horizon*
Ship Website:	www.shipsked.ucsd.edu/Ships/New_Horizon/
Marine Personnel Manager:	Ms. Mary Maldonado
Email:	mmaldonado@ucsd.edu
Telephone:	(858)-534-1633

Regional

Operating Institution:	University of Delaware
Ship:	*Hugh R. Sharp*
Ship Website:	www.ceoe.udel.edu/marine/rvSharp.shtml
Director, Marine Operations:	Mr. William M. Byam
Email:	byam@udel.edu
Telephone:	(302) 645-4341

Operating Institution:	Duke University/UNC
Ship:	*Cape Hatteras*
Ship Website:	http://www.rvcapehatteras.org
Executive Officer, R/V *Cape Hatteras:*	Beth Govoni

Email:	lg105@duke.edu
Telephone:	(252) 504-7559

Operating Institution:	Moss Landing Marine Laboratories
Ship:	*Point Sur*
Ship Website:	marineops.mlml.calstate.edu/PointSur
Operations Analyst:	Maria Ka'anapu
Email:	mkaanapu@mlml.calstate.edu
Telephone:	(831) 771-4133

Coastal/Local

Operating Institution:	Scripps Institution of Oceanography
Ship:	*Robert Gordon Sproul*
Ship Website:	www.shipsked.ucsd.edu/Ships/New_Horizon/
Marine Personnel Manager:	Ms. Mary Maldonado
Email:	mmaldonado@ucsd.edu
Telephone:	(858)-534-1633

Operating Institution:	Louisiana Universities Marine Consortium
Ship:	*Pelican*
Ship Website:	http://rvpelican.com/
Administrative Assistant:	Chuck Guidry
Email:	cguidry@lumcon.edu
Telephone:	(985) 851-2807

Operating Institution:	University of Miami
Ship:	*F.G Walton Smith*
Ship Website:	www.rsmas.miami.edu/resources/marine-department/fg-walton-smith/
Email:	Contact page
Telephone:	(305) 421-4000
Fax:	(305) 421-4711

Operating Institution: University System of Georgia
Ship: **Savannah**
Ship Website: skio.usg.edu/?form=resources/rvsavannah/index
Job Opportunities: About Us page

Operating Institution: University of Minnesota - Duluth
Ship: **Blue Heron**
Ship Website: http://www.d.umn.edu/llo/facilities/blueheron.html

Research Associate
& Marine Supt.: Doug Ricketts
Email: ricketts at d.umn.edu
Telephone: (218) 726-7826
Fax: (218) 726-6979

Operating Institution: University of Washington
Ship: **Clifford A. Barnes**
Ship Website: http://www.ocean.washington.edu/vessels/CAB/cab.html
Vessel button: Marine Employment

Dredges

Associated Marine Contractors, LLC
1473 Pioneer Rd., Suite C
Salt Lake City, UT 84104
Telephone: (801) 886-8887   Fax: (801) 886-8170
Email: bkelly@marinecontractors.com
Website: www.marinecontractors.com

Callan Marine LTD
P.O. Box 17017
Galveston, TX 77552
Telephone: (409) 762-0124   Fax: (409) 762-1915
Email: rvanantwerp@callanmarineltd.com
Website: www.callanmarineltd.com

Caribbean Marine Contractors Corp.
220 Western Auto Plaza, Suite 101
Trujillo Alto, PR 00979
Telephone: (787) 283-1779   Fax: (787) 283-0925
Email: adiaz@cmcpr.net   Website: www.cmcpr.net

Cashman Dredging and Marine Contracting Co., LLC
P.O. Box 692396
Quincy, MA 02269
Telephone: (617) 890-0600   Fax: (617) 890-0606
Email: jay@jaycashman.com
fbelesimo@jaycashman.com   Website: www.jaycashman.com

Cavache Inc.
3310 NE 33rd St.
Ft. Lauderdale, FL 33308
Telephone: (954) 568-0007   Fax: (954) 566-7401
Email: info@cavache.com   Website: www.cavache.com

Cottrell Contracting Corp
328 N. Battlefield Blvd.
Chesapeake, VA 23320
Telephone: (757) 547-9611   Fax: (757) 436-4659
Email: benv@cottrellcontracting.com
jmc@cottrellcontracting.com   Website: www.cottrellcontracting.com

Dredge America, Inc.
9555 NW Highway N
Kansas City, MO 64153
Telephone: (816) 330-3100   Fax: (816) 330-3103
Email: dan@dredgeamerica.com   Website: www.dredgeamerica.com

Durocher Marine, a Division of Kokosing Construction Co., Inc.
958 North Huron Street
Cheboygan, MI 49721
Telephone: (231) 627-5633   Fax: (231) 627-2646
Website: www.durocher.biz

Dutra Dredging Company
2350 Kerner Blvd., Suite 200
San Rafael, CA 94901
Telephone: (415) 258-6876   Fax: (415) 721-1377
E-mail: bdutra@dutragroup.com   hstewart@dutragroup.com
bgilfillan@dutragroup.com   wwallgren@dutragroup.com
Website: www.dutragroup.com

General Construction Company
33455 6th Ave. South
Federal Way, WA 98003
Telephone: (253) 943-4200
Email: Jeffrey.arviso@kiewit.com   michaelc.shaw@kiewit.com
Website: www.generalconstructionco.com

Great Lakes Dredge & Dock Company
2122 York Road
Oak Brook, IL 60523-1930
Telephone: (630) 574-3000   Fax: (630) 574-3007
Email: dbmackie@gldd.com
whhanson@gldd.com   Website: www.gldd.com

Kokosing Construction Co.
PO Box 226
17531 Waterford Road
Fredericktown, Ohio 43019-0226
Telephone: (740) 694-6315 or (800) 800-6315   Fax: (740) 694-1481
Website: www.kokosing.biz

Luedtke Engineering Company
P.O. Box 111
Frankfort, MI 49635
Telephone: (231) 352-9631   Fax: (231) 352-7178
Email: KurtLuedtke@charter.net   Website: www.luedtke-eng.com

Manson Construction Company
P.O. Box 24067
Seattle, WA 98124
Telephone: (206) 762-0850   Fax: (206) 764-8590
Email: : ehaug@mansonconstruction.com fpaup@mansonconstruction.
com ljuhnke@mansonconstruction.com
Website: www.mansonconstruction.com

> Manson Construction Company Florida Office
> 4309 Pablo Oaks Ct., Suite #1
> Jacksonville, FL 32224
> Telephone: (904) 821-0211   Fax: (904) 992-0811
> E-mail: dhussin@mansonconstruction.com
> hschorr@mansonconstruction.com

Marine Tech, LLC
716 Garfield Ave.
Duluth, MN 55802
Telephone: (218) 720-2833   Fax: (218) 525-9574
Email: tsmith@marinetechduluth.com
Website: www.marinetechduluth.com

Marinex Construction, Inc.
2008 Cherry Hill Lane
Charleston, SC 29405
Telephone: (843) 722-9083   Fax 843-722-9085
Website: www.marinexconstruction.com

Mike Hooks, Inc.
409 Mike Hooks Rd.
Westlake, LA 70669
Telephone: (337) 436-6693   Fax: (337) 433-8701
Email: dredge@mikehooks.com   Email: ashley@mikehooks.com
Mike McMahon, President   Ashley M. Kerns, Vice President
Website: www.mikehooks.com

Orion Marine Group
12000 Aerospace Ave.
Houston, TX 77034
Telephone: (713) 852-6500   Fax: (713) 852-6530
Mike Pearson, President & CEO
Email: mpearson@orionmarinegroup.com
Website: www.orionmarinegroup.com

Paul Howard Construction Company
P.O. Box 35227
Greensboro, NC 27425
Telephone: (336) 662-9050   Fax: (336) 662-9060
Email: rhoward@paulhowardconstruction.com
Website: www.paulhowardconstruction.com/

Pine Bluff Sand & Gravel Company
P.O. Box 7008
Pine Bluff, AR 71611
Telephone: (870) 534-7120   Fax: 870-534-2980
Email: phyllis.harden@pbsgc.com   Website: www.pbsgc.com

Portable Barge Service, Inc.
644 E. Bayfield St.
St. Paul, MN 55107
Telephone: (651) 248-2864   Fax: (651) 458-3619
Email: mike@portablebarge.com
Website: www.portablebarge.com

R.E. Staite Engineering, Inc.
2145 E. Belt Street
San Diego, CA 92113
Telephone: (619) 233-3697   Fax: (619)233-3697
Email: bonniem@restaite.net   Website: www.restaite.net

Ryba Marine Construction Co.
P.O. Box 265
Cheboygan, MI 49721
Telephone: (231) 627-4333 Fax: (231) 627-4890
Email: tmorrish@rybamarine.com   zmorrish@rybamarine.com
Website: www.rybamarine.com

Southern Dredging Company, Inc.
814 Main Rd.
Johns Island, SC 29455
Telephone: (843) 559-7500 Fax: (843) 559-0566
Email: sdredge@aol.com   Website: www.southerndredging.net

Vortex Marine Construction, Inc.
Livingston Street Pier
Oakland CA 94606
Telephone: (510) 261-2400 Fax: (510) 261-2444
Email: blaise@vortex-sfb.com   Website: www.vortex-sfb.com

Weeks Marine, Inc.
4 Commerce Drive
Cranford, NJ 07016-3598
Telephone: (908) 272-4010 Fax: (908) 272-4740
Website: www.weeksmarine.com

>Associates:
>**Gahagan and Bryant Associates, Inc.**
>P.O. Box 18505
>Tampa, FL 33679
>Telephone: (813) 831-4408   Fax: (813) 831-4216
>Email: gbryant@gba-inc.com   cmbryant@gba-inc.com
>Website: www.gba-inc.com

Appendix 2: Unions

Maritime Labor Unions

Seafarers International Union
P.O. Box 75
Piney Point, MD 20674
Telephone: (877) 235-3275 Website: www.seafarers.org

Sailors Union of the Pacific
450 Harrison Street
San Francisco, CA 94105
Telephone: (415) 777-3400 Website: www.sailors.org

Marine Firemen's Union
240 Second Street
San Francisco, CA 94105
Telephone: (415) 362-4592 Website: www.mfoww.org

American Maritime Officers
490 L'Enfant Plaza East, SW, Suite 7204
Washington, DC 20024
Telephone: (202) 479-1166 Website: www.amo-union.org

Marine Engineers' Beneficial Association
District No. 1-MEBA
444 North Capital Street N.W., Suite 800
Washington, DC 20001
Telephone: (202) 638-5355 Website: www.d1meba.org

International Organization of Masters, Mates and Pilots
700 Maritime Blvd.
Linthicum Heights, MD 21090
Telephone: (410) 850-8700 Website: www.bridgedeck.com

United Inland Group Offices

Cleveland, OH
Charlie Malue, Regional Representative
1250 Old River Road, 3rd Floor
Cleveland, OH 44113
Phone: 216-776-1667   Fax: 216-776-1668

Juneau, AK
Ron Bressette, Regional Representative
229 Fourth St.
Juneau, AK 99801
Phone: 907-586-8192   Fax: 907-789-0569
Email: rbressette@bridgedeck.org

Portland, OR
John J. Schaeffner, Regional Representative
2225 N. Lombard St.- No. 206
Portland, OR 97217
Phone & Fax: 503-283-0518
Email: jschaeffner@bridgedeck.org

San Francisco, CA
Raymond W. Shipway, Regional Representative
548 Thomas L. Berkeley Way
Oakland, CA 94612
Phone: 415-543-5694   Fax: 415-543-2533
Email: rshipway@bridgedeck.org

San Juan, PR
Eduardo Iglesias, Regional Representative
1959 Building Center
1959 Loiza St., Ste 200

San Juan, PR 00911
Hours: Monday-Friday
9:00am-1:30pm ET
Phone: 787-724-3600   Fax: 787-723-4494
Email: eiglesias@bridgedeck.org

Seattle, WA
Michael Murray, VP, United Inland Membership Group
Tim Saffle, Regional Representative
144 Railroad Ave., Suite 205
Edmonds, WA 98020
Phone: 425-775-1403   Fax: 425-775-1418
Email: mmurray@bridgedeck.org   tsaffle@bridgedeck.org

Wilmington, CA
Raymond W. Shipway, Regional Representative
533 N. Marine Ave.
Wilmington, CA 90744-5527
Phone: 310-549-8013   Fax: 310-834-6667
Email: rshipway@bridgedeck.org

Appendix 3: Training

Maritime Education and Training

Kingsborough Community College: Staten Island, New York. www.kbcc.edu.

This is the brown-water program for New York harbor. It is set up to prepare students for an inland maritime career in the northeast. The program has been around long enough now that many of its alumni do the hiring for local tug and ferry companies, a good place to be. Kingsborough is careful to consult with local tug and ferry companies and tailors its programs to meet their needs. For example: its graduates are all cross trained, a deck student will have studied welding and diesel engine repair as well as the expected splicing and navigation. The engine students know there way about the deck as well as the engine room. This is a lot more important on a boat with a three man crew than it is on a ship where each department has its own gang of specialists.

This is a mature program that continues to grow. It has its own four-station bridge simulator to train students in boat handling and bridge resource management. It boasts two training vessels: a former 54-foot buoy tender and a former 44-foot patrol boat. The 44-footer has been converted to run on retired French fry oil from the school cafeteria, which apparently serves a considerable amount of fried potatoes. Students then practice their boat handling skills by taking it out on the weekends to skim floating plastic out of the nearby harbors.

The program is set up so most of the students take an entry-level summer job at a local maritime company in the summer between school years. This allows the company and student to evaluate each other and if all goes well the student has an excellent chance on graduation of returning with a full-time position. It also provides the student with another 90 days of seatime and three months of well compensated employment; I think all college should work that way.

It grants 250 days of sea time, since each day of instruction counts as two days of seatime. A The program is two years, grants 60 college credits, and is half classroom instruction and half lab/boat work. A limited license requires 360 days of seatime, but those extra weekend days picking up plastic count, and so does the summer work. That gets you very close—within a month of the required seatime. You have a year after graduation to work the last few days needed to reach 360 and sit for your 200 GT license.

Clatsop Community College: Astoria, Oregon
www.clatsopcc.edu

The "go to" maritime community college in Oregon is Clatsop Community College. The school has a 50-foot training vessel and a very practical program. It offers a two-year AA degree in Applied Sciences in Vessel Operations, and a shorter Able Seaman program, but only offers deckside training. The two-year program grants 244 days of seatime, so some additional sea service is required prior to sitting for a license. They do offer a high school program so students can begin racking up seatime while still enrolled in secondary school.

This is what I keep nagging you about: Take responsibility for your career, do the research, document all of your seatime, and test for whatever endorsement you qualify for as soon as you can. Think about your potential resume:

- Began earning sea service time while still in high school.
- Worked summer jobs (taking advantage of Clatsop's connections) in maritime entry level positions.
- By the age of twenty, earned an AA degree in Applied Sciences in Vessel Operations.
- Simultaneously earned a Mates License.

That is a great resume. The world would have to be coming to an end before that resume wouldn't get you an excellent job at a top company. Skipper of a high end tug boat by 25 . . . . Don't get discouraged if you're already past 25. You can still easily catch up; you just have to get started and apply yourself. I keep hearing how short life is and how it goes by so fast. Bullshit. It takes forever. If you take a couple of years in the middle of your life to alter course to a career you truly desire, those few years will pass quickly and your life will become much better. I do it all the time.

Sorry, I got a little carried away. The classes at Clatsop are open entry/open exit and non-traditional in length to fit into an intense two-week period designed to accommodate a working student on a two week on, two week off job rotation. There are a lot of working students upgrading their endorsements, which makes for a really good learning environment.

The Coast Guard has approved Clatsop's Marine Licensing Program in lieu of testing for Master/Mate of 200 GT. The Celestial Navigation program is also approved in lieu of USCG testing for "Ocean" endorsements up to 1600 GT. This means the tests you pass in these particular programs will earn you your licenses and endorsements without having to retest at the Coast Guard facility. This cuts down on testing anxiety considerably.

The school offers Master/Mate license training, AB ticket training and a Master of Towing endorsement.

Once you get to the Clatsop Community College website, click on MERTS on the port side of the page. It will get you to the Marine Sciences Department web page. In case you didn't know, MERTS stands for Marine and Environmental Research and Training Station.

Seattle Maritime Academy: Seattle, Washington
www.seattlecentral.edu/maritime/

SMA offers a new one-year program, fully accredited by the USCG, which serves Alaska and Washington state with a

95 percent graduation rate and a 100 percent employment rate. The school offers both a deck and engine program directed toward the fishing, merchant marine, and workboat industries.

The academy offers a 64-unit certificate in Marine Deck Technology. Each graduate receives eight months of seatime toward a 100 GT Master or 200 GT Mate, which is two-thirds of the required time. If the student interns for 90 days rather than the required 30 days, he will have enough seatime for an AB—Special at graduation. Graduates will have fulfilled the written and practical examination requirements for both Able Seaman and the Lifeboat endorsements. They will also qualify for a STCW "Ratings Forming Part of a Navigational Watch" endorsement.

Bottom line: With a few extra months of seatime earned before, after, or even while completing the program, the graduate will come away with an AB Special endorsement, a Mate 200 GT license, and a Captain 100 GT license.

The Marine Deck Technology program requires students to go to sea once a week during the second and third quarters aboard the program's training vessels. The academic program is followed by a 30-day at-sea internship on a large commercial vessel. On completion of the program the students will have both the paperwork and the skills necessary for employment in the maritime Industry as professional mariners.

Total cost before grants and scholarships is $6,788 (in-state tuition.) Graduates seldom are carrying any school loans on graduation.

The Marine Engineering Technology program grants 77 credits, also takes 12 months, and satisfies the training requirements for QMED, provided the student shows 90 days of engine room sea service while enrolled in the program. This usually consists of 30 days on the training vessel and 60 days on a student at-sea internship. It also satisfies the training requirements for (STCW) Ratings Forming Part of an Engineering Watch. Students will also be eligible for the unlicensed ratings of oiler, junior engineer, electrician, and pumpman without further testing. They are also eligible for a Designated Duty Engineer Limited—1000 HP, once they generate four months of sea service as a QMED.

Candidates must have a TWIC, MMC, and a passport prior to enrollment. A placement test may be required as well, depending on previous college credit; official high school and college transcripts are required.

The campus is located in Ballard, Washington (adjacent to Seattle), which is the capital city of the Alaskan fishing fleet. It consists of classrooms, docks, labs, and several training vessels. The labs consist of a diesel lab, a hydraulic and refrigeration lab, an electrical lab, a rigging and trawl gear lab, a radar lab, and a computer lab. The training fleet consists of a 43-foot troller, an 83-foot cutter, and a 101-foot training ship.

San Jacinto College: Houston, Texas
www.sanjac.edu/maritime

We'd better go over how to find the Maritime Program page first. Go to the above website, hit the "Cont. and Prof. Development" button, hit the "Program Information" button, and hit the "Maritime" button.

San Jacinto Community College, near Houston, Texas, is a young program with big plans for the future. In time it plans to offer over 80 USCG and STCW approved courses and an AA Maritime degree program, but for right now it offers a hausepipe program where students attend the school for short periods of time to take the courses required to move up the ladder. Engineering classes are just coming on line as I write this.

Many of their students work on river tugs and are taking the courses to upgrade to Mate and Master. The school offers the courses needed by entry level personnel, as well as some of the courses required all the way up to master. They also offer courses that need to be renewed every five years by professional mariners.

Fletcher Technical Community College: Houma, Louisiana. www.ftcc.edu

In their Marine and Petroleum Department, Fletcher offers a number of professional mariner courses that are required in order to obtain various USCG documents, licenses, and endorsements. The courses are some of the most reasonable that I have seen. For instance, an Able-Bodied Seaman's Course (all categories) takes 44 hours and costs $212 (in-state tuition) and $363 (out-of-state tuition). A Master/Mate 200 GT, Near Coastal or Inland is 106.5 hours and costs $465 (in-state tuition) and $840 (out-of-state tuition.) Some of the classes, such as Rating Forming Part of a Navigational Watch ($175) or Tankerman Barge PIC ($280) are the same for in-state and out-of-state students. It's also located 57 miles to the southwest of my second favorite city in America. Are you thinking what I'm thinking?

The system isn't really set up for the novice wanting to get into the maritime industry. Instead, it services mariners who already have a job and want to move up in the industry or need to renew their credentials. The school works closely with many of the local supply boat and towing companies, providing the training for many of their employees. If you begin working in the Gulf on a supply or tug boat this may very well be where you'll go to take your classes to upgrade. Once you've worked the required number of days at sea and met all of the other requirements, you can complete the course work, pass the final exam, and the USCG will issue you a 100 Ton Master/200 Ton Mate's License.

The school does not have a school ship, but it does have a bridge simulator. Because of state budget cuts it no longer offers a two-year AA degree in Maritime Science, but it still offers the classes required by the USCG to upgrade—particularly in the supply boat and tow boat fleet—at a remarkably reasonable rate.

Delgado Community College: New Orleans, Louisiana. www.dcc.edu

Delgado has been training licensed mariners and industry personnel for over twenty years. It has classes in Basic Safety Training, Fire Fighting, Radars, and Communications, as well as for various limited deck licenses such as Western Rivers and Steersman, Apprentice Mate.

The Alaska Maritime Training Center at Avtec—Alaska's Institute of Technology: Seward, Alaska http://avtec.labor. State.ak.us/AMTC-Home.aspx

Alaska's Institute of Technology, (AVTEC) is a vocational/ technical school rather than a community college in that it provides certificates rather than units transferable to other colleges. It is located in Seward, Alaska, about 120 miles south of Anchorage and is funded by the state of Alaska to provide training for all of the vessels working the state's endless coastline, which is longer than the coastline of the rest of America. This program accepts both Alaskans and non-residents. Non-resident tuition is exactly double the amount listed for residents, while other costs (fees, tools, room and board) are the same as for Alaskan residents. Applicants may take a TAB test to measure their suitability/capability for the curriculum at no charge. Free support courses are also offered to those students needing extra help to meet the program's standards. For more information call Admissions at (800) 478-5389. Would I encourage Lower Forty-Eight citizens to relocate and establish residency in order to take full advantage of this fantastic program? Umm, no comment . . . .

AVTEC offers USCG/STCW compliant maritime training using a world-class ship simulator (their website offers an impressive virtual tour of the simulator.) This institution is supported by the richest state in the union and it shows. The program offers great deals on training for QMEDs and ABs that would cost about

$18,000 a la carte, but is offered as a package for around $10,000 for everything, including room and board. But the applicant must have the minimum sea service of 90 days toward QMED or 180 days toward AB to be considered for the reduced tuition rates as AVTEC's funding is based on their success rate (not how many they train, but how many they train who get jobs) and they want their graduates to gain USCG credential within one year of course completion. Anyone can train, but reduced rates are offered to those students who can train and certify quickly. A full range of courses to train unlicensed deck and engine crew members, up to and including a 500–1600 ton Mate/Master package and license prep course, is offered. Contact Shirley Cambell at (907) 224-6196 to create a personalized maritime training program to get you where you need to go. With the new Coast Guard regulations it really is both difficult and expensive for a hawsepiper to earn an unlimited license. AVTEC's maritime program is set up specifically to make hausepiping practical and economically feasible. I really commend them for this approach because I don't believe that unlimited licenses should come only from the four-year academies. The way it works is the student gets his sea time on his own, probably on some of the many vessels working Alaskan waters. The student then takes his license classes while on vacation.

The school has both extensive job placement assistance and a job search class that teaches writing resumes, completing job applications, refining career goals, and acing job interviews. Their job placement rate for graduates is over 94 percent, which is basically everyone who wants to work.

The school supplies dormitories for both single students and students with families. The rate for short-term classes less than 6 weeks for room and board is $45 a night in a brand-new (opens in January 2014) dorm complex. If you're an Alaskan and employed in the maritime industry, this is the place to go to upgrade your skills and training. You won't do any better than this.

Maritime-Themed Schools

Maritime programs are offered in various middle and high schools around the country. These programs provide rigorous academic programs with a focus on maritime studies, science, and technology. They also provide studies and opportunity to enter maritime careers upon graduation or to pursue further advanced maritime education at a vocational school, community college, service academy, or maritime academy.

Contact the U.S. Department of Education or the Association for Career and Technical Education for information regarding maritime-themed schools.

A list of high schools or associations with maritime–oriented programs is available online at www.madra.dot.gov. Once there, click on the "Education" heading.

Maritime Academies

There are seven maritime academies in the United States that educate and train individuals to become officers in the Merchant Marine. Graduates receive college degrees and U.S. Coast Guard Merchant Mariner Credentials with STCW endorsements as deck or engineering officers.

U.S. Merchant Marine Academy
Kings 300 Steamboat Road
Point, NY 11024
Telephone: (516) 773-5000   Website: www.usmma.edu

California Marine Academy
200 Maritime Academy Drive
Vallejo, CA 94590
Telephone: (707) 654-1000   Website: www.csum.edu

Great Lakes Maritime Academy
Northwestern Michigan College
1701 East Front Street
Traverse City, MI 49686
Telephone: (800) 748-0566, ext. 1200   Website: www.nmc.edu/maritime

Maine Maritime Academy
Castine, ME 04420-5000
Telephone: (800) 464-6565 (in state)
(800) 227-8465 (out of state)   Website: www.mainemaritime.edu

Massachusetts Maritime Academy
101 Academy Drive
Buzzards Bay, MA 02532
Telephone: (508) 830-5000   Website: www.maritime.edu

State University of New York Maritime College
6 Pennyfield Avenue
Throggs Neck, NY 10465
Telephone: (718) 409-7220   Website: www.sunymaritime.edu

Texas Maritime Academy
Texas A&M University at Galveston
P.O. Box 1675
Galveston, TX 77553-1675
Telephone: (877) 322-4443   Website: www.tamug.edu/corps

Maritime Industry-Affiliated Schools

The U.S. maritime industry operates high quality, state-of-the-art training facilities that provide a wide variety of courses for mariners entering the industry as well as those upgrading professional qualifications. These schools are union affiliated and are primarily concerned with training their own union members, although they sometimes train non-union students for a fee.

Calhoon MEBA Engineering School
27050 Saint Michaels Road
Easton, MD 21601
Telephone: (410) 822-9600   Website: www.mebaschool.org

Andrew Furuseth School of Seamanship
450 Harrison Street
San Francisco, CA 94405
Telephone: (415) 777-3400   Website: www.sailors.org

Maritime Institute of Technology and Graduate Studies (MITAGS)
692 Maritime Boulevard
Linthicum Heights, MD 21090
Telephone: (866) 656-5568   Website: www.mitags.org

Pacific Maritime Institute (PMI)
1729 Alaskan Way South
Seattle, WA 98134
Telephone (888) 893-7829   Website: www.mates.org

Paul Hall Center for Maritime Training and Education
Box 75
Piney Point, MD 20674-0075
Telephone: (301) 994-0010, (877) 235-3275
Website: www.seafarers.org/phc

Appendix 4: USCG Regional Exam Centers

Anchorage, AK
USCG RBC
800 E. Dimond Blvd., Ste. 3-227
Anchosrage, AK 99515

Boston, Massachusetts
USCG REC
455 Commercial Street
Boston, MA 02109

Charleston, SC
USCG RBC
196 Tradd Street
Charleston, SC 29401

Baltimore, Maryland
USCG REC
US Custom House Building
40 S. Gay Street, Room 420
Baltimore, MD 21202-4022

Houston, TX
USCG REC
8876 Gulf Freeway, Suite 200
Houston, TX 77017

Honolulu, HI
USCG REC
433 Ala Moana Blvd.
Honolulu, HI 96813-4909

Juneau, AK
USCG REC
9105 Mendenhall Mall Rd.
Suite 170, Mendenhall Mall
Juneau, AK 99801

Los Angeles, CA
USCG REC
501 W. Ocean Blvd.
Long Beach, CA 90802

Miami, FL
USCG REC
Claude Pepper Federal Building
6th Floor, 51 S.W. 1st. Avenue
Miami, FL 33130-1608

Memphis, Tennessee
USCG RBC
200 Jefferson Ave., Ste. 1301
Memphis, TN 38103

Oakland, CA
USCG REC
Oakland Fed. Building North Tower
1301 Clay Street, Room 180 N
Oakland, CA 94612-5200

Seattle, WA
USCG REC
915 Second Ave., Room 194
Seattle, WA 98174-1067

Toledo, Ohio
USCG REC
420 Madison Ave., Suite 700
Toledo, OH 43604-1265

New Orleans, LA
USCG REC
4250 HWY 22
Suite F
Mandeville, LA 70471

New York, New York
USCG REC
Battery Park Building
1 South Street
New York, NY 10004-1466

Portland, OR
USCG REC
911 NE 11th Ave., Rm. #637
Portland, OR 97232-4169

St. Louis, MO
USCG REC
1222 Spruce Street, Rm. 7.105
St. Louis, MO 63103-2846

Appendix 5:
Excerpt, USCG Marine Safety Manual

Chapter 2:
Equivalent Service for Licenses/Merchant Mariner's Documents

A. Military Service.

Sea service requirements for original licenses and raises of grade are stated in 46 CFR Part 10, and are based on service aboard U.S. merchant vessels. 46 CFR Part 12 gives the requirements for unlicensed ratings. Military sea service experience must be a reasonable equivalent to the service required of a merchant mariner who is seeking an identical license or MMD. Military personnel applying for a license or MMD represent a challenge to the REC evaluating their application. This is due to the wide range of ratings and duties they present as sea service. The evaluations are normally conducted by the REC. The REC may refer the more difficult or sensitive evaluations to NMC. In addition, to avoid the appearance of favoritism or undue influence, the REC should refer an evaluation to NMC for any applicant that is:

1. A Coast Guard officer senior to the OCMI;
2. A Coast Guard officer stationed at the MSO or Activity senior to the chief of the REC; or
3. A person assigned to work at the REC.

B. Criteria for Accepting Military Sea Experience.
    1. Application Evaluation.
    Evaluations of military experience are conducted when a Transcript of Sea Service or equivalent information is presented with an application (see Section B.2). At the discretion of the REC, additional information may be requested. Generally, additional information will be required to verify claims of a higher percentage of underway time than the 60% normally allowed by the regulations. In addition, the REC may require an official description of duties statement, letters of qualification, service record entries, or letters from former supervisors or commanding officers.

    2. Transcript of Sea Service.
    The Transcript of Sea Service provides the periods of assignment, name of vessel, and capacity (rate/rank) served. The application must contain a Transcript of Sea Service, not a shipboard generated letter or DD-214. Standard Form SF-180, Request Pertaining to Military Records, may be used by the applicant to obtain a transcript. This form lists the addresses of all the services where the request should be sent. The Federal Record Center, at St. Louis, MO, is not sending the ex-service person Transcripts of Sea Service. Instead, they are sending various pages from their personnel files which document when, where, rate, and duration of the applicant's sea service. Evaluators will have to become familiar with the various forms and how to extract the pertinent information. Because these forms are military in nature, MSO administration offices or PERSRUs could be of assistance in deciphering the information. The SIP may accept other documentation attesting to sea service if it has the same level of authenticity as a transcript. In other words, will it stand up to an audit?

    3. Tonnage.
    The majority of military vessels are not measured in gross or net tonnage. Therefore, it is necessary for the evaluating officer to estimate the gross tonnage of the vessels for which experience

is claimed. The formula "DISPLACEMENT x .57" provides an acceptable estimate of gross tonnage (use full load displacement). Jane's Fighting Ships is an excellent reference for finding the vital statistics of U.S. military vessels. It is likely that this source will provide the displacement for most military vessels. All Coast Guard high endurance cutters (WHECs), medium endurance cutters (WMECs) of the Bear class only (270 foot cutter), icebreakers (WAGBs), and the USCGC Eagle are over 1600 gross tons. All other Coast Guard vessels currently in service are less than 1600 gross tons. Former Coast Guard vessels of 255 feet (77 meters) and up were over 1600 gross tons.

4. Calculation of Service.
Military sea service shall be evaluated sequentially in the order obtained over the course of a military career, which reflects the same progression for a merchant mariner. Tonnage and horsepower limitations, if any, shall be calculated for each license level through the progression. It is not acceptable to average tonnage or horsepower over a career. Pay particular attention to the recency requirements in 46 CFR 10.202(e) because recency, or lack thereof, can also limit the tonnage or horsepower for an original license.

5. Description of Duties Evaluation.
The most troublesome aspect of the military evaluation is translating military duties to meet the experience requirements specified in 46 CFR Part 10. Based upon past evaluations, the following guidelines have been developed. See Figure 2-2 and 2-3 of this chapter for further explanations and examples.

    a. Officers. Deck watch officers' (DWOs) and engineering watch officers' (EWOs) duties are considered equivalent to the watchstanding duties performed by licensed mates and engineers respectively aboard merchant vessels. Therefore, this qualifying sea service may be used to satisfy the experience requirements for an original or raise of grade of a mate or assistant engineer license. For an original third's license, up to eighteen months service as DWO/EWO may be substituted for up to 36 months of unlicensed service. One day of service as a DWO or EWO is counted as 2 days of unlicensed sea service to meet the requirements of the regulations. When computing sea service toward a license grade above third, such as an original second, or a raise of grade, DWO/EWO time is creditable on a one-for-one basis. Service experience obtained as a junior officer of the deck (JOOD) is considered equivalent (on a one-for-one basis) to able seaman time. See examples at the end of this chapter.

b. Service as Commanding Officer (CO). To qualify as unlimited master, at least six months of the required creditable service must have been as CO. The CO Service must have occurred after the applicant had accumulated enough creditable service to qualify as chief mate. An applicant with military experience has not had exposure to merchant marine concerns such as cargo handling, payrolls, union relations, etc. Service as CO indicates that the applicant has experience in a position of responsibility which compensates, to some extent, for differences between the operation of military and merchant vessels.

c. Service as Engineer Officer (EO). To qualify as unlimited chief engineer, at least six months of the required creditable service must have been as EO. The EO service must have occurred after the applicant had accumulated enough creditable service to qualify as first assistant engineer. An applicant with military experience has not had exposure to merchant marine concerns such as payrolls, union relations, etc. Service as EO indicates that the applicant has experience in a position of responsibility which compensates, to some extent, for differences between the operation of military and merchant vessels.

d. Enlisted Personnel Applying For Licenses. Evaluation of sea service is more complex for enlisted personnel than it is for officers. This is due to the great variety of specialized duties that enlisted personnel perform. When evaluating underway sea service, use the following guidelines:

(1) Service as a seaman apprentice (SA) or seaman (SN) is equivalent to sea service as an ordinary seaman or deckhand;

(2) Service as fireman apprentice (FA) or fireman (FN) is equivalent to sea service as a wiper or coal passer;

(3) Service as a petty officer in the deck department is considered equivalent to that of an AB; and

(4) Service as a petty officer in the engineering depart ment is considered equivalent to that of a QMED.

(5) Deck rating of E-4 and above with qualifications as DWO is equivalent to licensed mate time.

(6) Service experience obtained as a junior officer of the deck (JOOD) is considered equivalent (on a one-for-one basis) to able seaman time.

(7) Engine rating of E-4 and above with qualifications as EWO is equivalent to licensed assistant engineer time.

Note: The above are only guidelines. Applicants furnishing time as a petty officer in charge of a navigational watch should have that time counted towards a licensed officer.

e. Ratings Accepted Toward Licenses.
Certain ratings due to their nature are usually disqualifying on their face for a license. Figure 2-1 is a guide for evaluating service in various ratings. Suggested acceptance of service is indicated by "XXX." When evaluating military ratings, if the military service is found to be closely related to the duties of AB or QMED, then RECs are authorized to grant up to 50% of the service towards the applicable license

[To see the full chart displayed in Fig. 2.1, please visit www.
uscg.mil/directives/cim/16000.../CIM_16000_8B.pdf]
f. Ratings Accepted Toward MMDs.

    (1)   Deck Service. Enlisted service, regardless of rating,
must meet the definition in 46 U.S.C. 7301 of "service on deck" in order for it to be accepted toward
any of the able seaman classifications.

    (2)   Engineer Service. Any enlisted service which
can be equated to wiper or to any of the qualified
member of the engine department (QMED)
ratings may be accepted toward meeting the
service requirements for all the QMED
endorsements except deck engine mechanic and
engineman. Qualifications for deck engine
mechanic and engineman must be evaluated
separately since these two ratings have specific
qualification requirements which must be met.

g. Submarine Service

    (1)   Enlisted Service. Care should be taken when
applying Figure 2-1 to submarine service. Often on
submarines non-traditional ratings such as YNs or
SKs stand operational watches. Watchstanding
qualifications and interviewing the applicant should
help the evaluator determine what is acceptable
submarine service.

    (2)   Deck Service. Only 75 percent of the total
creditable sea service required for a deck license
may be obtained aboard submarines. The
remaining creditable sea service must have been
obtained aboard surface vessels.

(3)   Example. An applicant for an unlimited third mate license has a total of 20 months of creditable sea service on board submarines as DWO. The applicant is required to present 18 months of creditable sea service as DWO. Only 75% may be on submarines,; therefore, only 13.5 months (18 months x .75) can be used toward the third's license. The additional 4.5 months must be obtained as a DWO on surface vessels.

(4)   Engineering Service. In contrast, underway engineering service aboard submarines is considered equivalent to engineering service obtained aboard surface vessels.

(5)   See 46 CFR 10.213(d) for further information.

h.   Service On Vessels Other Than Underway.
46 CFR 10.213(c) discusses the application of a 25% credit factor for periods of assignment to vessels at times other than underway. Creditable sea service for this category applies to vessels, whose sea service has not been previously used, that spend the vast majority of their time moored. An example would be a submarine tender or a vessel undergoing an extended shipyard visit. The vessel status would not be reflected on the Record of Sea Service but might be established during the evaluator's interview of the applicant.

i.   Credit for Military Schools.
Unless the school is NMC approved, training received at a military school will not be granted sea service credit nor be accepted as meeting mandatory training requirements (e.g. radar observer, firefighting).

C. Experience Aboard Dredges.
Self-propelled dredges may conduct their operations upon inland waters. Service on board dredges should be evaluated to ensure appropriate ocean or near coastal service. Daily operations that include at least one voyage

beyond the boundary lines for the disposal or mining of dredge material shall be credited as ocean service.

D. Evaluating Coast Guard Personnel for Licenses.
Coast Guard personnel who apply for a license shall comply with all the regulations for the license. Officers senior to the OCMI, shall request permission from the district commander to apply for a license. In granting such requests, the district commander may require the applicant to comply with certain additional conditions. Some of these conditions may include submitting applications and taking examinations at a Regional Examination Center (REC) in another district.

E. Examining Coast Guard Marine Safety Personnel for Licenses.
Coast Guard marine safety experience does not equate to shipboard service and may not be used to qualify for an original or raise of grade of a license. Such experience is generally helpful in preparing for a license examination; however, the only military service creditable towards eligibility for a license is underway service (except as discussed in paragraph 2.B.4.h. above). To prevent criticism or charges of Coast Guard favoritism in the licensing process, Coast Guard marine safety personnel must obtain permission to apply for a license from their district commander. The district commander may apply the restrictions listed above. However, under the present examination system, a separate randomly produced examination can allow the applicant to sit at the local REC. The applicant's file shall contain the letter of request and the district commander's letter of approval. Headquarters personnel should apply to the district commander in whose jurisdiction the REC resides. Refer to paragraph A.2. Of this chapter for instances when applications must be sent to Commandant to be evaluated. Coast Guard personnel who have passed a rules of the road test as an end of course test or as a Deck Watch Officer examination will not be exempted from taking the rules of the road portion of any Coast Guard license examination.

F. Examining Coast Guard Regional Examination Center Personnel for Licenses.
Special examinations should be requested from the examinations branch at the National Maritime Center for REC personnel. See Chapter 5 for further details.

G. Time-and-one-half Sea Service Credit.

The time-and-one-half provision was put in the regulations to take into account the additional experience mariners obtain when they stand watches on a six-on, six-off watch schedule. Time-and-one-half credit will not be given for overtime nor for other work days that do not involve six-on, six-off watchstanding even if the work days are more than eight hours long. The six-on, six-off watch schedule should be proven to the satisfaction of the OCMI or their representative before the time and a half credit is applied. The following sources express this intent.

1.   The Notice of Proposed Rulemaking (for the current licensing system), FR 35926, August 8, 1983, stated, "Many comments expressed concern about obtaining additional credit for 12 hour days in the case of people that work six on/six off watches. A statement has been added to a new definition section in the proposed regulations whereby any persons standing watches on any vessels upon which the six on/six off watch schedule may be used, will be given credit for 1.5 times each 12 hour day of service in that capacity."

2.   House Report No. 96-1075 on Public Law 96-378 [H.R. 5164], which created our current system of Able Seaman ratings, states on page 27, "The eight-hour provision is primarily intended to assure that those mariners who work a two-watch system (that is, six hours on duty and six hours off duty for a total of twelve hours a day) will receive a day and a half of credit for each twelve-hour day worked."

3. Some inland vessels not subject to the 2 or 3 watch system have in place a 12 hour watch rotation. If the REC can verify that such a schedule is practiced and legal, day and a half credit may be granted.

Note: The service presented must be equivalent to that required of a merchant mariner. The following methods of evaluation apply. All the sea service times referred to below are after all the appropriate deductions have been made.

Original Third Mate (Except Academy Graduates)

Officer Sea Service:

Each day of DWO sea service is counted as two days of the required service for an original third mate's license. As an example 18 months sea service as DWO is equal to the 36 months of unlicensed sea service. Service as DWO is equivalent to licensed merchant marine watchstanding service rather than unlicensed service; therefore, more sea service credit can be given.

Officer sea service as other than a DWO is counted day-for-day towards an original third mate's license. The following are some examples of this type of deck service: CIC Officer, Navigator, JOOD, Assistant Navigator, 1st Lieutenant, Gunnery Officer and other duties associated with the operation of the vessel on deck.

This time cannot be used to duplicate service during the same time period that is being counted as watchstanding. When the non-watchstanding time exceeds that of the watchstanding time, the difference in the times may be used as 1 for 1 service. For example, if the Transcript of Sea Service shows 20 months as operations officer and 16 months as DWO during the same time period, the difference of four months can be credited, after applying a 60% reduction, on a 1 for 1 basis.

Enlisted Sea Service:

Most of the ratings are explained in 46 CFR 10.213(b). The Navy has combined some ratings into operations specialist. Operations specialist is a combination of the ratings quartermaster, radar man, sonar man, and signalman. The evaluator must be careful when evaluating the operations specialist to ascertain the type of duties the applicant performed as it relates to the navigation and control of the vessel.

Combining Sea Service: When computing the 36 months (1080 days) required for a third's license, you may use a variety of service in combination.

Care must be taken not to allow excess service when computing the license. Service is computed in the chronological order in which it was served. The following is an example:

Sample Transcript of Military Sea Service

NAME: CDR Joe Goodship

CGC GALLATIN (WHEC)	SA/SN	8 MONTHS
	GM3	24 MONTHS
CGC POINT HURON (WPB)	GM3/2	24 MONTHS
CGC TACKLE (WYTL)	GM2/1	28 MONTHS
CGC POLAR STAR (WAGB)	ENS/LTJG	15 MONTHS
	DWO (Underway)	10 MONTHS
	1ST LT.	12 MONTHS
	OPS OFFICER	3 MONTHS
CGC SASSAFRAS (WLB)	LT	12 MONTHS
	OPS OFFICER	12 MONTHS
	DWO	8 MONTHS

The following is an example of how to compute the sea service time for the aforementioned transcript:

Computation of Sea Service

Sea Service Reduced by 60% (Days) = Total Sea Service (Months) X .6 (60%) X 30 Days

1. 46 CFR 10.213(b) allows SA/SN sea service as equivalent to ordinary seaman service.

2. Section 2.B.4.d. allows up to 180 days of non-deck rating time (as defined in 46 CFR 10.213(b)) toward a Third Mate license.

3. The remainder of the 432 days after the 180 days is allowed can be given

50% credit as indicated in Figure 2-1 (432 - 180 = 252. 252 x 50% = 126). [NOTE: Had the GM3 service been a deck rating, such as BM3, the sea service would be equivalent to the able seaman sea service required by 46 CFR 10.407(a)(1).]

(2). CGC Point Huron GM3/2   24   432   0

(3). CGC Tackle   GM2/1   28   504   0

Both vessels are under 200 gross tons, therefore the sea service cannot be used for this license.

(4). CGC Polar Star   DWO   10   180   360
(over 1600 GT)   1ST Lt   5   90   90

Since the time here was as a DWO, each day of DWO sea service is counted as two days of required service or double the accrued time. As stated previously, this sea service is considered equivalent to watchstanding mate service.

(5). CGC Sassafras   DWO   8   144   288
(over 200 GT)   OPS Officer   4   72   72

TOTAL 1260

The *Sassafras* is under 1600 but it is over 200 gross tons so it can be used for up to 50 percent of the service required for an unlimited third's license.

If more than 50 percent of the required service was on vessels under 1600 gross tons, a tonnage limitation would be computed for the third's license.

Examples of Military Evaluations (Deck) (Cont'd)

EXAMPLE OF ORIGINAL MASTER CALCULATIONS (ACADEMY)
TRANSCRIPT OF MILITARY SEA SERVICE

NAME: CDR B. JONES

Summary of Service:

Vessels	Service	Days Assigned	Credit
Graduated CG Academy: Cadet			
('77)Northwind (WAGB)			
>1600	DWO	700	420
('78)Burton Is. (WAGB)			
>1600	DWO	369	221
('84)Laurel (WLB)			
<1600	DWO	723	434
('91)Sedge (WLB)			
<1600	DWO	1067	640
('97)Acushnet (WMEC)			
<1600	CO	822	493

Sequential Evaluation

For 3rd Mate:

Vessels	Credit	Notes
CG Academy		
Northwind:		Qualified DWO

Qualifies as third mate: 46 CFR 10.407 (a) (1) (iii)

For 2nd Mate:

Vessels	Credit	Notes
Northwind		360

TOTAL: 360 days/360 >1600

<u>For Chief Mate</u>

Vessels	Credit	Notes
Northwind	60	Carry over
Burton Is.	221	
Laurel	79	
Total:	360 Days/281 >1600	

CDR Jones meets the sea service for chief mate AGTs. However, he has not served aboard a vessel of over 1600 gross tons since Burton Island in 1978. The recency provisions of 46 CFR 10.202(e) apply. He must have three months' qualifying experience on vessels of appropriate tonnage (all over 200grt, half over 1600grt) within three years of application.

<u>For Master:</u>

Vessels	Credit	Notes
Laurel	355	
Sedge	640	
Acushnet	493	CO
Total:	1488 < 1600	

CDR Jones qualifies for Master 1600 gross tons because he does not have sufficient service on vessels of over 1600 gross tons. However, he may be permitted to sit for Master Unlimited with a 2,000 gross register ton restriction as permitted by 46 CFR 10.402(b).

1. Mariner qualifies for third mate after completing the Coast Guard academy and qualifying as a deck watch officer under, 46 CFR 10.407(a)(1)(iii).

2. Service is evaluated sequentially, in the order obtained over the course of the career. In this case, the mariner "uses up" service on vessels of over 1600 gross tons early in the career. In effect, the higher tonnage service was used

to qualify at second and chief mate levels.

3. To qualify for an original master's license, the mariner must serve as Commanding Officer for at least 180 days, 46 CFR 10.213(a).

Examples of Military Evaluations (Engine)

Note: The service presented must be equivalent to that required of a merchant mariner. The following methods of evaluation apply. All the sea service times referred to below are after all the appropriate deductions have been made.

Original Third Assistant Engineer (except academy graduates)

Officer Sea Service:
Each day of EWO sea service is counted as two days of the required service for an original Third Assistant Engineer's licenses. As an example, 18 months sea service as EWO is equal to the 36 months creditable sea service. Service as EWO is equivalent to licensed merchant marine watchstanding service rather than unlicensed service; therefore, more sea service credit can be given.

Officer sea service as other than a EWO is counted day for day towards an original third's license. The following are some examples of this type of engineering service: Main Propulsion Assistant, Electrical Officer, Auxiliary Officer, Damage Control Officer and any other duties associated with the engineering plant.

This time cannot be used to duplicate service during the same time period that is being counted as watchstanding. When the non-watchstanding time exceeds that of the watchstanding time, the difference in the times may be used as 1 for 1 service. For example, if the Transcript of Sea Service shows 20 months as main propulsion assistant and 16 months as EWO during the same time period, the difference of four months can be credited, after applying the 60% reduction, on a one for one basis.

Enlisted Sea Service: Most of the ratings are explained in 46 CFR 10.213(b). The Coast Guard has the rating of Machinery Technician (MK) that combines the Boiler Technicians (BT), Machinist Mate (MM), Damage Control man (DC) and Engineman (EN).

Combining Sea Service: When computing the 36 months (1080 days) required for a third's license, a variety of service may be used in combination. Care must be taken not to allow excess service when computing the license. Service is computed in the chronological order in which it was served. The following is an example:

Examples of Third Assistant Engineers (Non-Academy)

TRANSCRIPT OF MILITARY SEA SERVICE

NAME: CDR Joe Goodship

CGC Gallatin (WHEC)	FA/FN	8 Months
	DC3	24 Months
CGC Polar Star (WAGB)	CWO2 (Eng)	15 Months
	EWO (Underway)	10 Months
	Main Propulsion Asst.	12 Months
	Auxiliary Officer	3 Months
CGC Tamaroa (WMEC)	CWO2 (Eng)	12 Months
	Auxiliary Officer	12 Months
	EWO (Underway)	8 Months

The following is an example of how to compute the sea service time for the above transcript.

COMPUTATION OF SEA SERVICE

Sea Service Reduced by 60% (Days) = Total Sea Service (Months) x .6(60%) x 30 Days

	Rank/Rate	Total Sea Service (Months)	Sea Service Reduced By 60% (Days)	Sea Service Allowed (Days)
CGC Gallatin	FA/FN	8	144	144^1
7000 hp (5300 kW)	DC3	24	432	180^2

1. 46 CFR 10.213(b) allows FA/FN sea service as equivalent to ordinary seaman service.

2. Section 2.B.4.d. allows up to 180 days of non-engine room rating time (as defined in 46 CFR 10.213(b)) toward a Third Assistant Engineer's license. The computation gives 432 days but only 180 days can be used. [NOTE: In this example DC3 Goodship was not an engine room Watch Stander so per Figure 2-1, the service is not credited as engineer service. Had the DC3 service been as a Watch Stander or had it been an engine room rating such as MM3, the sea service would be equivalent to the QMED sea service required by 46 CFR 10.516(a) (1).]

CGC Polar Star	EWO	10	180	360
18,000 hp	Dept. Head	5	90	90
(13,500 kW)				

Since the time here was as an EWO, each day of EWO sea service is credited as two days of required service or double the accrued time. As stated previously, this sea service is considered equivalent to watchstanding engineering service.

CGC Tamaroa	EWO	8	144	288
3000 hp	Aux. Officer	4	72	72
(2200 kW)				

TOTAL 1134

The Tamaroa is under 4000 hp (3000 hp) so it can be used for up to 50% of the service required for an unlimited third's license. If more than 50% of the required service was on vessels under 4000 hp (3000 kW), a horsepower (power rating) limitation would be computed for the third's license.

Appendix 6

Excerpt USCG Title 46 CFR 10.219, Mariner's Fees Manual

Mandatory Fees for MMCs and Associated Endorsements

	Evaluation Fee	Examination Fee	Issuance Fee
MMC with officer endorsement:			
Original:			
Upper level	$100	$110	$45
Lower level	100	95	45
Renewal:	50	45	45
Raise of grade:	100	45	45
Modification or			
removal of limitation of scope			
	50	45	45
Radio officer endorsement:			
Original:	50	45	45
Renewal:	50	n/a	45
Staff officer endorsements:			
Original:	90	n/a	45
Renewal:	50	n/a	45
MMC with rating endorsement:			
Original endorsement for ratings other than qualified ratings			
	95	n/a	45
Original endorsement			
for qualified rating	95	140	45
Upgrade or raise of grade	95	140	45
Renewal endorsement for ratings other than qualified ratings			
	50	n/a	45
Renewal endorsement for qualified rating			

	50	45	45
STCW certification:			
Original	No fee	No fee	No fee
Renewal	No fee	No fee	No fee
Reissue, replacement, and duplicate			
	n/a	n/a	1$45

1 Duplicate for MMC lost as result of marine casualty—No Fee.

    (b) Fee payment procedures. Applicants may pay:

        (1) All fees required by this section at the time the application is submitted; or

        (2) A fee for each phase at the following times:

            (i) An evaluation fee when the application is submitted.

            (ii) An examination fee before the first examination section is taken.

            (iii) An issuance fee before receipt of the MMC.

    (c) If the examination is administered at a place other than an REC, the examination fee must be paid to the REC at least one week before the scheduled examination date.

    (d) Unless the REC provides additional payment options, fees must be paid as follows:

        (1) Fee payment(s) must be for the exact amount.

        (2) Payments may be made by cash, check, money order, or credit card.

        (3) Payments submitted by mail may not be made in cash. Mailed payments should specify the type of credential sought and the type of fee (e.g., evaluation, examination, issuance) being paid. The address for sending payment by mail can be found at http://www.uscg.mil/stcw/ldcr-userfees.htm.

        (4) Checks or money orders are to be made payable to the U.S. Coast Guard, and the full legal name and last four digits of applicant's security number must appear on the front of each check or money order.

        (5) Fee payment may be made by electronic payment in a manner specified by the Coast Guard. For information regarding current forms of electronic payment, go to http://www.uscg.mil/stcw/ldcr-userfees.htm.

(e)   Unless otherwise specified in this part, when two or more endorsements are processed on the same application:

    (1)   Evaluation fees. If an applicant simultaneously applies for a rating endorsement and a deck or engineer officer's endorsement, only the evaluation fee for the officer's endorsement will be charged. If an applicant simultaneously applies for a staff officer or radio officer endorsement along with the deck or engineer officer's endorsement, only the evaluation fee for the deck or engineer officer's endorsement will be charged. No evaluation fee is charged for an STCW endorsement.

    (2)   Examination fees. One examination fee will be charged for each exam or series of exams for an original, raise of grade, or renewal of an endorsement on an MMC taken within one year from the date of the application approval. An examination fee will also be charged to process an open-book exercise used to renew an MMC. If an officer endorsement examination under part 11 of this chapter also fulfills the examination requirements in part 12 of this chapter for rating endorsements, only the fee for the officer endorsement examination is charged.

    (3)   Issuance fees. Only one issuance fee will be charged for each MMC issued, regardless of the number of endorsements placed on the credential. There is no fee for a Document of Continuity.

(f)   The Coast Guard may assess additional charges to anyone to recover collection and enforcement costs associated with delinquent payments, failure to pay a fee, or returned checks. The Coast Guard will not provide credentialing services to a mariner who owes money for credentialing services previously provided.

(g)   Anyone who fails to pay a fee or charge established under this subpart is liable to the United States Government for a civil penalty of not more than $6,500 for each violation.

(h)   No-fee MMC for certain applicants.

    (1)   For the purpose of this section, a no-fee MMC applicant

is a person who is a volunteer, or a part-time or full-time employee of an organization that is:

(i) Charitable in nature;

(ii) Not for profit; and

(iii) Youth oriented.

(2) Determination of eligibility.

    (i) An organization may submit a written request to U.S. Coast Guard National Maritime Center, 100 Forbes Drive, Martinsburg, WV 25404, in order to be considered an eligible organization under the criteria set forth in paragraph (h)(1) of this section. With the written request, the organization must provide evidence of its status as a youth-oriented, not-for-profit, charitable organization.

    (ii) The following organizations are accepted by the Coast Guard as meeting the requirements of paragraph (h)(1) of this section and need not submit evidence of their status: Boy Scouts of America, Sea Explorer Association, Girl Scouts of the United States of America, and Young Men's Christian Association of the United States of America.

(3) A letter from an organization determined eligible under paragraph (h)(2) of this section must also accompany the person's MMC application to the Coast Guard. The letter must state that the purpose of the person's application is solely to further the conduct of the organization's maritime activities. The applicant then is eligible under this section to obtain a no-fee MMC if other requirements for the MMC are met.

(4) An MMC issued to a person under this section is endorsed restricting its use to vessels owned or operated by the sponsoring organization.

(5) The holder of a no-fee MMC issued under this section

may have the restriction removed by paying the appropriate evaluation, examination, and issuance fees that would have otherwise applied.

Glossary

abaft: Behind the center of the vessel.

able-bodied seaman: A journeyman deck seaman who has all the skills of an experienced seaman. He may also be called an AB or able seaman.

ABS: American Bureau of Shipping, a classification society that does vessel inspections in concert with the Coast Guard.

aft: Toward the back or stern.

AIS: Automatic identification system, an electronic device that gives the name and other information on radar contacts.

alongside: Refers to the side of the ship. A barge coming alongside is approaching the side of the ship.

amidships: The center of the vessel, or towards the center of the vessel.

AMO: American Maritime Officers, a licensed officers union.

Articles of Agreement: A document that lays out the agreement between the vessel's master and the ship's crew. Usually called ship's articles or shipping articles.

astern: Moving backwards

automatic pilot: An electronic device that steers the ship automatically along a predetermined course.

ballast: Heavy items, often water, used to load down an empty or partially empty ship to improve stability, sea-keeping, speed, vessel stress or other factors.

ballast tanks: Tanks built into the vessel to carry sea water when extra ballast is required. Double hulled tankers usually have a layer of ballast tanks between the cargo tanks and the sea.

bare boat charter: A charter where the ship is chartered without a master or crew.

barge: A flat-bottomed vessel with no engine or crew quarters. Used to transport various cargos and powered by an attached tug boat.

barge carriers: An unusual type of ship designed to carry barges and containers on board. LASH and SEABEE are two types of this vessel.

barritry: A crime committed by a master or crew against their vessel.

beam: Width of the vessel.

bill of lading: A document used to accept the cargo by the master that binds him to deliver the cargo in the same condition to its destination.

Black Gang: Crew members who labor in the engine room.

boatswain (bosun): Senior member of the deck gang, supervises the deck gang under the direction of the chief officer.

boilers: Steam generating units used to provide heat or occasionally propulsion.

bow: Front of vessel.

bow thruster: A propeller all the way forward, situated at right angles to the vessel, able to move the bow sideways. Usually used for docking.

breakbulk: A number of small lots of cargo packed into a single container, or an entire ship loaded with different lots of cargo without the benefit of containers.

bridge: Vessel nerve center. Area where the vessel is conned.

bulk: Large volume of cargo shipped without packaging in a loose condition, such as grain, ore, or oil.

bulk carrier: Ship designed to carry bulk cargos.

bulkhead: Vertical wall.

bunkers: Fuel.

buoy: Floating navigation marker, used to mark dangers or aid navigation.

cable ship: Ship designed to lay or repair telephone cables.

cabotage: The business of carrying by water cargo or passengers to ports of the same country.

cargo: Freight loaded on a vessel.

cargo handling: Loading and unloading the vessel.

cargo manifest: A list of the cargo on board the vessel.

cargo preference: Requires a portion of the nation's cargo to be carried on the nation's flagged vessels.

carriers: Companies or ships that carry cargo.

catamaran: A vessel constructed by joining two or three hulls together, usually very stable.

catwalk: A raised walkway on deck that provides access in a cluttered world.

Certificate of Inspection (COI): Issued by the U.S. Coast Guard, certifies the American-flagged vessel complies with all laws and regulations.

Certificate of Registry: States the country where the vessel is registered.

chandlery: A store that supplies vessels.

charterer: The organization that hires the ship for a stated time and purpose.

Charter Party: A contractual agreement between a ship's owner and a cargo owner for the use of the vessel.

chief engineer: Senior engineer aboard, responsible for all of the ship's machinery.

chief mate: Second in command, responsible for the deck department, cargo, ship's stability, and deck maintenance. Usually very busy.

Classification Society: A respected private society that supervises the vessel from its construction and during its life with inspections and advice. It helps keep the vessel seaworthy and safe for both her sailors and the ports that the vessel calls on.

clean ship: Tankers that have removed all traces of previous cargo.

coastwise: Domestic shipping routes up and down the coast.

collier: Ship used for the carriage of coal.

collision avoidance system: An electronic device used by the deck watch officer to avoid collisions.

COLREGS: Convention on International Regulations for Preventing Collisions at Sea; Rules of the Road.

combi: Combination ship designed to carry passengers and cargo, cargo may be containerized or breakbulk.

common carrier: Ship available to carry cargo for anyone. Must post rates and cannot discriminate against any cargo owners.

complement: Total number crewmembers aboard vessel.

consignee: To whom the cargo is sent.

consignor: From whom the cargo is coming.

container: A van, open top trailer, flatrack, or tank in a frame into which cargo is loaded. It is transported without a chassis and has a double door on one end. Some containers have refrigeration capability.

container terminal: A large area with easy access by truck and often rail, used to store, gather, and distribute containers as they are loaded onto or discharged from a ship.

containerizable cargo: Cargo that fits in a container.

container ship: A ship able to stack containers on top of each other, both under deck and on deck. Using large shoreside cranes, these ships can be simultaneously loaded and unloaded in different holds. These ships can generally carry between 25,000 and 60,000 tons of cargo. Older breakbulk vessels used to spend as much as 70 percent of their time in port loading or unloading cargo, while container ships spend less than 20 percent of their time in port.

contraband: Prohibited cargo

contract carrier: Not a common carrier, but carries passengers or freight for compensation.

crew: The personnel who run the ship, not counting the captain.

crew list: List of crew prepared by the captain which gives the pertinent details of the captain and crew. This list is always required by customs and immigration on arrival.

cross-trades: Cargo carried by ships from a nation neither importing nor exporting the cargo.

crude oil washing: An oil tanker technique of tank cleaning using the cargo shot through a nozzle to clean the tank.

D&H: Dangerous and hazardous cargo.

dangerous cargo: Substances that are dangerous to transport, may be flammable, explosive, poison, or dangerous in other ways. They have special stowage rules that must be followed during their carriage.

dangerous liquids: Liquids that give off flammable vapors.

davits: Lifesaving equipment used to stow, lower, and retrieve lifeboats.

deadweight: A measure of cargo carrying capacity. The number of long tons of cargo, stores, and fuel that a given vessel can carry.

deck gang: The unlicensed deck sailors aboard ship.

deckhand: Member of the deck gang.

deck house: Superstructure above the main deck, usually the hotel spaces and bridge of the vessel.

deck log: A record of the deck watch, written up at the end of each watch by the watch officer.

deck officer: Licensed officers who navigate the vessel and supervise cargo operations.

demurrage: A fee the port is liable for if the ship isn't loaded or unloaded by a contracted deadline.

disabled ship: A ship that is unable to sail because of mechanical problems, crew shortages, or other damage.

discharges: An essential document that gives the sign on and sign off dates of a seaman on a particular ship.

displacement: The total weight of the vessel and everything on her.

DOD: Department of Defense.

DOT: Department of Transportation.

double bottom: Consists of water-tight spaces between the outer hull and the cargo spaces. More important on tankers where they make an oil spill more unlikely in case of a collision or grounding.

draft: The depth of the ship beneath the water.

dry cargo: All cargo that is not bulk liquid cargo.

dry cargo ship: Ship that carries cargo other than bulk liquids.

dry dock: A ship construction or repair facility where the ship can be towed in, the door behind can be secured, and the water can be pumped out, leaving the vessel high and dry.

dunnage: Wood, cardboard, or other material used to protect the cargo in the ship's holds.

DWT: dead weight tons.

EEZ: exclusive economic zone, extends 200 miles off shore.

even keel: The ship is flat, the fore and aft drafts are the same.

fart locker: Buttocks.

feeder: A grain reservoir that automatically adds more grain should a void space develop in the cargo hold.

feeder service: Smaller ships deliver cargo to a centralized port to be consolidated and shipped on a larger vessel on a longer voyage.

FEU: forty-foot equivalent units (containers).

flags of convenience (FOC): The registration of ships in a country where the taxes are lower and the regulations for crewing and safety are more lax. All ships must be registered in a country that provides some level of oversight but it can be any country the ship's owner chooses.

floating oil storage: Laid-up tankers are sometimes used as oil storage tanks.

FMC: Federal Maritime Commission.

fore and aft: The long axis of the vessel.

forecastle: The raised section of the bow, often used for deck storage.

forward: Toward the bow.

freight: Either the cargo carried or the charge for carrying the cargo.

freighters: Container ships, breakbulk ships, roll on/roll off ships, barge carriers.

full container ships: Ships with cell guides for the containers and no space for breakbulk cargo.

gangway: A narrow ramp providing access to the vessel.

general cargo: A non-bulk oil cargo of various goods.

GMDSS: Global Maritime Distress and Safety System, a communications system.

GPS: Global Positioning System, common navigational system.

Great Lakes ports: American or Canadian ports on the Great lakes. Canadian ports include Port Arthur and Fort William on Lake Superior; Hamilton, Kingston, Toronto, and Prescott on Lake Ontario. American ports include Chicago, Milwaukee, on Lake Michigan; Duluth and Superior on Lake Superior; and Toledo on Lake Erie.

Great Lakes ship: Ships developed to carry raw materials across the Great Lakes, almost always a bulker.

gross registered tons (GRT): A common measurement of volume. 100 cubic feet is equal to 1 GRT, the total of the enclosed spaces within a ship expressed in tons.

grounding: Contact of the ship's hull with the bottom.

gun deck: Cheat, claiming to do inspections without doing them.

gyro pilot: A steering system where the course from the gyro compass is dialed in and automatically followed.

harbor dues: Local charges paid by all ships entering a harbor to cover harbor maintenance.

Harbor Master: The person responsible for administering all of the shipping movements within a given harbor.

hard aground: A grounded vessel that cannot refloat itself; always a bad thing.

hatch: A rectangular opening in the deck providing access to the hold below.

hausepipe: Tunnel through which anchor chain passes as it is dropped. Ships officers who never attended an academy, but earned their licenses on their own.

hawser: Large, strong line used to tie ships to the dock or to tow them.

HAZ MAT: Hazardous material.

head: Toilet.

helm: Wheel or tiller installed on bridge used to steer the vessel.

hold: The cargo storage spaces located below the main deck; called tanks on a tanker.

hopper barge: Used in conjunction with a dredge, loaded through the top and dumped at the spoils area through the bottom.

Hovercraft: A vessel that rides on a cushion of air, rather than through the water; very fast and used for ferries and by the Navy.

hull: Shell of the vessel.

hydrofoil: Similar to the Hovercraft. A non-displacement vessel, however supporting legs remain in contact with the water even when the vessel is up to speed.

IBU: Inland Boatman's Union of the Pacific.

IMDG: International Maritime Dangerous Goods Code. International rules for transporting D&H cargo.

IMO: International Maritime Organization. Works through the UN for international maritime safety and related procedures.

inert gas system: A system where the ship's exhaust gas is piped into the cargo tanks, displacing any oxygen and making explosions impossible. The tank must then be "gas freed" before personnel are able to enter the tank.

inland carrier: A transportation company that hauls cargo around from ports to points inland.

inland waters: Navigable waters extending from harbor entrances inland.

INMARSAT: International Maritime Satellite System

integrated tug barge: A barge constructed so that a pusher tug locks securely into its stern so that the two vessels become one.

intercoastal: Domestic shipping routes servicing both East and West Coasts.

intermodalism: Door to door service, using trucks, ships ,and rail to provide the most efficient transport possible.

international load line: Gives details of the ship's freeboard after the ship has been surveyed, painted on the side of the ship amidships.

intracoastal: Domestic shipping routes along a single coast.

ISM code: The IMO adopted the International Safety Management Code in 2002 for most ships. It is designed insure these vessels are operated in a safer manner.

ISPS code: The International Ship and Port Facility Code of 2002 increases the security regulations for ships and port facilities.

Jacob's ladder: A rope ladder hung from the side of the ship to permit boarding.

jettison: To throw cargo or equipment over the side in an emergency to increase the seaworthiness of the vessel.

Jones Act: Merchant Marine Act of 1920, Section 27, requires all American domestic cargo to be shipped on U.S.-flagged, U.S.-built, U.S.-manned vessels.

keel: The lowest longitudinal strength member of the vessel, on which the frame of the entire vessel is built.

knot: Nautical mile per hour; 6080 feet per hour.

laid-up tonnage: Surplus ships not working, awaiting better market conditions or refitting.

laker: Ship designed to sail only on the Great Lakes; usually a bulker carrying grain, ore, coal, and the like.

LASH: Lighter Aboard Ship, a specialized container ship that carries barges used to transport the containers from the vessel to the shore. The barges are moved around by local tugs.

LCL: Less than a container load, a quantity of cargo too small to fill a container, will be combined with other cargo.

lifeboat: A heavy double-ended boat stowed onboard to be used if abandoning ship becomes necessary.

lifeboat drill: Ships are required to drill monthly with their lifeboats in case of an emergency.

liftboat: A vessel used in the offshore oil industry. It is a self-propelled vessel able to lift itself clear of the water on its own legs. Usually used as a repair platform.

lighter: Small vessel used to transport cargo from a ship at anchor to shoreside.

liner: A cargo ship that runs on a published schedule.

list: The amount in degrees the vessel tilts from the vertical.

LNG: Liquefied natural gas, or a vessel that carries LNG.

LNG carrier: A very sophisticated tanker that costs about double what a similar sized conventional tanker would. It carries gas cooled to -285 degrees to reduce the volume of the gas. Often uses the LNG boil off to power the vessel.

load line: The mark on the hull showing the maximum draft of the vessel.

long ton (L/T): 2240 pounds.

longshoreman: Person whose job it is to load and unload the vessel.

lookout: Crewmember stationed on the bow or the bridge to watch for other vessels or other dangers coming into sight.

main deck: The highest continuous deck running from bow to stern.

manifest: A full list of the ship's cargo.

manning scales: The minimum number of crewmembers required to sail the ship.

marine insurance: Covers loss or damage of cargo or the vessel at sea.

maritime: Business dealing with commerce or navigation on the sea.

Maritime Administration (MarAd): Government agency that oversees subsidy programs that permit American ships to compete with flag of convenience vessels.

masthead light: White light over the center line of the vessel.

MEBA: Marine Engineers Beneficial Association.

MM&P: Masters, Mates, and Pilots Union

MODU: Mobil Offshore Drilling Unit

mooring line: A cable or heavy line used to tie up a ship.

MSC: Military Sealift Command, civilians working for the Navy.

MSP: Maritime Security Program; maintains a nucleus fleet of military useful American cargo vessels.

M/T: metric tons, 1000 Kg.

National Cargo Bureau: A private organization that assists shippers by insuring cargo is stowed properly by inspection.

national flag: The flag of the country of registry.

nautical mile: One minute of longitude at the equator, or 6,076 feet.

net tonnage: Gross Tonnage minus deductions showing volume available for cargo.

NVOCC: Non-vessel-operating common carrier, a ship's agent. Conducts business for the vessel but doesn't operate the vessel.

OBO: A flexible bulk carrier able to carry different cargos such as oil, ore, and grain that is more expensive to build than less capable bulkers but able to carry a different cargo on the return trip.

officer: Licensed member of the ship's complement.

off-load: Discharge cargo from the vessel.

oiler: Unlicensed member of the engine department who used to do a lot of oiling and greasing. Now the work is mostly done automatically, so the oiler mainly just checks that it is done. Most oilers have been replaced by QMEDs.

oil record book: A log where a record of every oil transfer is recorded.

oil tanker: A ship designed to carry oil in bulk. The cargo is moved by pumps or gravity.

open top container: A container with either no roof or a removable roof. Can be loaded from above.

ordinary seaman: Entry level member of the deck department.

pallet: A flat wooden tray designed for cargo to be stacked on, facilitates the use of forklifts.

Panamax: The biggest ship that can fit through the Panama Canal.

passenger ship: A ship able to carry more than 12 passengers legally.

personal flotation device (PFD): Usually a life jacket.

pilot: A person licensed to assist the Master entering and leaving port.

pilot house: The bridge, or wheel house.

Plimsoll mark: A series of painted horizontal lines that must be kept above the water line under different circumstances. Prevents overloading of ships; hence the toast "God Bless the United States Coast Guard and Samuel Plimsoll."

PMA: Pacific Maritime Association.

port: Left side of the ship when facing forward.

POL: Petroleum, oil, and lubricants

pooling: The sharing of cargo by members of a liner conference.

port of call: Port where a ship loads or discharges cargo.

port state control: The inspection of foreign ships in port to insure they are being manned, operated, and maintained in accordance with international law. Done all over the world.

PR 17: Public Resolution that U.S. Government financed cargo must be shipped 100 percent on American flag ships, but sometimes reduced to 50 percent.

product carrier: A smaller tanker used to transport refined products, able to carry different products simultaneously.

pumpman: Member of the engine department who tends the pumps on a tanker.

purser: A ship's officer in charge of paperwork, usually on a passenger ship.

qualified member of the engine department (QMED): Unlicensed engine department rating who tends to a fully automated engine room.

quartermaster/helmsman: An Able Seaman engaged in steering the vessel.

quarters: Berthing areas, accommodations.

quay: A structure attached to the shore, parallel to the shore line, to which a ship is moored.

reefer: A ship with a refrigerated hold.

reefer box: A container with a refrigeration unit built in.

return cargo: Cargo that allows a ship to return loaded to the port where it had previously loaded out.

RFPEW: Rating forming part of an engineering watch; certificate required to work as a watchstander in the engine room.

rolling cargo: Cargo on wheels, such as cars, allowing it to be driven or towed aboard.

RO/RO ship: Freighter set up for rapid loading and discharging of rolling cargo.

RRF: Ready Reserve Fleet.

salvage: Recovery of lost cargo or a damaged vessel.

Seebee: Obsolete system of barge carrier, uses rollers to bring the giant barges back aboard.

sea trials: After the ship is built, the buyer and builder run the ship through a series of trials to insure it meets its specifications.

seaworthiness: Meaning the vessel is properly built, maintained, and crewed to safely participate in a particular trade.

self-propelled barge: A barge with its own engine.

self-sustaining ship: A container ship that can load and unload itself with its own cranes.

self-unloader: A bulk carrier able to load and unload itself with its own cargo gear.

shifting: Accidental cargo movement in the vessel, can be very dangerous. A movement in port from one berth to another.

ship's tackle: All rigging and cranes on a ship used to load and unload cargo.

shippers: Those who purchase transportation services to move their goods.

ship's agent: A person or business who does business in port on behalf of the ship owner or charterer.

ship's stability: The seaworthiness of a vessel in regard to its ability to return to an upright position.

short ton (S/T): 2,000 pounds

sister ships: Vessels of the same design.

SIU: Seaman's International Union.

slip: A berth or the distance a ship made compared to the distance it should have made.

slop tank: A tank used to hold a mixture of oil and water, usually pumped ashore.

SOLAS: Safety of Life at Sea Convention.

spot voyage: A charter for a single voyage in the immediate future.

S.S.: Steam ship.

starboard: Right side of a ship when facing forward.

station bill: A list of the ship's crew and details their emergency duties.

STCW: International Convention on Standards of Training, Certification and Watchkeeping for Seafarers, 1978.

stern: Back of vessel.

sternway: The vessel's movement aft.

stevedore: Person or business who contracts to load or unload a ship with hired longshoremen.

store: A general term for supplies.

stripping: Unloading a container.

stuffing: Loading a container.

tail shaft: The aft end of the propeller shaft.

tank barge: A barge designed to carry liquid cargos.

tank cleaning: Removing all traces of previous cargo, usually by high pressure washing with either water or product.

territorial waters: Usually about 3 miles, or the length of a muzzle-loaded cannon shot. The country's sovereignty extends over this water.

T.E.U. twenty foot equivalent unit (container): A measurement of cargo-carrying capacity on a containership, referring to a single twenty-foot container.

time charter: A charter for a specified length of time.

top-off: To fill completely a partially loaded ship.

tow: Pulling through the water by means of a rope, when one vessel tows another, or some other floating object.

tramp service: Vessels operating without a fixed schedule.

transship: Transfer goods from one ship to another, or one transportation line to another.

trim: The relationship between the forward and after draft.

tug: A small, powerful vessel used to move larger vessels. They are used to land much larger vessels alongside a berth. They are also used to push large numbers of barges on rivers and inland waters.

ULCC: Ultra large crude carriers, tankers larger than 300,000 dwt.

unmanned machinery spaces: A space covered by alarms that sounds should an engineering failure occur. The engineers answer the alarm and solve the problem, which eliminates the need for a round the clock engineering watch.

USCG: United States Coast Guard.

U.S. effective controlled fleet: A large number of merchant ships owned by American citizens or corporations but not U.S. flagged.

VLCC: Very large crude carrier, between 200,000 and 400,000 dwt.

watch: The day at sea is divided into six four-hour watch periods. The three watches each stand two watches a day with eight hours off between each watch. Work done between watches is overtime.

About the Author

Born and raised in the San Francisco Bay Area, Captain Jonathan Allen is a graduate of California Maritime Academy, where he earned a B.S. in Nautical Industrial Technology, a Naval Reserve Commission, and a Third Mate's License (Unlimited Tonnage). Upon graduation he worked on a variety of merchant ships, including tankers, research ships, and ro/ro ships for almost ten years.

As the eighties came to a close, commercial fishing in Alaska was booming and Allen headed north looking for adventure. He found it onboard trawlers, crabbers, and longliners, working up to eleven months out of the year as he learned his new trade. Eventually he worked his way up to captain aboard the F/V *Lilli Ann*, F/V *Blue North*, the *Arctic V* and the *Unimak Enterprise*. Eventually too much of a good thing proved to be too much of a good thing, and Captain Allen headed south to the lower forty-eight, where he began raising children with his wife Tammy and resumed working in the American merchant fleet.

Today he works as a chief officer for APL and on vacation watches his children play basketball, football, baseball, hockey, and cheerleading. He and his family live in the middle of the Rocky Mountains where no one knows or cares much about going to sea. He has an Unlimited Masters license, a couple of Alaskan pilotages, and hopes someday to become a better elk hunter and powder skier.

Other Books by Captain Jonathan Allen

The Big Bucks Guide to Commercial Fishing in Alaska

also see

Captain Allen's Blog

www.thebigbucksguide.com